Racism and Resistance among the Filipino Diaspora

Filipino migrants constitute one of the largest global diasporas today. In Australia, Filipino settlement is markedly framed by the country's ongoing nation-building project that continues to racialise immigrants and delineate the possibilities and limits of belonging to the national community. This book explores the ways in which Filipino migrants in Australia experience, understand and negotiate racism in their everyday lives. In particular, it explores the notion of everyday anti-racism – the strategies individuals deploy to manage racism in their day-to-day lives. Through case studies based on extensive fieldwork the author shares ethnographic observation and interview material that demonstrate the ways in which Filipinos are racially constituted in Australian society and are subject to everyday racisms that criss-cross different modes of power and domination. Drawing on theoretical approaches in critical race scholarship and the sociology of everyday life, this book illuminates the operation of racism in a multicultural society that persists insidiously in exchanges across a range of public and private spaces. More importantly, it explores the quotidian ways in which 'victims' of racism cope with routine racialised domination, an area underdeveloped in anti-racism research that has tended to focus on institutional anti-racism politics. Shedding light on a neglected corner of the global Filipino diaspora and highlighting the complexity of lived experiences in translocal and transnational social fields, this book will be of interest to academics in the field of diaspora and migration studies, the study of race and racism and ethnic minorities, with particular reference to the Asian diaspora.

Kristine Aquino is Lecturer in Global Studies at the University of Technology Sydney, Australia. Her research interests are in the study of global migration, transnationalism, race and ethnicity, and everyday multiculturalism in urban life.

Routledge Series on Asian Migration

Series Editors: Yuk Wah Chan (*City University of Hong Kong*), Jonathan H. X. Lee (*San Francisco State University, US*) and Nicola Piper (*The University of Sydney, Australia*)

Editorial Board: Steven J. Gold (*Michigan State University, US*), David Haines (*George Mason University, US*), Pei-Chia Lan (*National Taiwan University*), Nana Oishi (*University of Melbourne, Australia*), Willem van Schendel (*University of Amsterdam, The Netherlands*), Biao Xiang (*University of Oxford, UK*), Brenda Yeoh (*National University of Singapore*)

Racism and Resistance among the Filipino Diaspora
Everyday Anti-racism in Australia
Kristine Aquino

Racism and Resistance among the Filipino Diaspora
Everyday Anti-racism in Australia

Kristine Aquino
University of Technology Sydney, Australia

LONDON AND NEW YORK

First published 2018
by Routledge
2 Park Square, Milton Park, Abingdon, Oxon OX14 4RN

and by Routledge
711 Third Avenue, New York, NY 10017

Routledge is an imprint of the Taylor & Francis Group, an informa business

© 2018 Kristine Aquino

The right of Kristine Aquino to be identified as author of this work has been asserted by him/her in accordance with sections 77 and 78 of the Copyright, Designs and Patents Act 1988.

All rights reserved. No part of this book may be reprinted or reproduced or utilised in any form or by any electronic, mechanical, or other means, now known or hereafter invented, including photocopying and recording, or in any information storage or retrieval system, without permission in writing from the publishers.

Trademark notice: Product or corporate names may be trademarks or registered trademarks, and are used only for identification and explanation without intent to infringe.

British Library Cataloguing-in-Publication Data
A catalogue record for this book is available from the British Library

Library of Congress Cataloging-in-Publication Data
Names: Aquino, Kristine, author.
Title: Racism and resistance among the Filipino diaspora / Kristine Aquino.
Description: New York : Routledge, 2018. | Series: Routledge series on Asian migration | Includes bibliographical references and index.
Identifiers: LCCN 2017016408 | ISBN 9781138707931 (hardback) | ISBN 9781315201306 (ebook)
Subjects: LCSH: Filipinos—Australia—Social conditions. | Immigrants—Australia—Social conditions. | Racism—Australia. | Australia—Race relations. | Australia—Emigration and immigration. | Filipino diaspora.
Classification: LCC DU122.F5 A78 2018 | DDC 305.800994—dc23
LC record available at https://lccn.loc.gov/2017016408

ISBN: 978-1-138-70793-1 (hbk)
ISBN: 978-1-315-20130-6 (ebk)

Typeset in Times New Roman
by Apex CoVantage, LLC

For my parents, Lita and Augie

Contents

	List of figures	viii
	Acknowledgements	ix
1	Introduction	1
2	Histories of the 'Filipino' in Australia and beyond	17
3	Coping with honorary whiteness: aspirant middle-class Filipino migrants	43
4	Reclaiming rights, morality and esteem: the dignity of working-class Filipino migrants	66
5	'Mail order bride' or loving wife? Revisiting the experience of Filipina 'marriage migrants'	87
6	More than a game: embodied resistance among young Filipino-Australian street ballers	111
7	Conclusion	133
	Index	140

Figures

2.1	Parade of traditional Filipino costume, Philippine Cultural Day, St Marys, May 2009	40
2.2	Filipino Seniors Sonata Concert, Memorial Hall, St Marys, 2010	40
2.3	Filipino *turo turo* (point point) restaurant on Main Street, Blacktown	41
2.4	Filipino business hub in Main Street, Blacktown	41
2.5	Grand Final contention at the 2011 New South Wales Filos Championship Cup, Auburn	42
2.6	Filipino symbols inscribed as tattoos among young Filipino basketball players	42

Acknowledgements

There are many people who deserve my sincerest gratitude.

First and foremost, while their real names are not revealed in this book, I thank all of the Filipinos who shared their time and lives with me. Their journeys have touched me in so many ways and I hope to do their stories justice here.

This book was researched and written during my time at Macquarie University, Sydney, which was my intellectual home for close to ten years. It began as a doctoral thesis at the Centre for Research on Social Inclusion and completed as a book manuscript while I was Associate Lecturer at the Department of Sociology. I am grateful for the support of my senior colleagues and also for the Macquarie Research Excellence Scholarship that enabled me to undertake the research. Most especially, a big thank you goes to my mentors, Amanda Wise and Selvaraj Velayutham, who have both been so generous in nurturing my academic abilities. Their intellectual guidance through this work and complete belief in my potential have sustained me over the past few years and I am incredibly grateful for their continued support. I truly look forward to working together again and to many more years of friendship. I also thank Harry Blatterer, Alison Leitch and Justine Lloyd for all of their kind and reassuring encouragement. Thank you to my wonderful peers who shared the PhD journey with me, Sudheesh Bhasi, Laavanya Kathiravelu, Kylie Sait and Banu Senay. I cherish all of the serious and silly chats we shared about our research and our lives outside, amid piles of reading or bottles of wine. I am also grateful for the support of Peter Rogers, Barbara Beard, Niro Kandasamy, Edgar Liu and Vincent Suarez at Western Sydney Regional Information and Research, where I worked while completing my studies, who all helped me navigate the rich complexities of Western Sydney. As I begin the next stage of my academic career at the University of Technology Sydney, I look forward to sharing this book and collaborating with my new colleagues at the School of International Studies, Faculty of Arts and Social Sciences.

For their enthusiasm in pursuing the publication of this book, I thank the editors of Routledge's Series on Asian Migration, Nicola Piper, Yuk Wah Chan and Brandon H. X. Lee. Many thanks also to Routledge editors Dorothea Schaefter and Lily Brown, who made publishing my first book a really easy and friendly experience. Several scholars whose work I admire have provided helpful feedback throughout various stages of peer examination of the manuscript – Trevor

Hogan, Catriona Elder, Michele Lobo, Rick Bonus and Caroline Knowles. I thank them for their kind recommendations. A version of Chapter 3 appears as a journal article in *Ethnic and Racial Studies* (2016), Vol. 39, No. 1, pp. 105–122, as is the case for Chapter 6, which appears in the *Journal of Intercultural Studies* (2015), Vol. 36, No. 2, pp. 166–183. I thank the respective journals for granting permissions to reprint the material here and also the anonymous peer reviewers, whose feedback strengthened these chapters. The photograph and tattoo featured on this book's cover belong to Wayne and the tattoo's design is credited to the talented tattoo artist Murphy Aloda. I thank them both for permitting the use of the image and bringing the book title to life.

Of course, I extend my love and gratitude to my amazing group of friends and extended family in Sydney, my beautiful siblings, Dustin, Kat, Tim, James and Angeli, and my loving partner, Frankie Aesquivel. Their unwavering support and patience through the late nights, missed weekends and emotional ups and downs while I wrote this book mean the world and more. Last but certainly not least, I dedicate this book to my mother, Lita, and my father, Augie. My parents left the Philippines and migrated to Australia thirty years ago in order to provide their four children with a better future. I know the experience of dislocation and rebuilding has not always been easy and so I am forever indebted to their love and sacrifice.

1 Introduction

> I am very proud of Filipinos. In the hospital there are so many nurses! They love to hire Filipina nurses because they are *masipag* (hard-working). I have a Filipino friend and she's working in a factory and she asked, 'Why is it that no Australians work in the factory?' You know why? Because they cannot work hard like Filipinos. White people, they don't want. It's below them. . . I don't know, I'm not trying to criticise (slightly whispers), but the way we are treated, you really can feel it. Even now, it's okay. It's better now than before. But there's still discrimination. But it's up to us. If you want to be discriminated then they can get away with it. But you have to show them, stand up to them. You must not put up with it!
> —Melinda, 55-year-old Filipina migrant from Sydney

I met Melinda, a small and outspoken Filipina woman in her fifties, through my grandmother's Filipino senior citizens group. We were introduced when I escorted my Mama to a community hall in the south-western suburbs of Sydney for an annual Seniors Valentine's Day celebration. Semi-retired and much younger than the other elderly Filipino members, I found Melinda in the middle of the action, busily organising the potluck and the program. Despite her tiny stature, she was bursting with contagious energy, speaking at an excited pace and animating the other seniors to life. I remember my Mama explaining to me in the way only grandmothers know how, "That's Melinda, my friend. She talks too much. *Always* talking. But she has many stories to tell."

As I lent a hand here and there for the group's very busy social calendar, I got to know more of Melinda and invited her to sit down with me to share her story. I eagerly revealed that I was writing a book about Filipino migrants in Sydney. Less readily, I added that I was particularly interested to find out about their experiences of racism. Many other Filipinos who I had approached about the subject were often hesitant to impart painful and uncomfortable accounts about their migration. But Melinda had responded with gusto, "Oh, yes, yes. I have a lot to say!"

Melinda migrated on a spousal visa to Australia in the 1970s after a long-distance courtship with an Australian citizen from an Irish background. Introduced to each other by her hairdresser, they met in the Philippines during his business travels when she was thirty-three while he was much older, by fifteen years. At the time, she was working as a bookkeeper, which she eventually gave up to move to Australia. Sadly, her husband died after only a few years of marriage after suffering a stroke and Melinda fondly spoke about his kind-hearted nature as she remembered their time together. She admitted that he left her with some money from his business, which has allowed her a little bit of luxury to work part-time as an accounts clerk and dedicate most of her days helping Filipino senior citizens. But, more so, Melinda recounted to me quite vividly her regular experiences of prejudice prompted by her status as a Filipina wife of a much older white man. Upon moving to Australia, she complained of being unfairly judged often not by strangers but in intimate settings among her husband's family and friends. Melinda recalled, "Some of his friends accepted me, some friends not . . . They are thinking Filipinas are not good. They think we are maids. His family talk behind my back. They are thinking he just got me from the Philippines like a property." She has also endured other incivilities, usually slight and indirect, such as being stared at in public spaces when out with her partner and ignored or mocked by sales attendants: "Just in general here, when they see a white person with a Filipina – they think 'mail order', that girl is with him for money." While these experiences are uniquely painful to Melinda, at the same time, I could see she was attuned to how commonplace it might be for other Filipinas in her position. Melinda's personal experience is implicated in a popular discourse which featured in Australian media in the 1980s and 1990s about 'mail order brides' and particularly targeted Filipina women after a proliferation of advertisements marketing 'Filipina brides' to Australian men. This label remains conspicuous even today, producing a range of racialised (and sexualised) stereotypes about the Filipina: the 'opportunistic predator', the 'fragile victim', the 'submissive object'.

The manner in which the 'Filipino' must always look at herself 'through the eyes of others' and 'through the revelation of the other world', to borrow from Du Bois (1903), is a palpable struggle.[1] It is estimated that 10.4 million Filipinos reside outside of the Philippines – the largest numbers are composed of permanent settlers, followed by low-wage labourers, and a small proportion are living abroad undocumented (International Organization for Migration, 2013). Local and global imaginings of the diaspora remain deeply problematic: from demeaning conceptions of the 'Filipina bride' to storylines of exploited Filipino migrant workers, to benevolent but silencing labels such as the 'model migrant' assigned to longer-settled middle-class Filipino migrants. Beyond discursive archetypes, these categories speak to material positionings produced by larger webs of structural power and get played out in routine encounters of racism which exclude and marginalise Filipinos in the places that they call 'home'.

This book explores the ways in which Filipino migrants in Australia experience, understand and negotiate racism in their everyday lives. Filipino settlement to Australia is markedly framed by the country's ongoing nation-building project that continues to racialise immigrants and delineate the possibilities and limits of belonging to the national community. Moreover, this racial order intersects in complex ways with the racial regimes from Western colonisation of Philippine society, in which Filipino bodies and subjectivities have long been implicated even before the event of migration. I explore how historical, sociocultural, political and economic forces racially constitute these migrants and produce experiences of everyday racisms which criss-cross structural and quotidian, national and transnational modes of power and domination. There is, though, something even more profound in Melinda's story. The opening quote from our interview communicates a narrative about 'hard-working' Filipinos. It acts as a source of pride and respect – a representation about what it means to be 'Filipino' in Melinda's eyes. In particular, it is offset against a narrative constructed about privileged white Australians. While Melinda encourages Filipinos to directly confront prejudice and discrimination, coping with marginality and domination includes not only reordering the material world through practice and action but also representational processes of managing the self. This book also brings to light how racially devalued personal and collective identities are reworked in the face of powerlessness. It reveals the ways in which these individuals attempt to *resist* every day, often through unremarkable means, being subjugated and victimised.

Researching Filipino migrants in Sydney

In 2014, there were 225,110 Philippine-born persons living in Australia (Australian Bureau of Statistics, 2015). Despite being the fifth largest overseas-born group in the country, there is still little comprehensive research on Filipino migrants in the extensive scholarly study of immigrant settlement to Australia. There is also little to be found in the established area of research on international Filipino migration. Filipina women in Australia once occupied the centre of local scholarly enquiry in the advent of an influx of Filipinas migrating as spouses of Australian citizens in the 1980s and 1990s (Roces, 2003; Cuneen and Stubbs, 2003; Saroca, 2006; Khoo, 2001; Jackson, 1989; Woelz-Stirling et al., 1998; Robinson, 1996). This correlates with the broader international research agenda, where Filipina women figure significantly in the analysis of the feminisation of global labour migration. Research in these contexts has exposed the pervasive exploitation endured by low-wage and low-skilled Filipina migrants, such as domestic helpers, care workers or hostesses, particularly in Hong Kong, Singapore and the continents of the Middle East and Europe (Parrenas, 2001; Pratt, 1996; D. McKay, 2007; Gibson et al., 2001; San Juan Jr., 2001). Recent attention has been paid to the plight of male low-wage Filipino workers labouring as construction workers and seamen in the Middle East (S. McKay, 2007). In Australia, emergent research into Filipino labour migration has contributed knowledge about the experience of Filipina nurses and Filipino temporary workers (Siar, 2013; Hawthorne, 2001) and in the context of Filipino male experiences the identity politics among gay Filipino men have formed the basis of critical examination (Caluya, 2006). Aside from the 'mail order bride' controversy, however, Filipino migrants in Australia could be easily understood as a relatively 'unpanicked' community (Noble, 2009a) when canvassing the tendencies for academic enquiry to be conducted on groups who are most vulnerable or those who are at the centre of popular moral panics. Australia's Filipino immigrant demographics are most similar to that of America's – the majority are permanent settlers, a significant proportion has achieved middle-class status and the second generation is often considered well integrated.[2] However, North American scholarship is much more developed as imperial relations between the US and the Philippines have necessitated close scrutiny of Filipino settlement in America to reveal nuanced modes of neocolonial domination (Vergara, 2008; Espiritu, 2003; Bonus, 2000; Espana-Maram, 2006; Manalansan, 2003). I take encouragement from these exceptional works researching Filipino global migration and settlement to offer a closer look at the Filipino diaspora in this corner of the world.

The fieldwork for this book was carried out in Sydney, which is located in the east coast state of New South Wales (NSW) and is the most populous city in Australia. Almost half of the total population of Philippine-born immigrants in Australia reside in NSW and approximately 80 per cent of this number is concentrated throughout metropolitan Sydney (ABS, 2015). Between 2008 and 2012, I met and talked with Filipinos living and working across the vast suburban sprawl of the city. In particular, Sydney's 'Filipino heartland' is found in the locality of Blacktown, in the outer western suburbs (see Figures 2.1 to 2.4). I spent time observing and participating in Filipino community events and devoted countless hours at sites which Filipinos frequent for work and leisure, getting to know their day-to-day lives and routines. This was not so much unfamiliar terrain for me. I am a second-generation migrant Filipina and grew up in a suburb not too far from Blacktown, and I spent my childhood attending many Filipino community events with my family. Admittedly, this study was perhaps always a work in progress. For personal reasons, I have been interested in understanding the experience of immigrants and the phenomena of racism as a way to make sense of my own life lived in Australia, where I constantly confront the multitude of racialised positionings to which I am relegated – 'Filipino', 'Asian', 'Australian', 'Filipino-Australian', 'immigrant', 'non-white'. This has roused a political and theoretical interest in larger questions around race, migration, citizenship and nationhood, particularly in the context of a 'multicultural' society.

To be sure, many Filipinos I encountered are quite happy and content with their lives in Australia. Migrating has afforded most with a sense of economic security that the Philippines can no longer provide. For first-generation migrant Filipinos the sacrifices of migration have opened up even bigger opportunities for their children, although it is expensed by their own mobility. For others who migrated for love, settling in Australia has fulfilled the desire for a family. For those who migrated to join their kin, the anxieties of uprooting are well worth it in order to be reunited. For a growing number of newly arrived Filipinos, meanwhile, migration to Australia is just another stop in their multiple border crossings around the world for contracted labour, though there is a general sense that Australia is the land of the 'fair go'. Nonetheless, amid the steady hum of ordinary life, I found accumulated experiences of racism – signalling how these migrants can never take their migration or settlement for granted. From the numerous people I met and conversed with over the course of four years, I sat down with forty-five Filipino migrants for in-depth interviews who ranged from their late twenties to their early sixties, male and female, and are composed of first-generation migrants, second-generation migrant children and those newly arrived, often on temporary working visas. Their experiences are reconstructed here and demonstrate the subtleties of racial formations in lived contexts.

While my interviews probed into life histories, at the centre of my enquiry were questions specifically about encounters of racism and as well the means of coping with racism. This book, therefore, presents knowledge of racism and resistance that emerge from Filipino migrants themselves. I use 'experience' as sociological data to value individuals as interpretative actors who actively construct realities about their lives and the social world in which they are situated. My methodological approach is purposeful in the broader context in which these experiences are located. Racism in Australia, if not completely relegated to some bygone past, has become a topic of 'debatability' and it is a conversation which mutes the voices of those whose lives continue to be distressed by racism (Lentin, 2016). The experience of Filipino migrants detailed in this book respects the accounts from the marginalised and dominated as imperative to telling us about how racism might operate on the ground and its connection to larger racial structures.[3] In particular, the stories of racism I came across are not the violent or dramatic kind, but take the form of what Essed (1991) calls *everyday racism* – racism inscribed in taken-for-granted practices and experienced in the course of routine exchanges. Filipino migrants experience racism as mundane aggression, like bullying, harassment and intimidation, and also quiet hostility, like social distance, condescension or small acts of exclusion. These encounters occur in the everyday spaces they traverse and inhabit, such as the workplace, public spaces like shopping centres, restaurants, bars and sporting arenas, and even the private sphere involving social situations with friends. Such everyday racisms have tangible effects, like the denial of mobility because of being constantly passed over for promotions at work or having to limit one's movements to certain spaces. Moreover, it has affective penalties as the wear and tear of routine yet subtle racism can slowly eat away at one's dignity through being regularly made to feel uncomfortable, embarrassed, humiliated and rejected. Despite connotations of mundanity, these experiences signal acute systems of domination in everyday life.

Undertaking social enquiry among 'your own kind' is not as easy as some may think. Throughout the course of my research I discovered the difficulty that is defining a 'community'. For the most part, many Filipinos were welcoming of my interest in their lives and the issues 'we' were facing 'together'. In the beginning, admittedly, I struggled to intellectualise some things as 'issues' because they did not resonate instantly with my own life experience as a 'Filipino' in Australia. Having been an 'insider' by virtue of being 'Filipino' sometimes led me to miss the tiny details that make some lives different from my own, making me more of an outsider than I thought. On the other hand, the more I became immersed in people's lives, the more it became difficult to remove myself as an objective observer as I genuinely developed a sense of belonging to this 'community' like never before. I came to empathise with its pains and struggles, became angered by the different injustices and inequalities it endured, and also shared in its collective hopes and dreams. But again, on different occasions, my feelings of being completely absorbed were not always permitted. Some Filipinos I encountered expressed aversion to my investigation of the 'Filipino experience' of racism. This was not because they denied that racism existed or because the issue did not need attention. Some of them believed that I was not the person for this job. Not only am I middle-class with fluent English and a well-regarded education but also I am a light-skinned Filipina. I soon discovered that I represent to some Filipinos the racial (and class) system that produce some of their experiences of racialised marginalisation. For some of these migrants, while not denying my membership to the 'community', my preoccupation with the issue of racism was to them strange and perhaps even a little insulting. I was delving into a painful issue that they felt I knew little about.

I use these obstacles as important points of reflection throughout the book to capture the varied histories that make up Filipino settlement in Sydney and attempt to bring about an understanding of this migrant group in the most sincere and honest way. 'Identity' is never one-dimensional nor fixed and 'community' rarely homogenous. Race, class and gender overlap in intricate ways to shape the kinds of racisms experienced by different Filipino migrants and elicit varying styles of resistance. These categories also meet with other points of difference around religion, linguistic dialect, route of migration and migrant generation. In an endeavour to capture such intersections with some analytical depth, the main contents of this book are structured into four case studies. I explore the lives of aspirant middle-class Filipino professionals, working-class Filipinos labouring as cleaners and construction workers, Filipina women married to white Australian men, and young Filipino men struggling to succeed in some of Sydney's most disadvantaged neighbourhoods. These cases did not frame my research sample but have instead been selected from the breadth of data I collected, with the aim of interrogating thematically some of the textures of different lives carved out against forces of racism.

Matters of 'race', racism and anti-racism in everyday life

The mode of social analysis I employ to make sense of the experience of racism and the ways in which it is negotiated attempts to make some modest contributions to the larger political and theoretical contexts in which this study is situated.[4] Theorisations of 'race', racism and anti-racism are now fraught with contestation about definitions and methodological approaches and have become increasingly disconnected from the complexity of lived struggles against racism. Drawing on recent work that grounds the examination of racism in everyday life (see in particular Knowles, 2003; Alexander and Knowles, 2005; Essed, 1991; Wise and Velayutham, 2009), this book unpacks how the historical and structural dispersion of power along racial lines is translated as *lived* experiences of racism in social relationships and day-to-day interactions and which shape (and reshape) identities in the process. In tracing the operation of 'race', racism and anti-racism in the lives of Filipino migrants, I show how the 'everyday' is an important arena where we can uncover the intricate reproduction of racial ideologies and practices and open up critical interrogation of larger social systems that produce racialised inequality.

More importantly, it is a space that sheds light on how structures of domination are adapted or defied by ordinary individuals.

In part, this approach attempts to address some lingering questions about racism in Australia. The country's history is marked by British colonisation of the Indigenous population, invading in 1778, and setting out to eradicate the original inhabitants of the land. Settlement was further consolidated at Australia's Federation in 1901 through the establishment of what came to be known as the 'White Australia' policy – a suite of racially exclusive immigration controls that long restricted non-European settlement to the country and later, after large post-war immigration flows, extended to ideals of assimilation which required non-Anglo migrants to discard the distinctiveness of their ethnic identity and adopt the dominant Anglo-Saxon way of life. In particular, 'anti-Asian' sentiment has been a fixture of Australia's nation-building project as the country's geopolitical positioning in the Asian region has been a persistent source of racialised anxiety among the state and populace (Ang, 2000).[5] The contours of the country's nation-building project are complex and so I dedicate more time to detailing this history in Chapter 2 and link it with a discussion of the past and present situation of Filipino migration to Australia. I wish to signal from the outset, however, that the prolonged defence of a 'white nation' positions contemporary narratives of a 'multicultural Australia' as a decisive (and divisive) break in the framing of 'Australian identity'. Adopted by the state in the 1970s, in part as a strategy for ideological transformation, multiculturalism has enabled Australians to now reconceptualise race relations as progressing from an exclusionary 'White Australia' to a society predicated on the notion of 'unity in diversity' (Stratton and Ang, 1994). Indeed, while multiculturalism has deepened an appreciation for diversity in Australian society, at the same time, recognition continues to operate under an overarching set of dominant values where difference is welcomed but not unconditionally (Dunn et al., 2004). More precisely, in the new multicultural order, racism has come to be framed as a "*deviant* from the non-racist norm" (Ang and Stratton, 1998: 39). Today, when scholars, commentators and even 'victims' speak out about racism, they are commonly met with deflection, distancing and denial (Lentin, 2016: 34).

But that racism is now seen as something of an anomaly is a trend apparent in other Western multicultural democracies. Beyond the specificities of the Australian context exists a far-reaching debate as to how to understand contemporary processes and experiences of racism. A central starting point is the supposed 'end of "race"'. In the early twentieth century, the system of 'race' as a mode of human classification based on physiological and intellectual distinctions was scientifically discarded but also challenged by social movements from long-oppressed racial minorities. Today, 'culture' (customs, beliefs, traditions and ways of life) has become the principal marker of differentiation. The term 'ethnicity', for example, is more ubiquitously used in everyday life to describe old racial categories. On a formal political level, this culturalist discourse has provided the basis of multicultural policies in states like Britain, Canada and Australia to understand determinants of group membership and, more importantly, promote the coexistence of culturally distinct yet *equal* groups. The ideological shift has played a vital role in the transition from explicit regimes of racial domination to egalitarian modes of incorporating racial and ethnic minorities (Stratton and Ang, 1994). In the US, culturalist discourse finds its equivalence in 'colour-blind' policies that have ushered in proclamations of a 'post-racial' era (Bonilla-Silva, 2006). However, 'the end of race' has not led to 'the end of racism'. As Winant (1994: 987) states, "a significant consensus exists among scientists (natural and social), and humanists as well, that race lacks an objective basis. Yet the concept persists, as idea, as practice, as identity, and as social structure. Racism perseveres in these same ways."

Ultimately, the language of culture and ethnicity continues to be haunted by the history of 'race' (Balibar, 1991; Lentin, 2000). Articulations of racism are now rationalised around the insurmountability of cultural differences; only the subtlety of this domination is largely allowed to go unchecked in the mainstream (Essed, 1991). The 'cultural turn' has also produced structuralist critiques which, on the other hand, argue that racial disparity and racism are rooted in economic relations and not in distinctions of phenotype or culture nor questions related to recognition (Jakubowicz et al., 1984; Wilson, 1998; Miles, 2009). This has, however, led to simplistic definitions of integration that equate socio-economic mobility as a buffer against racism (Raj, 2003; Feagin and Sikes, 1994). Feminist accounts in cultural studies have attempted to counter reductionism to highlight the different positionalities of the racialised subject which produce varying experiences of social life (hooks, 1992; Crenshaw, 1991). But along with other forms of identity politics, such as the study of diasporic identities, it is criticised for being too fixed on the representational and detached from structure, practice and lived experience (Knowles, 2003). As Goldberg (2004: 211) reminds us, in refusing 'race', the "residues of racist arrangement and subordination . . . linger unaddressed and repressed in singularly stressing racial demise". The call to abandon 'race' prima facie involves the abandonment of "the word, the concept, the category, at most the categorising". More profoundly, however, it results in "forgetting, getting over, moving on, wiping away the terms of reference", leaving us with little memory and recollection of the "legacy, the roots, the scars of racism's histories, the weights of race" (Goldberg, 2004: 225).

In Australia, there is a general belief that "a 'white Australia' is no longer current in the national imaginary" (Ang and Stratton, 1998: 31). The racialised order that continues to structure material and symbolic inequalities is fervently denied as racism is increasingly ahistoricised. While 'old racisms', such as public displays of explicit racist abuse, are condemned, these incidents are cast as the actions of singular individuals (or extremists groups) and understood as isolated 'events' which disconnect these expressions from enduring racial structures (Lentin, 2016). Outside of framing difference as 'cultural' or 'economic' which supress the historical racialisations of immigrant subjects in the national space, the erasure of 'race' has silenced the claims of Indigenous Australians who particularly mobilise 'race' discourse to distinguish themselves from being just another 'ethnic minority' group (Cowlish and Morris, 1997). It has also homogenised the diversity of 'Anglo' subjects and produced a supressed fantasy of preserving white supremacy as a response to the sense of 'Anglo decline' that emerged in the pluralist narrative of multiculturalism (Ang and Stratton, 1998). It is a fantasy not only pursued by the seemingly 'backward' few who are assumed to lack the cosmopolitanism to embrace difference but can be unconsciously maintained by 'good white multiculturalists' whose discourse of tolerance entails a process of enrichment where the non-white Other awaits to be appreciated in a white-centred conception of multiculturalism (Hage, 1998).

One of the central analytical trajectories of this book is to (re)locate how 'race' operates in everyday encounters of racism and examine the manner in which it is constructed as a category of difference (or sameness) in lived contexts. To be sure, I agree that 'race' as a biological fact does not exist and acknowledge that re-engaging with 'race' discourse is sensitive terrain that risks reifying essentialised understandings of human difference (see Gilroy, 1988; Miles, 1996). But I argue that there remains a reality to the idea of race which needs to be better understood as it continues to take shape in structural orders, everyday life and identity articulations. Following the work of Knowles (2003 and 2010), the analysis in this book focuses on *how 'race' is made* in day-to-day life. What it means to be 'Filipino', to be 'Australian' and to be 'Filipino-Australian', I show, remain anchored to racial systems that are symbolically and materially ascribed on bodies and subjectivities across varying spatial and temporal contexts. 'Race' continues to operate through corporeality where the body endures as a tangible base through which power is inscribed. But racialising processes also transcend the surface differences of skin colour, hair and eyes. The spaces in which the body inhabits, works, plays – and how the body manoeuvres in these spaces – produce complex meanings of racialised difference (or sameness) which intersect with gender and class orders. Throughout the book, with respect to terminology, the concept of 'race' refers to historically complex and changing socially generated categories that hierarchise different types of bodies and capacities based on perceived physical and cultural distinctions (Omi and Winant, 2002). The related term 'racialisation' points to the processes that produce racial meanings (Barot and Bird, 2001). The notion of 'everyday racism' also has a particular definition, not merely referring to interpersonal encounters of racism but denoting racism at the intersection of micro and macro social fields that situates racial domination in both the active nature of human conduct and the activation of structural power (Essed, 1991).

I also extend a discussion of the acute manner in which racial regimes from Philippine society impact on the bodies and subjectivities of Filipino migrants even before migration. While my research began its life trying to understand how Filipinos negotiate the racial order of Australian society, talking with these migrants led me to realise the complex multi-routedness of racial ideologies and structures. 'Race' matters to Filipino migrants not only in the course of migration but also because the colonisation of the Philippines by Spain and America long ago racially constituted the 'Filipino' in violent and measured ways. I also detail this history in Chapter 2 to engage a more nuanced understanding of Filipino settlement in Australia that cannot be understood outside of the Philippines' history of colonisation. Whiteness, for example, is not an alien concept encountered only upon migration. It is a system within which they are implicated as a result of

European/Western subjugation of the Philippines and continues to be unsettled in the nation's postcolonial and globalising trajectory. In the migratory and diasporic context, the dynamics of this racial system interact with the racial order of Australian society, which is equally characterised by its own postcolonial condition. The notion of *transnational racial formations* is little explored in current racism and anti-racism theory, which limits understanding immigrant experiences of 'race', racism and racialisation within nation-state borders (Pugliese, 2007). Again, I am inspired by the work of scholars critically re-engaging with 'race' and who remind us of the ways in which local articulations of 'race' and racism are "tied to larger transnational projects of colonialism, imperialism, and empire" (Enakshi et al., 2005). Economic, cultural and political transnational processes, furthermore, shape expressions of identity, nationality and citizenship. I advance this paradigm in hope of disrupting constricted debates around assimilation and integration in Australia (and beyond) and give emphasis to bodies and subjectivities that cross transnational social fields.

Against systematic, multi-circuited and seemingly overwhelming forces, how then do individuals recover their agency? In many ways, the fight against racism is often seen as part of the 'routine' and the 'ordinary' for the Filipino migrants I met. Some certainly appeal to formal institutional aids, such as anti-discrimination laws and tribunals, especially in the workplace, as a means of redress. More significantly, however, routine racism is managed by accumulating habits and orientations that negotiate racialised exclusion and repair spoiled identities. Studies have traditionally focused on anti-racism deployed by governments, international human rights institutions and grass-roots organisations, through policy, laws and campaigns (see Pollock, 2008; Hollinsworth, 2004; Bonnett, 2000). These formal organised projects address structural formations of power through a re-education of society, targeting institutions of socialisation like schools and the media, and attempting to transform law enforcement and the allocation of resources and services (Lentin, 2004). While institutional responses are critical to combatting racism, outside of this arena, ordinary people engage in their own struggles for equality and respect. My respondents' stories reveal a range of material resources and rhetorical devices from which they draw to position and reposition themselves in the world. Everyday racism is negotiated across different temporal and spatial contexts and through varying identity struggles. For example, depending on the intersections of race, gender and class, degrees of equality can be achieved through socio-economic mobility, including intergenerational and transnational mobility, rights can be reclaimed by using legal avenues of redress, esteem recuperated by upholding moral ground, or the internalisation of racial stereotypes can be resisted through embodied protest that engages with popular cultural symbols.

Recent research has deployed the term *everyday anti-racism* to broadly describe how individuals respond to racism in their day-to-day lives. At the simplest level, everyday anti-racism is action that addresses racism experienced in micro spheres in interpersonal and/or individual contexts and often separated from formal institutional action. This can come in the form of victims confronting racism (Lamont and Fleming, 2005) or witnesses speaking out against racism in routine encounters

(Pederson et al., 2005; and Pedersen et al., 2011). Aestheticised commodities found in popular culture that challenge racism, such as forms of music, youth cultures and media, have also been listed in the inventory of everyday anti-racism (Bonnett, 2000), along with the varying ways 'victims' of racism reposition their identities to counter racist stereotypes (Lamont et al., 2002; Lamont and Askartova, 2002; Fleming et al., 2012). Following the work of Lamont, I examine the 'cultural supply' from which my respondents draw to respond to racism.[6] This includes material or symbolic resources used to counter stigmatisation and also the rhetorical devices employed to understand subjective positionings (Lamont and Mizrachi, 2012: 370). Such everyday resistance against racism, in the tradition of writers like Scott (1990), Abu-Lughod (1990) and de Certeau (1980), is understood as reflecting and reconfiguring larger ideological and structural forces. I hope to show that domination and resistance, in the realm of everyday life, have important things to teach us about the complex operation of power from 'above' and 'below'.

Outline of the book

I begin in Chapter 2 by detailing the histories of the 'Filipino'. I outline the process of European/Western colonialism and imperialism in the Philippines that sees racialised domination take root in Filipino lives before migration and is further complexified in the diasporic and transnational context. I then specify the history of Filipino migration to Australia set against the state's unfinished racialised nationhood formation and its particular struggle with its geopolitical positioning in the Asian region. I conclude with a discursive analysis of local and global representations of the 'Filipino' in Australia and beyond. This chapter sets the scene for the kinds of racial interpellations that Filipino migrants endure and that compel the struggle for resistance and recognition.

In Chapter 3, I commence the analysis of my empirical case studies with the experience of middle-class Filipino migrants in Sydney. Here, I unpack the concept of whiteness as central to the organisation of racialised bodies in Australian society. I focus in particular on the operation of middle-class whiteness and examine how Filipino middle class professionals negotiate this racialising force through socio-economic mobility, consumption practices and middle-class cultural capital. I explore how a status of 'honorary whiteness' can be accumulated to distance middle-class Filipinos from being an othered subject and draw attention to the complex hierarchies of power within and across migrant groups in a multicultural order. But 'honorary whiteness' fundamentally entails conditional respect and the chapter details the moments of everyday racism when such recognition is revoked or threatened. Further, I examine how negotiating whiteness also takes root in Philippine racial systems shaped by the legacies of colonisation.

Chapter 4 speaks to the chapter before it and provides a comparative analysis of Filipino working-class stories. While the middle class achieves levels of recognition through social mobility, Filipinos working as cleaners, construction and factory workers are, in comparison, treated as subordinate racialised labour and encounter everyday racisms which attempt to 'keep them in their place' at the bottom of the social and economic ladder. I also expand on how middle-class strategies of coping with racism impact on working-class Filipinos, who must also negotiate the intra-ethnic othering carried out against them by their more economically mobile counterparts. But the working class are far from being helpless 'victims'. They use formal systems of redress and discourses of morality but also engage in transnationalising their cultural and economic capital.

In Chapter 5, I revisit the experience of Filipina women married to white Australian spouses, which is the most developed area of research on Filipino migration to Australia. Studies have mainly focused on discursive and textual representations of the Filipina 'marriage migrant', and so I turn to the lived everyday racism encountered by Filipina women in my study who are married to white Australians. The discussion of racism and resistance in this chapter shifts its focus from public domains, like the workplace, to the private spheres of the home, marriage and family. Specifically, I examine how the 'mail order bride' stereotype is anchored by racialised norms around love and intimacy. Filipina women who marry older Australian men for economic security or agree to being 'housewives' are seen as practicing 'illegitimate' modes of love. I explore how these women rewrite their spoiled identities by reclaiming sensibilities of love and care as a resource for anti-racism.

In Chapter 6, I turn my focus on the intersection of race and masculinity, which is little explored in the Filipino diasporic context, by looking at the experience of young Filipino men interviewed in my research. Specifically, I share the sporting experiences of young Filipinos who play basketball in Sydney's disadvantaged outer suburbs and who report everyday racism that draws on paradoxical stereotypes of feminised and uncivil 'Asian masculinity'. I extend a discussion of the racialising force of hegemonic whiteness into the sporting arena to examine how male Filipino bodies are disciplined and subjugated on the basketball court and in other everyday spaces. But instead of avoiding their stigmatised bodies, these young men confront racism by directly engaging with their corporeality through the playing style of 'street ball' as a mode of embodied resistance that attempts to loosen the grip of whiteness.

Engaging with the quandary of racism compels reflection on the personal and political. In the final concluding chapter, I contemplate what quotidian experiences of racism and resistance might imply for broader racism theory and anti-racism politics. I raise some questions and draw attention to the possibilities around what private individual struggles could mean for the public sphere. More importantly, I reflect on what kind of value this book might have to the Filipino migrants who shared their stories with me. I re-emphasise that the lives laid bare in these pages endeavor to give voice to some of the everyday struggles and victories experienced in the Filipino diaspora, which are too often silenced and denied.

Notes

1 Filipino is the general term to describe both males and females from the geographical location of the Philippines. The term 'Filipina' is the specific term for females and 'Filipino' is for males. In this book, I use the general term 'Filipino' when speaking across

genders but will use 'Filipina' and 'Filipino' when distinguishing between gendered experiences. But I also deploy the term 'Filipino' with inverted commas when I refer to the more complex discursive construct of this collective identity.
2 In Sydney, where the fieldwork presented in this book is based, much of the population displays this middle-class stability. According to the 2011 Census, 21 per cent of Filipinos in Sydney work in the professional sector and a further 7 per cent are employed in managerial professional occupations. Twenty-nine per cent of the population indicated earning an individual weekly income between $1,000 and $1,999 (considered in the top three percentile bands), and a further 5 per cent earning in the highest income bracket ($2,000 or more a week). The majority of the population have also successfully completed a secondary school education (73.8 per cent), with a significant number having some form of tertiary qualification – 61 per cent having a bachelor degree. The socio-economic mobility promised by the second generation – high rates of educational attainment and proficiency in English – is taken as an even stronger indication of the continuing middle-class stability of Filipino migrants.
3 'Folk' understanding of racism is often not as ordinary as we might assume; for those who experience racism throughout their life, they generate complex ways of evaluating racism based on negotiated systems of knowledge. Essed (1991) suggests that there are two forms of knowledge that make up ordinary people's systems of understanding racism in everyday life. The first is *situational knowledge* of acceptable behaviour in given situations learnt through accumulated experiences of the same contexts and also derived from the media and education. The other form is *general knowledge of racism* – a cognitive system of assessing racism through accumulated experiences of racial episodes. One continues to test and modify and rebuild this system upon new experiences.
4 There are, therefore, two intersecting voices that can be heard in this book. I communicate my respondents' 'understanding' of their experiences and my own 'Understanding' of their accounts (Essed, 1991). The former refers to folk comprehension while the latter is 'Understanding' in a sociological sense, where I have grasped the data against wider sociological and historical reading around the issues. In this book, neither is privileged, but they work together to describe the operation of racism and the struggle against it in day-to-day life.
5 Throughout the book I deploy the term 'Asia' in two ways. Asia without the inverted commas refers to the geographically bounded region and 'Asia' with inverted commas refers to the discursive category of the peoples who originate from this region.
6 Lamont's extensive empirical work is focused on the experience of African American workers in the US and North African immigrants in France (Lamont et al., 2002; Lamont and Fleming, 2005; Lamont and Askartova, 2002; Fleming et al., 2012). Her recent collaborations illuminate cross-cultural comparisons of migrant and minority responses to racism in the context of Israel, Brazil, Sweden and Canada. For the latter see 'Special Issue: Responses to Stigmatisation in Comparative Perspectives: Brazil, Canada, France, South Africa, Sweden and the United States', *Ethnic and Racial Studies*, Vol. 35, No. 3, 2012.

References

Abu-Lughod, L. (1990) 'The romance of resistance: Tracing transformations of power through Bedouin women', *American Ethnologist*, vol. 17, no. 1, pp. 41–55.
Alexander, C. and Knowles, C. (2005) 'Introduction', in Alexander, C. and Knowles, C. (eds.), *Making Race Matter: Bodies, Space and Identity*, New York: Palgrave Macmillan, pp. 1–16.
Ang, I. (2000) 'Introduction: Alter/Asian cultural interventions for 21st century Australia', in Ang, I., Chalmers, S., Law, L. and Thomas, M. (eds.), *Alter/Asians: Australian Identities in Art, Media and Popular Culture*, Annandale: Pluto Press, pp. xiii–xxx.

Ang, I. and Stratton, J. (1998) 'Multiculturalism in crisis: The new politics of race and national identity in Australia', *Canadian Journal of Cultural Studies*, vol. 2, pp. 22–41.

Australian Bureau of Statistics. (2015) *Migration: Australia, 2014–15*, Cat. No. 3412.0, ABS, Canberra.

Balibar, E. (1991) 'Is there a neo-racism?', in Balibar, E. and Wallerstein, I. (eds.), *Race, Nation, Class: Ambiguous Identities*, London: Verso, pp. 17–28.

Barot, R. and Bird, J. (2001) 'Racialisation: The genealogy and critique of a concept', *Ethnic and Racial Studies*, vol. 24, no. 4, pp. 601–18.

Bonilla-Silva, E. (2006) *Racism without Racists: Color-Blind Racism and the Persistence of Racial Inequality in the United States*, Lanham, MD: Rowman & Littlefield.

Bonnett, A. (2000) *Antiracism*, London: Routledge.

Bonus, R. (2000) *Locating Filipino Americans: Ethnicity and the Cultural Politics of Space*, Philadelphia: Temple University Press.

Caluya, G. (2006) 'The (gay) scene of racism: Face, shame and gay Asian males', *Australian Critical Race and Whiteness Studies Association E-Journal*, vol. 2, no. 2.

Cowlish, G. and Morris, B. (1997) *Race Matters: Indigenous Australians and Our Society*, Canberra: Aboriginal Studies Press.

Crenshaw, K. (1991) 'Mapping the margins: Intersectionality, identity politics, and violence against women of colour', *Stanford Law Review*, vol. 43, no. 6, pp. 1241–99.

Cuneen, C. and Stubbs, J. (2003) 'Fantasy islands: Desire, race and violence', in Tomsen, S. and Donaldson, M. (eds.), *Male Trouble: Looking at Australian Masculinities*, Victoria: Pluto Press, p. 69.

de Certeau, M. (1980) 'On the oppositional practices of everyday life', *Social Text*, vol. 3, pp. 3–43.

Du Bois, W.E.B. (1903/1969) *The Souls of Black Folk*, New York: New American Library.

Dunn, K., Forrest, J., Burnley, I. and McDonald, A. (2004) 'Constructing racism in Australia', *Australian Journal of Social Issues*, vol. 39, no. 4, pp. 409–30.

Enakshi, D., Razack, N. and Warner, J. (2005) 'Race, racism and empire: Reflections on Canada', *Social Justice*, vol. 32, no. 4, www.socialjusticejournal.org/SJEdits/102Edit.html accessed 7 July 2016.

Espana-Maram, L. (2006) *Creating Masculinity in Los Angeles's Little Manila: Working Class Filipinos and Popular Culture, 1920s–1950s*, New York: Columbia University Press.

Espiritu, Y.L. (2003) *Home Bound: Filipino American Lives across Cultures, Communities, and Countries*, Berkeley: University of California Press.

Essed, P. (1991) *Understanding Everyday Racism: An Interdisciplinary Theory*, Newbury Park: SAGE.

Feagin, J. and Sikes, M. (1994) *Living with Racism: The Black Middle-Class Experience*, Boston: Beacon Press.

Fleming, C., Lamont, M. and Welburn, M. (2012) 'African Americans respond to stigmatisation: The meanings and salience of confronting, deflecting conflict, educating the ignorant and managing the self', *Ethnic and Racial Studies*, vol. 35, no. 3, pp. 400–17.

Gibson, K., Law, L. and Mckay, D. (2001) 'Beyond heroes and victims: Filipina contract migrants, economic activism and class transformations', *International Feminist Journal of Politics*, vol. 3, no. 3, pp. 365–86.

Gilroy, P. (1998) 'Race ends here', *Ethnic and Racial Studies*, vol. 21, no. 5, pp. 838–47.

Goldberg, D. (2004) 'The end(s) of race', *Postcolonial Studies*, vol. 7, no. 2, pp. 211–30.

Hage, G. (1998) *White Nation: Fantasies of White Supremacy in a Multicultural Society*, New York: Routledge.

Hawthorne, L. (2001) 'The globalisation of the nursing workforce: Barriers confronting overseas qualified nurses in Australia', *Nursing Inquiry*, vol. 8, no. 4, pp. 213–29.

Hollinsworth, D. (2004) *Race and Racism in Australia*, Victoria: Thomson Press.

hooks, b. (1992) *Black Looks: Race and Representation*, Boston: South End Press.

International Organization for Migration. (2013) *Country Migration Report: The Philippines 2013*, Manila: International Organisation for Migration.

Jackson, R.T. (1989) 'Filipino migration to Australia: The image and a geographer's dissent', *Australian Geographical Studies*, vol. 27, no. 2, pp. 170–81.

Jakubowicz, A., Morrissey, M. and Palser, J. (1984) *Ethnicity, Class and Social Policy in Australia*, SWRC Reports and Proceedings, No. 46, University of New South Wales.

Khoo, S. (2001) 'The context of spouse migration to Australia', *International Migration*, vol. 39, no. 1, pp. 111–31.

Knowles, C. (2003) *Race and Social Analysis*, London: SAGE.

Knowles, C. (2010) *Theorising Race and Ethnicity: Contemporary Paradigms and Perspectives*, London: in SAGE Handbook of Race and Ethnic Studies, SAGE.

Lamont, M. and Askartova, S. (2002) 'Ordinary cosmopolitanisms: Strategies for bridging racial boundaries among working class men', *Theory, Culture and Society*, vol. 19, no. 4, pp. 1–25.

Lamont, M. and Fleming, C. (2005) 'Everyday antiracism: Competence and religion in the cultural repertoires of the African American Elite', *Du Bois Review*, vol. 2, no. 1, pp. 29–43.

Lamont, M. and Mizrachi, N. (2012) 'Ordinary people doing extraordinary things: Responses to stigmatisation in comparative perspective', *Ethnic and Racial Studies*, vol. 35, no. 3, pp. 365–81.

Lamont, M., Morning, A. and Mooney, M. (2002) 'Particular universalisms: North African migrants respond to French racism', *Ethnic and Racial Studies*, vol. 25, no. 3, pp. 390–414.

Lentin, A. (2000) '"Race", racism and antiracism: Challenging contemporary classifications', *Social Identities*, vol. 6, no. 1, pp. 91–106.

Lentin, A. (2004) 'Racial states, antiracist responses: Picking holes in "culture" and "human rights"', *European Journal of Social Theory*, vol. 7, no. 4, pp. 427–43.

Lentin, A. (2016) 'Racism in public or public racism: Doing anti-racism in "post-racial" times', *Ethnic and Racial Studies*, vol. 39, no. 1, pp. 33–48.

Manalansan Jr., M.F. (2003) *Global Divas: Filipino Gay Men in the Diaspora*, Durham: Duke University Press.

McKay, D. (2007) 'Sending dollars shows feelings: Emotions and economies in Filipino migration', *Mobilities*, vol. 2, no. 2, pp. 175–94.

McKay, S. (2007) 'Filipino seamen: Constructing masculinities in an ethnic labour niche', *Journal of Ethnic and Migration Studies*, vol. 33, no. 4, pp. 617–33.

Miles, R. (1996) 'Does "race" matter? Transatlantic perspectives on racism after race relations', in Amitalia, V. and Knowles, C. (eds.), *Resituating Identities: The Politics of Race, Ethnicity and Culture*, Peterborough: Broadview Press, pp. 26–46.

Miles, R. (2009) 'Apropos the idea of "race" again', in Solomos, J. and Back, L. (eds.), *Theories of Race and Racism: A Reader*, London: Routledge, pp. 125–38.

Omi, M and Winant, H. (2002) 'Racial formation', in Goldberg, D. and Essed, P. (eds.), *Race Critical Theories*, Oxford: Blackwell, pp. 123–145.

Parrenas, R. (2001) *Servants of Globalisation: Women, Migration and Domestic Work*, Stanford, CA: Stanford University Press.

Pedersen, A., Paradies, Y., Hartley, L. and Dunn, K. (2011) 'Bystander anti-prejudice: Cross-cultural education, links with positivity towards cultural "out-groups" and preparedness to speak out', *Journal of Pacific Rim Psychology*, vol. 5, no. 1, pp. 19–30.

Pederson, A., Walker, I. and Wise, M. (2005) '"Talk Does Not Cook Rice": Beyond anti-racism rhetoric to strategies for social action', *Australian Psychologist*, vol. 40, no. 1, pp. 20–31.

Pollock, M. (2008) 'Introduction: Defining everyday anti-racism', in Pollock, M. (ed.), *Everyday Antiracism: Getting Real about Race in School*, New York: The New Press p. 1.

Pratt, G. (1996) 'Inscribing domestic work on Filipina bodies', in Nast, H. and Pile, S. (eds.), *Places through the Body*, London: Routledge, pp. 283–304.

Pugliese, J. (2007) 'White historicide and the returns of the Souths to the South', *Australian Humanities Review*, no. 42.

Raj, D. (2003) *Where Are You from? Middle Class Migrants in the Modern World*, Berkeley: University of California Press.

Robinson, K. (1996) 'Of mail order brides and "Boy's Own" tales: Representations of Asian-Australian marriages', *Feminist Review*, vol. 52, pp. 53–68.

Roces, M. (2003) 'Sisterhood is local: Filipino women in Mount Isa', in Roces M. and Piper N. (eds.), *Wife or Worker? Asian Women and Migration*, edn. Lanham, MD: First, Rowman & Littlefield, pp. 73–100.

San Juan Jr., E. (2001) 'Interrogating transmigrancy, remapping diaspora: The globalisation of labouring Filipinos/as', *Discourse*, vol. 23, no. 3, p. 52.

Saroca, N. (2006) 'Filipino women, migration, and violence in Australia: Lived reality and media image', *Kasarinlan: Philippine Journal of Third World Studies*, vol. 21, no. 1, pp. 75–110.

Scott, J.C. (1990) *Domination and the Arts of Resistance: Hidden Transcripts*, New Haven: Yale University Press.

Siar, S.V. (2013) From highly skilled to low skilled: Revisiting the deskilling of migrant labour. *Philippine Institute for Development Studies Discussion Paper Series*, (2013–30), Philippine Institute for Development Studies, Manila, Philippines.

Stratton, J. and Ang, I. (1994) 'Multicultural imagined communities: Cultural difference and national identity in Australia and the USA', *Continuum: The Australian Journal of Media and Culture*, vol. 8, no. 2.

Vergara Jr., B.M. (2008) *Pinoy Capital: The Filipino Nation in Daly City*, Philadelphia: Temple Press.

Wilson, W.J. (1998) *The Declining Significance of Race: Blacks and Changing American Institutions*, Chicago: University of Chicago.

Winant, H. (1994) *Racial Conditions*, Minneapolis: University of Minnesota Press.

Wise, A. and Velayutham, S. (2009) *Everyday Multiculturalism*, Houndsmill, England: Palgrave Macmillan.

Woelz-Stirling, N., Kelaher, M. and Manderson, L. (1998) 'Power and politics of abuse: Rethinking violence in Filipina-Australian marriages', *Health Care for Women International*, vol. 19, no. 4, pp. 289–301.

2 Histories of the 'Filipino' in Australia and beyond

Historical, structural and discursive processes underlie the experience of everyday racism. In this chapter, I begin with a discussion of Philippine colonisation and highlight the forces that racially interpellated the 'Filipino' in early Philippine history. I move on to trace the stages of Filipino migration to Australia and contextualise their settlement against the country's racialised project of nationhood formation. Such intersecting histories are crucial to exploring meanings ascribed to the 'Filipino' – constituted in varying ways throughout the Philippines' history of subjugation and fight for freedom and in the diasporic contexts in which millions of Filipino migrants around the world now live. I conclude with an analysis of contemporary popular representations of Filipino migrants in Australia that speak to other globally circulating discourses on Filipinos. In tracing the imaginings of the 'Filipino', this chapter shows how 'race' operates as "fluid, unstable and de-centred . . . constantly being transformed by political conflict, (shaping) the individual psyche . . . and furnishing an irreducible component of collective identity and social structures" (Winant, 1994: 54). These material and discursive processes display what Omi and Winant (2002) call racial formations – the socio-historical construction of racial systems and meanings. Such multi-routed transnational circuits filter down into processes of everyday race-making (Knowles, 2003), shaping lived experiences of racism but also subsequent identity negotiations that challenge and rework material and subjective positionalities in new and complex ways.

"Three centuries in a Catholic convent and fifty years in Hollywood": the early history of the 'Filipino'

The Republic of the Philippines is located in South-East Asia.[1] Who we call 'Filipinos' today are said to be principally made up of descendants of the Malayo-Polynesian racial group; early Chinese traders who arrived in the Spanish colonial period; and also Spanish conquistadores who colonised the country for three centuries. The indigenous population, known as Negritos, are mainly descendants of ancient Malaysian, Borneo and Sumatra tribes and are today represented by indigenous groups, like the Aeta, who live in isolated parts of mainland Luzon. There is immense diversity in the regional languages spoken throughout the Philippines, which is a primary classificatory system among Filipinos.[2] Presently, as a remnant of American imperialism, English sits beside Filipino as one of the co-national languages. Filipino is primarily based on Tagalog, which is the dialect with the most borrowings from the Spanish language.

The earliest contact Spain had with the archipelago was through Portuguese explorer Ferdinand Magellan (flying under the Spanish flag), who discovered the islands in 1521 in an attempt to establish influence in the roaring spice trade. It was not until 1543, however, that Spain took "conceptual possession" of the territory and named it *las islas Filipinas* after King Philip II of Spain and in 1565 set up the first colonial settlement in Cebu in the country's south (Rafael, 2000: 5). The islands proved to have inferior spices and instead the 'galleon trade' emerged, allowing Spain to use the Philippines as a way to acquire Chinese products, like silks, celadon and porcelain, to re-export back to the Spanish in Mexico. By the eighteenth century, the galleon trade transformed Manila into one of the most celebrated cities of the world (Karnow, 1989: 57). This period saw the influx of Chinese brokers, who grew in population and would later have a foothold over the Philippine economy in spite of being stigmatised as foreigners (Karnow, 1989: 62). Meanwhile, native *indios* were essentially seen as labour, captured and exploited as slaves by conquistadores despite the king illegalising slavery in Spain. *Indios* were eventually recruited into the 'polo system' of legalised forced labour and worked in quarries, gold mines, ship building, artillery casting and even in the provision of 'personal services' to officials and clergymen (Tubangui et al., 1982: 72–74).

The Spanish were selective in introducing Spanish cultural practices and institutions to native Philippine society. The first universities in the country were set up as training grounds for future Spanish clergy and refused to admit natives as education was not a key dimension to Spain's colonial endeavour and as the Spanish feared that *indios* would rebel. As a result, the colonised subjects of the Philippines – unlike the natives oppressed in Latin America by Spain – were the only Spanish colony who did not become Spanish speakers. The *enconmienda* system was also implemented to distribute land as rewards to Spanish bureaucrats and troops and, in the early nineteenth century, evolved into a *hacienda* system, which redistributed land as vast estates for cash crop production. *Indios* were left to become tenants and labourers of land owned by Spanish officials and religious orders and became another means for the Spanish to exploit the native population. The legacy of these land policies live on today, wherein the most profitable land ownership has been inherited by Filipinos from mestizo ancestry, who retain most of the country's political, economic and social power (Karnow, 1989). Filipino mestizos are those from Filipino-Spanish or Filipino-Chinese ancestry and came to dominate the upper class of Philippine society through their land ownership, business entrepreneurism and esteemed education.[3] Distinct in its occupation of the islands was also the manner in which its conquerors largely closed off the Philippines from foreign trade and investment until the nineteenth century, in turn crippling the growth of the colonial economy. Instead, the manner in which Spain wished to assimilate its colonised subjects was through Christianity. Catholic missionaries were given rule on the islands to evangelise the *indios* (Rafael, 2000; Perdon, 1998; Karnow, 1989) and by the end of the sixteenth century about half the conquered territory had been baptised and the Philippines soon became known as the only Christian nation in Asia (Tubangui et al., 1982). To this day, the Catholic Church exercises its influence in the daily lives of Filipinos and also on the Philippine government. Further, this Christian background remains intact across the global diaspora, including among Filipinos in Australia, who are predominantly of Roman Catholic or Christian faith.

Espiritu (2003: 52) reminds us that there are "intimate connections between racialism and colonialism", in that justifying domination is achieved "in part through racial modes of differentiation". In the Spanish period, a complex racial hierarchy was established to "distinguish the relationship of the colony's inhabitants to the motherland" (Rafael, 2000: 7). Native *indios* were the lowest on the racial ladder and perceived by the Spanish as a primitive 'race'. However, once they converted to Christianity, *indios* sat above un-Christianised Negritos or Islamised Moros from the south. Catholicism, therefore, was a primary marker of civilisation for the Spanish colonisers. The Chinese migrants – or 'Sangleys' as they were commonly referred to – were also seen as lesser equals of the Spanish settlers because of their cultural difference despite being valued for their contribution to the colonial economy. These Chinese traders were allowed to stay in the country and engage in economic transactions only if they converted to Christianity and married a native *indio* woman. The Spanish were so intent on distinguishing their position of power that differences were also made among the settlers themselves. The name 'Filipino' emerged as a reference to sons and daughters born in the Philippines to Spanish settlers and was a way to create a distance between the Spanish in or from the motherland and those who occupied the Spanish colony of the Philippines (Rafael, 2000). Spaniards in the homeland commonly associated being 'Filipino' with primitive *indios* because the colonies were seen as the "dumping ground for misfits and dregs of Spanish society" (Quimpo, 2003: 5). But despite not being seen as equals with settlers born in Spain, Filipinos enjoyed a more privileged position compared to *indios* or Chinese migrants and also sat above the wealthy mestizos of mixed *indio*-Spanish or *indio*-Chinese blood. Mestizos may have had wealth; however, any drop of *indio* blood was still considered a 'blemished birth' by the Spaniards.

Hence, the 'Filipino' of the colonial period was not the 'Filipino' we have come to know now. The term was rearticulated to include all inhabitants of the Philippines only in the 1900s by the educated mestizo elite, who were instrumental in the Philippine Revolution. After solidifying their economic status in the colonial society, mestizos took on the name of 'Filipino' as their own. Led by national hero Jose Rizal, the revolutionaries unified all of the country's colonised subjects as 'Filipinos' in the fight for equal status. While this moment is generally celebrated as the emergence of *indio* national consciousness, contemporary Philippine nationalists and postcolonial theorists remind us that the modern-day identification of 'Filipino' is rooted in a history of identification with "the oppressor, the coloniser, the white man" because, in its emergence, the category of 'Filipino' referred to a Philippine-born Spaniard (Quimpo, 2003: 5). This is further evidenced by the desire among the mestizo elite to accomplish Filipino integration into Spanish society but *not* an overthrow of its colonisers. And so, even in its early history, conceiving of the 'Filipino' or 'a Filipino people' was driven by the more privileged inhabitants of the land.

While identification as 'one Filipino nation' strengthened among mestizos and those formerly known as *indios* throughout the Philippine Revolution, the search for independence did not end with the overthrow of Spanish colonisers. As US forces helped Filipino rebels defeat Spanish armies, sovereignty was transferred from the Spanish to Americans in the 1900s and saw the Philippines and Filipinos being fashioned by another power. At the height of its imperialistic era, America took interest in the Philippines, seeing it as a "source of raw materials, a market for American goods, a strategic naval base, and as the Spanish had done nearly three and half centuries earlier, a gateway to China" (Tubangui et al., 1982: 110). Colonisation, however, was again something beyond economic expansion but also a subject-constituting project. Just as the Spanish attempted to mould native Filipinos in their own Catholic image, the US aimed to civilise the Philippines into its own Western reflection.

Unlike Spanish conquistadores, who essentially desired to distinguish the *indios* as 'different' from themselves through discriminatory practices, the US strongly aimed for the assimilation of Filipinos into a Western system. US president William McKinley proceeded with a policy of *benevolent assimilation*, which promoted to the Filipino people that the US did not come as invaders or conquerors but as friends and instilled the belief that US occupation would restore the rights and freedom of Filipinos. US imperialism would 'better' the society through Americanisation of its government, schools and public systems.[4] This benevolent assimilation was, however, essentially underscored by the racist assumption that Filipino people were incapable of self-government (Espiritu, 2003; Rafael, 2000; Bonus, 2000). Historical analysis indicates that Filipinos were often characterised as "children" to buttress the US's civilising efforts and rationalise the "power of 'civilised' white men, who shouldered the 'white man's burden' of protecting the weak" (Espiritu, 2003: 50). Consequently, Filipinos were positioned as subordinate 'wards of the state'. The first US census of the Philippines became a way to 'recode' race and divided inhabitants of the Philippines into language groups, types of citizenship, locations of birth and a graduation of five skin colours from 'white' to 'black' (Rafael, 2000: 9). Moreover, "official and popular discourse racialised Filipinos as less than human, portraying them as savages, rapists, uncivilised beings, and even as dogs and monkeys" (Espiritu, 2003: 51).

Back in the US mainland, images of Filipinos – who became popularly known as America's 'little brown brothers' – depicted their inferiority in newspapers, books and museums as 'tree-dwellers' or 'dog-eaters' (Espiritu, 2003: 58). Despite being a 'brown brother', state legislations and policies in 1917 actively discriminated against Filipino migrants in the US, where they were refused citizenship and denied the right to vote, establish businesses, hold any office and own property. They were, instead, classified as 'US nationals', which allowed them to travel freely in the country to work (Espiritu, 2003: 60). Filipinos, in turn, became a source of cheap labour to bolster the US economy but were not granted the recognition of US citizenship. Espiritu (2003: 47) has described this process as *differential inclusion* "whereby a group of people is deemed integral to the nation's economy, culture, identity and power – but integral only or precisely because of their designated subordinate standing". Not surprisingly, the granting of independence to the Philippines by the Americans in 1934 was not a decision based on the view that Filipinos were finally capable of self-rule but a decision based on certain economic interests in the US, such as local farmers and producers who wanted to keep out Philippine imports like sugar and also as a result of labour unions who desired to restrict Filipino migration into America (Tubangui et al., 1982; Schirmer and Shalom, 1983). Jenkins (2003) argues that the granting of independence was a move to shift formal dependency to an informal dependency on the US and therefore moving the Philippines on to a neocolonial status.[5]

Fervent nationalist Constantino (1976: 5) sees colonisation as ultimately "undermin[ing] the efforts of Filipinos to develop a highly liberated national consciousness". He calls Filipinos a "confused people" who in their search for identity "look to an idealised indigenous past and to the Hispanicised culture of their colonial forbears and who in their desire to solve the problems of the present dream of a future anchored on western concepts and values" (Constantino, 1976: 5). In a posthumous essay published two years after he was assassinated in 1983, the late national hero and Marcos's political rival Benigno 'Ninoy' Aquino similarly described Filipinos as being "bewildered" about their identity: "They are an Asian people not Asian in the eyes of their fellow Asians and not Western in the eyes of the West" (Aquino, 1985). Despite nationalistic revolutions – from the original revolt in 1896 to the one that rallied for independence from America in the 1930s and to the more recent People Power movements of 1986 and 2001 – laying the ghosts of colonialism to rest has had "uneven success and unsettling effects" (Rafael, 2000: 9). The country's history of colonisation is now entwined with contemporary trajectories of globalisation that propel Filipinos into volatile circuits of international migration and, further, into the highly exclusionary racial orders of the societies that receive them. Since the 1970s, the country has witnessed phenomenal rates of outmigration of Filipinos as permanent settlers and temporary migrant workers who live and labour in every corner of the globe (Tyner, 2009). The ways in which the 'Filipino' is imagined and constituted are further complicated and continue to be underscored by the symbolic and material violence of racialisation that is exercised by those with the most power.

From Manila men to the 'mail order bride', from the middle class to the migrant worker: Filipino migration to Australia

Australia's history is equally marked by the process of colonisation and a subsequent nation-building endeavour. European explorers came across Australia as an unknown southern land as early as the 1600s. In 1778, it was invaded by British lieutenant Captain James Cook, who claimed the east coast under instruction from

King George III of England with aims of establishing a penal colony. Attempts to settle the territory began with efforts to eradicate the Indigenous population. Direct and violent conflict began immediately and disease-related deaths (brought by the British) saw the Indigenous population almost wiped out in the early days of invasion. A long violent period ensued in the battle for the frontier and eventually led to the institutionalisation of the surviving Indigenous population. It is important to acknowledge that the manner in which the Australian state and populace have managed other non-white subjects takes root in Indigenous dispossession. In the discussion to follow, I allude to but also refrain from conflating the intersecting histories of racialised domination experienced by Indigenous people and non-white immigrants in Australia. I focus primarily on Australia's racialised immigration policies and, moreover, long-held 'anti-Asian' sentiment as the pertinent context in which Filipino immigrants have been received. Australia-Asia relations occupy a distinctive place in Australian history as the country's geopolitical positioning in the Asian region has been a persistent source of racialised anxiety as a result of being both *included* in the margins of Asia but also *excluded* because of its desire to remain a British outpost (Ang, 2000). This has seen 'Asians' historically homogenised as a pan-racial category in the Australian imaginary, which serves to reinforce these peoples as threatening company and also functions to silence the distinctive voices that emerge from the diverse geographical, cultural and political histories in the region (Lo, 2006).

Convict transportation remained the central mode of British (and Irish) settlement to Australia after 1778 and lasted for over 50 years across the varying states (Jupp, 2002). Freed convicts and military personnel were granted land and became the core of the New South Wales settlement. As colonies expanded throughout Australia, the control of immigration became a principal concern among colonial leaders. The discovery of gold in 1851 brought a large influx of foreign immigration from all over the world. In particular, Chinese gold miners entered Australia to work in the gold mines and over the next 20 years numbered approximately 40,000 persons (Jupp, 2002). The growth of the sugar industry in Queensland also saw the arrival of Pacific Islanders as indentured workers. Filipino migration to Australia as well commenced during this time. The Philippines' 'Manila Men' – the generation of Filipino men from colonial Philippines who were recruited as labour for work mainly to the Americas – arrived around 1869 to fill the country's shortage of pearl divers (Perdon, 1998). They worked as crew members and divers and eventually went on to become supervisors and owners of fishing fleets. The first sizeable population of Filipino migrants was on Thursday Island, which reached a total of 147 persons in 1885. Filipino migration expanded to other locations of the pearl diving industry, including Western Australia, when a major mining boom occurred on the west coast (Perdon, 1998).

Immigration was a prominent topic in the lead-up to Australia's Federation and was bound to labour disputes and anxieties around maintaining racial and ethnic homogeneity (Jupp, 2002). Local unions rallied against cheap foreign (non-British) labour. In particular, competition between white and Chinese miners led to a series of violent riots between the two groups (Markus, 1979). In 1901, the first pieces of legislation instituted by the newly formed government came to be known as the 'White Australia' policy, which was characterised by the firm restriction of non-Anglo European immigration. This policy wove together the aim of protecting local workers and their employment conditions and a common-sense racial-nationalism at the time to preserve whiteness, British-ness and Australian-ness as the determinants of citizenship (Hage, 1998). The *Immigration Restriction Act* and the *Pacific Islanders Labourers Act* were passed to control immigration, particularly of neighbouring 'Asiatics'. Immigration restriction entailed methods such as dictation tests in any European language designed to disadvantage non-European applicants and the creation of racial categories for entry, such as 'half-cast and mixed descent', where a 75 per cent blood rule was imposed on mixed-descent arrivals (Jupp, 2002). For decades onwards, immigration was successfully kept at a low level, with anti-Asian sentiment a persistent character of government policies and labour union protests. Only through the campaigning of wealthy land and business owners was a small flow of 'Asiatic' labour sustained, including Filipino migrants, who continued to fill labour shortages in the pearl diving industry (Perdon, 1998).

Small amendments were made to immigration restriction only as World War II increasingly displaced populations, which produced mixed reactions across the populace. For example, Japanese expansion in the Pacific saw the relatively unquestioned settlment of Anglo refugees fleeing the Dutch East Indies (now Indonesia) while Jewish refugees persecuted by the Hitler regime were accepted by the state but received with ambivalence by the public (Jupp, 2002). Filipinos too arrived in Australia, seeking asylum during the Japanese occupation of the Philippines between 1941 and 1944 (Perdon, 1998), and faced direct racism, along with other Asian groups, as the Pacific War made more real the threat of 'Asian invasion'. British migration remained a priority and in 1945 formed the basis of the *Assisted Passage Migration Scheme* to respond to a growing industrial sector. This saw hundreds of thousands cross the seas from the British Isles and southern parts of Ireland and other Anglo settlers from British colonies. But ultimately, migration through this program failed to meet the country's population needs. In the 1950s, the government began to offer assisted passage from non-Anglo-Saxon European countries, such as Italy, Greece and Malta, and also resettled thousands from war-torn Eastern and Central Europe and the Middle East, such as Turkey, through *The Displaced Persons' Resettlement Scheme*. These migrants, seen as 'factory fodder', filled labour shortages in industrial factories in the big cities of Sydney and Melbourne (Colic-Peisker, 2011). Immigration from the Asian region remained limited and restricted flows occurred through schemes like *The Colombo Plan*, which sponsored student exchange between Australia and South-East Asia as part of economic bilateral exchange agreements.

These post-war migration flows produced significant change to the demographic composition of Australia and have since seen the state pursue a range of policies that have expanded from immigration restriction to the management of growing racio-ethnic diversity *within* its borders. By the beginning of the 1950s, the policy of assimilation was implemented to address the settlement of non-Anglo immigrant communities (Jupp, 2002). Set against the decline of policies explicitly based on racial exclusion, assimilation emerged as an ideology of incorporation underscored by the idea that socialisation would maintain modes of cultural uniformity amid difference. This response has important roots in state attempts to absorb Indigenous people into 'white society' that saw the forced removal of Indigenous children from their families. Applied to newly arrived migrants – particularly non-Anglo Europeans who assumed the target of popular racism at the time – it entailed discarding the distinctiveness of their ethnic backgrounds by adopting the language and discouraging the creation of 'ethnic ghettos'. Assimilation policy was adopted by successive governments for almost a whole decade and operated as a de facto extension of the White Australia policy to maintain a hegemonic Anglo core. This was promised in political rhetoric to foster some level of acceptance among the public that an expanded immigration program was necessary to Australia's nation-building project. Assimilation policy, however, failed to successfully incorporate ethnic minorities into Australia's economic and social life. By the end of the 1950s, the state initiated a range of reforms to extend citizenship to certain categories of non-British migrants and also established Good Neighbour Councils to provide volunteer-based grass-roots community support to help new migrants become *a part of* 'Australian society'. In 1959, an official policy of integration was announced and acknowledged the need to provide migrants with a transitional period during which they could maintain their cultural identity after their arrival, but it was expected that they would come to adopt the dominant culture. Ethnic-specific services, such as English classes, and resettlement services, like assisted housing, were funded across ethnic communities as a means to facilitate integration into the 'mainstream'.

But the policy of integration was largely a brief venture. It is, instead, most noted for paving the way for a more 'radical' approach. Underpinned by the liberal ideology of cultural pluralism spreading across political institutions in other immigrant-receiving states in the North, the discourse of 'multiculturalism' espoused that cultural difference was to be not only acknowledged but also actively embraced as a positive thing. By the 1970s, the 'White Australia' policy was 'officially' discarded and saw further liberalisation of Australia's immigration controls (Jupp, 2002). Reforms under the policy of multiculturalism opened the gates to the country's first significant period of 'mass Asian immigration', particularly from East and South-East Asia. In 1975, the fall of Saigon and the fall of East Timor saw a large wave of Vietnamese and East Timorese refugees resettled by the Fraser government. Chinese immigrants also migrated as students in large numbers. The first sizeable influx of Filipino migrants also arrived and consisted mainly of skilled Filipina nurses but also Filipina women on spousal visas (Soriano, 1995; Jackson, 1993). The characteristics of the Filipino population in Australia soon transformed from a predominantly male-oriented migration to a female one. This was in direct correlation with the immigration policies of the Philippine president Ferdinand Marcos at the time which oriented the economy towards labour export that took on a decidedly female character as demand grew for labour in domestic work, hospitality and health care in advanced industrial societies (Tyner, 2009). By the 1980s, Australia's immigration policy prioritised skilled migration and saw a large proportion of Filipinos migrating to Australia from highly skilled and educated backgrounds and who also spoke very proficient English. Within this same period, Filipinos also sponsored their families through the popular family reunion scheme. Over half of the Filipino population in Australia today is recorded to have arrived during this period (ABS, 2007d).

Extending beyond changes to immigration sanctions, moreover, multiculturalism policy embarked on an ideological transformation of how Australia was to see its 'national identity'. Promoting the preservation of cultural difference, multiculturalism discourse reconceptualised the country's race relations as progressing from an exclusionary 'White Australia' to a society predicated on the notion of 'unity in diversity' (Stratton and Ang, 1994). The opportunity to apply for citizenship was extended to all permanent migrant settlers, ethnic-specific services were enhanced, and anti-racial vilification laws were put into place. Multiculturalism, however, was not received without controversy. The policy transition sharpened public debate on the immigration program and the 'national interest'. In particular, in the 1980s, backlash surfaced against the 'Asianisation of Australia' as the state began to see the growth of the Asian economy driven by Japan, Singapore and Hong Kong as a source of motivation to strengthen its own place in the global economy. By the 1990s, the sitting Labour government led by Paul Keating vocally advocated for Australia to 'enmesh', 'integrate' and 'engage' with Asia (Ang, 2010). A part of this discourse entailed projecting a 'cosmopolitan' image of Australia as a 'multicultural nation in Asia'. Educational policies included the teaching of Asian languages, and cultural exchanges with East and South-East Asia were advanced to increase Australians' literacy regarding 'Asia'. While embraced by the elite, white middle class, multiculturalism was not so well received among the 'old Australia' of white, working-class 'battlers'. Criticism of Asian immigration heightened with the rise of right-wing politician Pauline Hanson (1996), who infamously claimed in her 1996 maiden speech to Federal Parliament, "We are in danger of being swamped by Asians . . . They have their own culture and religion, form ghettos and do not assimilate . . . A truly multicultural country can never be strong or united." Other conservatives also reasserted the primacy of 'Australian values and traditions'. Many Filipino migrants I interviewed, reflecting on their experience during this time, recalled vivid memories of racist encounters as Asians became the target of widespread racial attacks.

Two decades on, however, multiculturalism has produced some very real positive outcomes. Australians now publicly celebrate racial and ethnic diversity as an essential part of the fabric of Australian life. Recent quantitative research affirms that a large number of ordinary Australians hold positive attitudes towards ethnic diversity (Dunn et al., 2004; Forrest and Dunn, 2010). Some notable qualitative scholarship also teases out the day-to-day forms of conviviality and solidarity negotiated in moments of intercultural encounter (Wise, 2005 and 2010; Harris, 2009; Ho, 2011; Ho and Burridge, 2011; Butcher and Harris, 2010; Noble, 2009a). Indeed, in many of my interviews with Filipino migrants, they made clear that Australia is a far better place to live as a non-white person than it was "back then". Even during the 2000s when John Howard's Liberal government retreated from multiculturalism policy to champion Australia's cultural allegiance to its Anglo-Saxon roots, there remained high levels of acceptance of a 'multicultural norm'. And so, Australia today finds itself at a particular historical conjuncture – acclimatised to its new multicultural order but continually tested in how it navigates living with difference. Tolerance and recognition now coexist with everyday prejudice and institutional racism. Further, racialised anxieties have heightened against a 'new' threat post–September 11: Muslim Arabic migrants. This includes dramatic events on Cronulla beach in Sydney in 2005 – now infamously known as the Cronulla Riots – which saw mob violence initiated by a mass gathering of white Australians protesting against the incompatibility of Muslim Arabic immigrants to 'Australian' society (Noble, 2009b; Poynting and Noble, 2004). The riots were especially unsettling for Sydney – often priding itself as the country's most 'global' and 'cosmopolitan' city. As the 'war on terror' escalates, these migrants continue to be surveilled in the fight against 'home-grown terrorists'. Anti-Muslim sentiment has also become entangled with moral anxieties towards 'boat people' – asylum seekers from countries like Afghanistan and Iran – who are arriving unannounced on Australia's shores. The state has pursued a tough stand through offshore detention centres while social media debates are conflicted about the cruelty of such policies (which include the locking up of children) versus the view that these migrants are 'queue jumpers' manipulating the system. Amid these struggles, the inequity between the life chances of Indigenous Australians and non-Indigenous Australians remains the most systematic form of racial disparity that exists in the country and for which present-day generations resist being held accountable.

On the other end of the spectrum, from explicit modes of anti-Asian attitudes emerge new forms of acceptance for some Asian immigrants, especially those from the middle class via the social mobility of second and third generations (Colic-Peisker, 2011). State policies over the last decade have also re-emphasised Australia's future as being bound to 'The Asian Century', engaging mostly economic goals, like free trade agreements with India and China, but also attempting cultural engagement through educational exchange between Australia and countries from the Asian region (Fozdar, 2015). The prioritisation of skilled or educational migration has, furthermore, seen increased migration flows from countries like India, China, Bangladesh, Malaysia, Taiwan and the Philippines (Colic-Peisker, 2011). Aside from arriving as permanent settlers, many Filipinos now enter through the temporary visa channel as contract workers before applying for Australian citizenship in high rates (Department of Immigration and Citizenship, 2010). In contrast to earlier migration schemes prioritising skilled professionals, the current skilled migration program attempts to address skills shortage in the construction, manufacturing, health care, hospitality and mining industries, and currently many Filipinos arrive as welders, metal fabricators, motor mechanics, fitters and registered nurses. This migration pattern has diversified the class structure of the Filipino migrant population in Australia from a predominantly middle-class diaspora to one with a growing working-class sector. Research, however, cites the challenges in acquiring work in skilled fields for these migrants as English proficiency or the 'accent ceiling' and the devaluing of overseas qualifications remain persistent modes of institutionalised racism (Ho and Alcorso, 2004). There lurks an unease about relations with 'Asia' and the idea of 'Asians in Australia' that continues to draw from historical conceptions about Otherness and remain entwined with broader economic and political questions.

Competing representations: local and global imaginings of the 'Filipino'

Set against the broader historical and structural processes I have outlined, a range of racialised imaginings of Filipinos in Australia have materialised in local and global media, international research literature, and narratives from the Filipino 'community' about Filipino settlement in Australia. These metaphors are by no means distinct from each other but are connected in a multitude of ways. Such imaginings are prescribed to or rejected, promoted or downplayed in varying ways across a range of actors: from the mainstream media to Filipino news-makers in the community; from the powers of the state to the resistance enacted by grass-roots Filipino organisations; and from the white Australian to the Filipino migrant herself.

Submissive and victimised

There is a distinctively feminised dimension to the global Filipino diaspora today. As a result of the large migration flows of Filipina migrants across the world's borders, being 'Filipino' has come to be racialised in accordance with this visibility and tends to project a narrative of victimisation. Controversially, in April 2009, Hong Kong columnist Chip Tsao was forced to make a public apology after calling the Philippines 'a nation of slaves' in what he claimed was a satirical article about Hong Kong residents' mistreatment of their hired maids (The Philippine Star, 2009; Guinto, 2009; Didace and Sisante, 2009). Speaking to the feminised migration trends that emerge from the Philippine government's economic policy, being labelled as 'slaves' confines Filipina women to their labour and they are positioned as subservient, submissive and docile subjects. Further, in the 1980s and 1990s, Filipina migrants also came to be commonly known as *abused* domestic help, therefore intertwining servitude with a victim status.[6] Cases of exploitation, violence and death in countries like Singapore and Honk Kong were reported in Australian media and became enmeshed with local representations of Filipinas who were arriving as spouses of Australian men.[7] The latter were labelled 'mail order brides' in accordance with the proliferation of advertisements marketing Filipina brides to local men. Although not 'domestic helpers', the media depictions of these Filipinas became increasingly dominated by their supposed servitude towards their often much older Anglo partners and a convenient connection was regularly made between these attributes and the subsequent abuse and, in some cases, tragic deaths suffered at the hands of the same men.[8]

Early activism from Filipino migrants in Australia attempted to address these media representations and emerged as the original forms of organised anti-racism undertaken by the community. The majority of the Filipino migrant services available during this time were primarily focused on the welfare of Filipina women. In 1989, a NSW Filipino Women's Working Party was established, comprising several organisations in an attempt to collectively lobby the plight of Filipina women – specifically brides of Australian men – to state and Commonwealth bodies. Aside from placing pressure on the Australian government to regulate introduction agencies and improve the availability of culturally appropriate services to both metropolitan and rural Filipina women, they also focused on addressing media portrayals of Filipina women (Ethnic Affairs Commission of NSW, 1992). Media skills seminars for Filipina women provided training on how to deal with the media, leading to a more vocal presence of Filipina activists in media features advocating for increased awareness of the violence Filipina women face. There was also increased visibility of Filipina women sharing their more positive experiences in Australia to promote an empowered image of the community (Bone, 1995; Dempsey, 1992; Pearce, 1992; M. Millett, 1991; S. Millett, 1991; Escio-Musson, 1989). This pioneering activism continues today in the lobbying work of NGOs, like the Centre for Philippine Concerns, based in Brisbane, and in the material support provided by community groups, like the Philippine Australian Community Services Inc. (PACSI), based in western Sydney.

The prominence of issues related to the 'mail order bride' has also influenced Australian scholarly research about Filipino migrants. This topic, by far, predominates the literature available on Filipinos in Australia (Cuneen and Stubbs, 2003; Khoo, 2001; Jackson, 1989; Woelz-Stirling et al., 1998; Robinson, 1996; Saroca, 2006). This corresponds with international enquiry concentrating on the experience of Filipina women in countries like Hong Kong and Singapore and the continents of the Middle East and Europe as abused domestic helpers, brides or trafficked sex workers (Tolentino, 1996; Pratt, 1996; Parrenas, 2001; San Juan, 2001; L. Brown, 2000). Recent studies, however, increasingly focus on the strategies of empowerment in which Filipina migrants engage to subvert their status as victims (Law, 2001; Parrenas, 2005; Ebron, 2002). These cases highlight Filipina migrant workers in countries like Canada, Singapore and Italy as a vocal community protesting unfair work conditions and attempting to rework racialised stigmas attached to their employment (Kelly, 2007).

Disempowered representations are, however, reworked in mainstream media reports on the exploitation of Filipino contract workers. The discourse of servitude and oppression underscoring the 'mail order bride' stereotype now reproduces itself in the migrant Filipina nurse who features prominently in Australian reports about labour migrants who become victims of exploitative working conditions, gross underpayment and corrupt recruiting agencies (Australian Associated Press, 2008). With increased Filipino migration through the skilled migration visas, activism from the community has evolved to include rallying for the rights of these new migrants. MIGRANTE Australia, for instance, is a major activist organisation advocating for the rights of Filipino temporary workers in Australia and has been active in trade union negotiations, lobbying both the Australian and Philippine governments, and providing material support to Filipino migrant workers. Further, these same discourses of victimhood are also applied to Filipino male labourers employed as construction workers, farmers or factory labour and increasingly figure in news reports about exploited migrant workers (SBS, 2008; Toohey, 2007; Australian Associated Press, 2007; Knox and Moore, 2007; Knox, 2007a, 2007b and 2007c). Like the Filipina brides of the 1980s and 1990s media coverage, these men are positioned as 'easy prey', desperately desiring to escape the impoverished conditions of the Philippines. This time, however, these migrants are targeted by crooked recruitment agencies or dishonest employers, with some lives also ending tragically in death.[9] Although such focus has been imperative to bringing attention to the injustices endured by these migrants, in many ways, it has produced a biased projection around the world of Filipinos as weak and victimised. This subordinate status essentialises the Philippines within the colonial paradigms of the feminine East – a weak nation by virtue of the emasculation of its economy and people – and continues to survive through the effeminate representation of a subservient, powerless and victimised diaspora.

Hostile and opportunistic

On the other end of the spectrum, there is a paradoxical imagining of the Filipino as hostile and opportunistic. In Australia, these discourses take root in conceptions of foreign Asian masculinity in early colonial Australia depicted in the notion of the 'Yellow Peril' invading Australian territory, particularly in the advent of migration of Chinese gold rush miners. Such metaphors were later reproduced in moral panics around Vietnamese gangs in ethnic enclaves, like Cabramatta, in Sydney's south-western suburbs, in the 1980s and 1990s (Dreher, 2007). Filipino men in Australia have rarely been the direct focus of these discourses. When applied to Filipinos, it has been done without discriminating across 'Asian' differences, in that only by virtue of being 'Asian' have Filipino men been included in such categorisations. Perdon (1998: 11–16), however, specifies depictions of the Philippines that surfaced in Australia in the 1950s and 1960s underlined by similar discourses around barbarism and violence. The very few Australian writers who first travelled to the Philippines conveyed in their commentaries a "Filipino 'tradition of violence'" and a general state of lawlessness on Manila's streets. Today, such representations endure in global media news through reporting of violent attacks against Western media in the country; the ongoing bloody war between the Philippine army and Muslim separatists in the islands of the South; kidnappings of foreign tourists or torturing of public officials; hijackings on public infrastructure; and the electoral fraud and frequent killings of political rivals (Sydney Morning Herald, 2010a, 2010b, 2010c, 2010d, 2011a, 2011b, 2009a and 2009b; The Australian, 2009). Further, with increased migration of Filipino male workers in the trades industry, aside from being framed as exploited victims, they are also perceived as 'invading' the local job market. In media reports, Filipino migrant workers are portrayed as shameless opportunists willing to work for cheap and brazenly stealing jobs from local Australians (Burrell and Perpitch, 2010; Burrell, 2010; Ryan, 2009; Knox, 2007b). The discourse of the hostile Other has also been applied in the media on Filipina women. Saroca (2006) describes the dichotomous representation of Filipinas as either 'woman in danger' or 'dangerous woman'. Such metaphors signal the perpetuation of orientalist discourse that continues to position the East as both weak and inferior, exotic and barbaric, generating fetishised desire and fear for the Other (Said, 1995).

It is, however, important to recognise that the fashioning of Filipinos along these paradoxical representations is not merely a matter of discourse. Structural forces, like a globalised economy and the policies of the Philippine government, shape the racialisations of Filipinos in such a manner. Parrenas (2001: 1129) argues that "the globalisation of the market economy" is the primary cause of "construct[ing] the Philippines as a nation gendered female". Neo-liberalism, global restructuring and the increasing demand for low-wage services in many industrial cities around the world operate together to integrate Filipina women *and* men into transnational economic circuits that make them vulnerable to tremendous forms of exploitation, abuse and victimisation (Parrenas, 2001; also see Tolentino, 1996; Gibson et al., 2001). Moreover, the Philippine government must also be held accountable due to its active role in developing and promoting an aggressive migration industry. In what was meant to be a temporary solution to the country's unemployment problems and economic downturn in the 1970s, outmigration of Filipino people (whether as temporary migrants or permanent settlers) and the remittances they send back to their families have become the chief means by which the government maintains the national economy.

Inferior and 'Third World'

The idea of the Philippines as 'Third World' further underwrites the second-class status of Filipino migrants in Australia. Filipinos as 'Third World' subjects draw on notions of poverty, inferiority and incivility, which are salient in myths surrounding the 'yellow hordes' invading the Australian job market; the violent Asian gangster; the submissive yet opportunistic and sexually conniving 'mail order bride'; and the helpless migrant worker undertaking the unwanted 'dirty jobs' of Australians. Perdon (1998) remarks that representations of the Philippines' poverty in travel observations have long been described specifically *in contrast to* the glimmers of affluence. According to Perdon (1998: 18–19), as early as 1966, Australian writer George Farwell penned his fondness for the country and people but "made a critical description" of the poverty and "scandalous opulence" displayed side by side in the nation's neighbourhoods. This conflicting imagery works to further position the Philippines and its people as 'Third World', where the polarity between the rich and poor is used as proof of the country's entrenched culture of corruption and its distorted East/West contradictions. More recently, in 2007, the popular American series *Desperate Housewives* caused international controversy for mocking the medical qualifications of one of the show's characters by asking if they were attained from the Philippines. Filipino-Americans, especially from the middle class and medical community, were quick to protest and initiated action across the global Filipino diaspora to pressure the studios to issue an apology. A writer in a Sydney Filipino newspaper called it a "racial slur" (Farmer, 2007) and agreed it was underpinned by stereotypes around the Philippines as a corrupt Third World country but, as well, a nation whose education and intelligence are much more inferior to that of the First World's (also see Morden, 2007; Laforteza, 2007b).

Moreover, 'Third World-ness' is articulated in the Australian government's position towards the Philippines. In spite of the government recognising the necessity of Australia's integration into the Asian region, Asia is still the 'alien' landscape rife with poverty, political turmoil and fleeing refugees. Analysis undertaken by Laforteza (2007a: 2) of Australian government documents and international programs indicates that there is a strong narrativising of "Australia as an authoritative regional power within the Asia-Pacific". In other words, the idea of the Philippines as an inferior 'Third World' subject is constantly reproduced through the positioning of Australia as a 'good neighbour', which Laforteza (2007a) argues is a form of neocolonial benevolence. Further, the economic value of migrants to the Australian government has always strongly underscored the country's immigration policies (Vasta, 1993). Such migration schemes have been read as neocolonial restructurings of power relations between the First World and the Third World. In other words, the economic positioning of Filipino migrants as labour to bolster Australia's economic growth contributes to the racialisation of Filipinos as second-class citizens whose bodies are needed but whose identities do not count. Accordingly, the same economic value designated by the Philippine government to its people's migration abroad remains at the forefront of criticisms towards its policies, in spite of state attempts to uphold these migrants as national heroes.

'Western', integrated and invisible

Again, in contradiction, the Philippines are also distinguished as less Other through imaginings of its 'Westernised' culture attributed to its colonisation by Spain and America. Perdon (1998) observed historical records indicating that impression of Filipinos in Australia as 'Westernised Asians' was apparent among the early Filipino pioneers in the pearl diving industry. According to Perdon (1998: 142), Filipinos on Thursday Island defied anti-Asian sentiment of the time and were "highly regarded as the only fully integrated Asians. They were considered good and permanent members of the community." Post-war migration flows from the Philippines to Australia further shape such conceptions with the migration of middle-class Filipinos in the 1980s and 1990s from skilled and educated backgrounds and who possessed high levels of English proficiency. Migrant social mobility is often equated with not only economic integration but also cultural assimilation and has been essential to how some scholars and policymakers (and even many migrants themselves) conceptualise how ethnic minorities become 'absorbed' into the majority society (Raj, 2003). Such 'successful' integration in societies where Filipinos have arrived predominantly as middle-class migrants has consequently deemed the population as relatively unimportant in conventional migrant research agendas. The achievement of economic integration by Filipino migrants in countries like the US and Australia has led to modes of invisibility in these states' multicultural imaginaries. In the US, Espiritu (1994) describes Filipinos as "the forgotten Asian Americans" due to the lack of research conducted on the Filipino community compared to other immigrant groups. Bonus (2000: 1) also observes that "Filipinos are largely invisible in most accounts of US history and in contemporary scholarship" and comprise "a 'silent minority'". This invisibility can preclude their ability to celebrate a distinctive racio-ethnic identity that has symbolic value in the cultural pluralist order.

At the same time, it can be welcomed through projections of the 'good integrated migrant'. The front pages of major Filipino-Australian newspapers in Sydney regularly feature headlines, stories and images of Filipinos 'making it' in the 'mainstream', such as Filipino entertainers, artists and sportspersons. Integration in the political sphere is also praised. During my fieldwork, 2008 was heralded by community leaders and Filipino media as monumental for Filipinos entering the mainstream political scene in NSW (Zaragosa, 2008; Philippine Community Herald, 2008; Bayanihan News, 2008). A record number of twelve Filipino migrant candidates ran in local elections, and *The Philippine Community Herald* (2008: 1) reported the efforts "significant because this is the first time that Filipino-Australians have exhibited interest and active involvement in Australian mainstream politics". Two of these candidates were successfully elected into local office. Such themes were constant in the various community events I attended. At the 2008 NSW Philippine Community Council's inaugural Independence Day Ball, held inside one of the grand ballrooms of the Hilton Hotel in Sydney, a visiting Philippine politician commended the crowd for achieving an "upper-class" status in Australia. The subject of achieving mainstream 'integration' and 'recognition' was also clearly present in all of the speeches of the night's honoured guests. The Philippine ambassador to Australia praised Filipinos for being "respectable citizens" – integrating successfully because of their hard work and cultural compatibility. A NSW state politician also celebrated the community for its successful and "trouble-free" adaptation into Australian life and listed prominent entertainment and sports celebrities of Filipino background as being exemplars of this 'success story'. In the same year, I attended the launch of a new community organisation specifically aimed at raising the profile of Filipinos in the 'mainstream' political spheres and in the media. The night's theme featured a tribute to 'Filipino achievers' in Australia, such as mainstream entertainers and sports stars who were of full or partial Filipino background. In the chair's impassioned opening speech, he communicated the intentions of the organisation:

> We are a lobby and advocacy group which aims to push Filipino-Australians beyond their comfort zones – to stand up and be counted – in the hope of building an image worthy of respect and admiration in a multicultural society that is Australia. . . . For only then can we truly say that we have arrived and we now belong. . . . I believe that by standing together, we can add value to ourselves as a people and be taken seriously as a community.

Conclusion

The fluctuating tropes of racialised visibility and invisibility and the movements to address them by different parts of the Filipino 'community' demonstrate articulations that speak back to the unfinished postcolonial project of the 'Filipino' in the Philippines and are pronounced in new ways in the diasporic immigrant context. In the case of Australia, these processes intersect with the country's own postcolonial condition, which remains conflicted between "a redemptive understanding of the past" as a British settler colony and that of a new 'multicultural society' that is at times specifically underscored by a "future-oriented discourse" that sees Australia's destiny as "part of Asia" in order to forge its place on the world stage (Ang and Stratton, 2006: 18). On the one hand, Filipino migrants in Australia are interpellated into negative racialised particularities that produce imaginings of submissiveness and victimisation and/or hostility and aggressive opportunism. Alternatively, positive gains around 'integration' and 'cultural compatibility' are underwritten by a "mis-interpellation" (Hage, 2010), hailed by the dominant group as belonging to the collectivity but ultimately involving conditional and revocable respect. And then, at times, Filipinos are rendered invisible where being 'Filipino' can intersect with being 'Asian', especially under the homogenising white gaze. It is a "non-interpellation" (Hage, 2010) that can deny their claims to a distinctive identity. These different processes damage bodies and subjectivity in profound affective ways and also raise questions about injustice deeply implicated in structures of inequality. But in foregrounding the overwhelming manner in which self-constitution can be denied, it is important to understand the 'Filipino' equally as a site of resistance. As the lives of Filipino migrants in these pages will disclose, racism also produces grounds for the fight for autonomy and that may lead to the negotiation of emancipatory spaces.

Notes

1. The Philippines is made up of approximately 7,100 islands. The islands are divided into three groups – Luzon, Visayas and Mindanao. Luzon is the largest and most populated island and is home to the country's capital of Manila and its population of 1.6 million people.
2. The largest language groups are the Tagalogs, Cebuanos, Illongos, Ilocanos, Bicolanos and Pampanguenos.
3. Filipino-Chinese were only later classified as part of the mestizo group after coming to dominate Philippine society economically (Rafael, 2000). In addition, the usage of the term 'mestizo' has changed in contemporary Philippine society. Whereas it might have traditionally referred to a Filipino-Spanish or Filipino-Chinese 'bloodline', it is now a general term used to describe men or women (mestiza is the term used for females) with light skin, fair hair and light eyes (Rafael, 2000).
4. The government, judicial system and police force were reorganised into American-style institutions that appointed many Filipinos but were administered by Americans (Tubangui, 1989: 114–118). Public infrastructure was repaired after deteriorating considerably as a result of war while ports, lighthouses and piers were modernised and an irrigation system constructed. In Manila, horse-car transportation and a steam train line were also replaced by the country's first electrical railway. Health and sanitation were addressed

through vaccination programs, construction of hospitals, application of modern American medical technology, and a nationwide health education campaign. Lastly, education became the signature trademark of American occupation in the country with the building of free public schools where teachers instructed in English.
5 For instance, the Bell Trade Act "tied the Philippine economy to that of the US by establishing a system of preferential tariffs between the two countries; it placed various restrictions on Philippine government control of its own economy and required the Filipinos to amend their constitution to give special position to US capital" (Schirmer and Shalom, 1987: 87). Furthermore, one of the more visible ways in which the US remained in the consciousness of the Filipino people was through the military bases America maintained in Subic Bay and Clark, which became the US's largest offshore naval and airbases between 1947 and 1991.
6 The most controversial was the hanging of Filipina maid Flor Contemplacion in Singapore in 1995, who many believed was framed by her employer for the murder of another Filipina maid (Sydney Morning Herald, 1995).
7 Filipinas have not come into Australia as domestic helpers like they have to Europe, Singapore, Japan or the Middle East as government migration schemes do not cover their assisted entry.
8 News reports centred on older Australian men using Internet and pen pal agencies to find Filipina wives and reported the seeming desperation and subserviency of Filipina women as the basis of their appeal coupled with their youth and beauty (Button, 1999). Furthermore, this image of servitude and submission was a frequent reason cited by mainstream media reports for the deaths of some Filipinas murdered by their Australian spouses (see Saroca, 2006). One of the most well covered of these cases was the double suicide-murder involving the Garrott brothers – world-renowned cartridge designers – and their Filipina wives, Teresita and Violeta, on an isolated outback farm. During the inquest into the deaths, headlines like 'Inquest Hears of Garrott's Authority' or 'Four Who Lived as One: Death by Cooperation' and much subsequent reporting frequently positioned the wives as being "controlled" by their husbands and therefore willing participants in the suicide (Brown, 1992; Curtin, 1992; Frith, 1991).
9 One of the more recent tragedies that received much media attention was the death of Pedro Balading in 2007, whose story appeared under headlines such as 'Bullied, Underpaid and Abused, with No Escape' (Knox, 2007a).

References

Ang, I. (2000) 'Introduction: Alter/Asian cultural interventions for 21st century Australia', in Ang, I., Chalmers, S., Law, L. and Thomas, M. (eds.), *Alter/Asians: Australian Identities in Art, Media and Popular Culture*, Annandale: Pluto Press, pp. xiii–xxx.

Ang, I. (2010) 'Australia, China, and Asian regionalism: Navigating distant proximity', *Amerasia Journal*, vol. 36, no. 2, pp. 127–40.

Ang, I. and Stratton, J. (2006) 'Asianing Australia: Notes toward a critical transnationalism in cultural studies', *Cultural Studies*, vol. 10, no. 1, pp. 16–36.

Aquino, B. (1985) 'What's wrong with the Philippines?', *Inquirer.net*, 21 August 2010, http://newsinfo.inquirer.net/inquirerheadlines/nation/view/20100821-287978/Whats-wrong-with-the-Philippines accessed 16 February 2011.

The Australian. (2009) 'Philippines most dangerous for media', 25 November, www.adelaidenow.com.au/news/world/philippines-worlds-most-dangerous-place-for-media/story-e6frea8l-1225803982212 accessed 22 April 2011.

Australian Associated Press. (2007) 'Filipino workers claim racial discrimination', *Australian Associated Press*, 15 October 2008, (online Factiva accessed 12 April 2011).

Australian Bureau of Statistics (ABS). (2007d) 'Country of Birth of Person (Full classification list) by sex, NSW', *2006 Census of Population and Housing*, Cat. No. 2068.0, ABS, Canberra.

Bayanihan News. (2008) '12 Fil-Aussies in local government elections', Bayanihan News, September, vol. 10, no. 9, p. 1.

Bone, P. (1995) 'Plight of the Filipina', *The Age*, 12 April (online Factiva accessed 12 April 2012).

Bonus, R. (2000) *Locating Filipino Americans: Ethnicity and the Cultural Politics of Space*, Philadelphia: Temple University Press.

Brown, L. (2000) *Sex Slaves: The Trafficking of Women in Asia*, London: Virago Press.

Brown, M. (1992) 'Brothers, wives in death pact', *Sydney Morning Herald*, 2 July (online Factiva accessed 12 April 2012).

Burrell, A. (2010) 'Fury as migrant workers keep jobs and Australians let go in Pilbara', *The Australian*, 2 March (online Factiva accessed 12 April 2011).

Burrell, A. and Perpitch, N. (2010) 'Sparks fly as locals sacked but foreign welders kept on', *The Australian*, 6 March (online Factiva accessed 12 April 2011).

Butcher, M. and Harris, A. (2010) 'Pedestrian crossings: Young people and everyday multiculturalism', *Journal of Intercultural Studies*, vol. 31, no. 5, pp. 449–53.

Button, D. (1999) 'Cliff finds a picture perfect bride', *Herald Sun*, 2 November, (online Factiva accessed 12 April 2012).

Colic-Peisker, V. (2011) 'A new era in Australian multiculturalism? From working class "Ethnics" to a "Multicultural Middle Class"', *International Migration Review*, vol. 45, no. 3, pp. 562–87.

Constantino, R. (1976) 'Identity and consciousness: The Philippine experience', *Journal of Contemporary Asia*, vol. 6, no. 1, pp. 5–28.

Cuneen, C. and Stubbs, J. (2003) 'Fantasy islands: Desire, race and violence', in Tomsen, S. and Donaldson, M. (eds.), *Male Trouble: Looking at Australian Masculinities*, Victoria: Pluto Press, p. 69.

Curtin, J. (1992) 'Four who lived as one: Death by cooperation', *Sydney Morning Herald*, 23 October (online Factiva accessed 12 April 2012).

Dempsey, D. (1992) 'From the struggle, an image of courage', *The Sunday Age*, 26 April (online Factiva accessed 12 April 2012).

Department of Immigration and Citizenship. (2010) *Country Profile: Philippines*, Canberra: Economic Analysis Unit, Department of Immigration and Citizenship, www.immi.gov.au/media/statistics/country-profiles/_pdf/philippines.pdf accessed 18 July 2010.

Didace, S. and Sisante, J. (2009) 'Chip Tsao apologises for 'maid country' remark', *GMA News*, 1 April, www.gmanews.tv/story/155062/HK-columnist-Chip-Tsao-says-sorry-for-racist-piece accessed 22 April 2010.

Dreher, T. (2007) 'Contesting Cabramatta: Moral panic and media interventions in "Australia's heroin capital"', in Morgan, G. and Poynting, S. (eds), *Outrageous! Moral Panics in Australia*, Hobart: Australian Clearing House for Youth Studies, p. 111.

Dunn, K., Forrest, J., Burnley, I. and McDonald, A. (2004) 'Constructing racism in Australia', *Australian Journal of Social Issues*, vol. 39, no. 4, pp. 409–30.

Ebron, G. (2002) 'Not just the maid: Negotiating Filipina identity in Italy', *Intersections: Gender, History and Culture in the Asian Context*, no. 8, http://intersections.anu.edu.au/issue8/ebron.html accessed 19 February 2008.

Escio-Musson, E. (1989) 'Now I have no regrets', *Sydney Morning Herald*, 11 December, (online Factiva accessed 12 April 2012).

Espiritu, Y.L. (1994) 'The intersection of race, ethnicity, and class: The multiple identities of second-generation Filipinos', *Identities*, vol. 1, no. 2–3, pp. 249–73.

Espiritu, Y.L. (2003) *Home Bound: Filipino American Lives across Cultures, Communities, and Countries*, Berkeley: University of California Press.

Ethnic Affairs Commission of NSW. (1992) *Filipino Women: Challenges and Responses (1989–1991)*, Ashfield: Ethnic Affairs Commission of NSW.

Farmer, L. (2007) 'Desperate housewives' racial slur spur global Filipino outrage', *The Philippine Community Herald*, October, p. 3.

Forrest, J. and Dunn, K.M. (2010) 'Attitudes to multicultural values in diverse spaces in Australia's immigrant cities, Sydney and Melbourne', *Space and Polity*, vol. 14, no. 1, pp. 81–102.

Fozdar, F. (2015) 'Asian invisibility/Asian threat: Australians talking about Asia', *Journal of Sociology*, vol. 52, no. 4, pp. 789–805.

Frith, D. (1991) 'Hi fi legends lived for love', *Sydney Morning Herald*, 13 May (online Factiva accessed 12 April 2012).

Gibson, K., Law, L. and Mckay, D. (2001) 'Beyond heroes and victims: Filipina contract migrants, economic activism and class transformations', *International Feminist Journal of Politics*, vol. 3, no. 3, pp. 365–86.

Guinto, J. (2009) 'HK columnist slammed over "servant' remark", *Inquirer.net*, 30 March, http://globalnation.inquirer.net/news/breakingnews/view/20090330-196976/HK-columnist-slammed-over-servant-remark accessed 22 April 2011.

Hage, G. (1998) *White Nation: Fantasies of White Supremacy in a Multicultural Society*, New York: Routledge.

Hage, G. (2010) 'The affective politics of racial mis-interpellation', *Theory, Culture and Society*, vol. 21, no. 7–8, pp. 112–29.

Hanson, P. (1996) *Maiden speech*, Commonwealth of Australia, Parliamentary Debates (1st Session-2nd Period), pp. 3860–3683.

Harris, A. (2009) 'Shifting boundaries of cultural spaces: Young people and everyday multiculturalism', *Social Identities: Journal for the Study of Race, Nation and Culture*, vol. 15, no. 2, pp. 187–205.

Ho, C. (2011) 'Respecting the presence of others: School micro-publics and everyday multiculturalism', *Journal of Intercultural Studies*, vol. 32, no. 6, pp. 605–21.

Ho, C. and Alcorso, C. (2004) 'Migrants and employment': Challenging the success story', *The Journal of Sociology*, vol. 40, no. 3, pp. 237–59.

Ho, C. and Burridge, N. (2011) 'Scaling up connections: Everyday cosmopolitanism, complexity theory & social capital', *Cosmopolitan Civil Societies: An Interdisciplinary Journal*, vol. 3, no. 3, pp. 47–67.

Jackson, R.T. (1989) 'Filipino migration to Australia: The image and a geographer's dissent', *Australian Geographical Studies*, vol. 27, no. 2, pp. 170–81.

Jackson, R.T. (1993) 'Recent migration to Australia from the Philippines', in Illeto, C. and Sullivan, R. (eds.), *Discovering Australasia*, Brisbane: James Cook University, pp. 144–7.

Jenkins, S. (2003) 'The independence lobby', in Schirmer, D. and Shalom, S. (eds.), *The Philippines Reader: A History of Colonialism, Neo-Colonialism, Dictatorship and Resistance*, Boston: South End Press, pp. 55–8.

Jupp, J. (2002) *From White Australia to Woomera: The Story of Australian Immigration*, New York: Cambridge University Press.

Karnow, S. (1989) *In Our Image: America's Empire in the Philippines*, New York: Ballantine Books.

Kelly, P. (2007) *Filipino Migration, Transnationalism and Class Identity*, Singapore: Asia Research Institute of the National University of Singapore, Working Paper Series No. 90.

Khoo, S. (2001) 'The context of spouse migration to Australia', *International Migration*, vol. 39, no. 1, pp. 111–31.

Knowles, C. (2003) *Race and Social Analysis*, London: SAGE.

Knox, M. (2007a) 'Death in the outback', *The Age*, 28 August 2007, (online Factiva accessed 12 April 2011).

Knox, M. (2007b) 'Hundreds ride the conveyer belt to fortune', *Sydney Morning Herald*, 28 August 2007, accessed 12 April 2011 from Factiva database.

Knox, M. (2007c) 'Bullied, underpaid and abused, with no escape', *Sydney Morning Herald*, 28 August 2007, accessed 12 April 2011 from Factiva database.

Knox, M. and Moore, M. (2007) 'Philippines calls for halt of abuse guest workers', *Sydney Morning Herald*, 29 August, accessed 12 April 2011 from Factiva database.

Laforteza, E. (2007a) 'White geopolitics of neo-colonial benevolence: The Australian-Philippine partnership', *Australian Critical Race and Whiteness Studies Association E-Journal*, vol. 3, no. 1, pp. 1–17.

Laforteza, E. (2007b) 'Desperate racist housewives', *The Philippine Community Herald*, October, p. 32.

Law, L. (2001) 'Home cooking: Filipino women and geographies of the senses in Hong Kong', *Ecumene*, vol. 8, no. 3, pp. 246–83.

Lo, J. (2006) 'Disciplining Asian Australian studies: Projections and introjections', *Journal of Intercultural Studies*, vol. 27, no. 1–2, pp. 11–27.

Markus, A. (1979) *Fear and Hatred: Purifying Australia and California 1850–1901*, Sydney: Hale and Iremonger.

Millett, M. (1991) 'Grim choice for migrants', *Sydney Morning Herald*, 15 August (online Factiva accessed 12 April 2012).

Millett, S. (1991) 'Filipina brides', *Sun Herald*, 14 July (online Factiva accessed 12 April 2012).

Morden, A. (2007) 'Desperate housewives, not so desperate Filipinos', *The Philippine Community Herald*, October, p. 2.

Noble, G. (2009a) 'Everyday cosmopolitanism and the labour of intercultural community', in Wise, A. and Velayutham, S. (eds.), *Everyday Multiculturalism*, Houndsmill, England: Palgrave Macmillan, pp. 46–65.

Noble, G. (2009b) *Lines in the Sand: The Cronulla Riots and the Limits of Multiculturalism*, Sydney: Institute of Criminology Press.

Omi, M. and Winant, H. (2002) 'Racial formation', in Goldberg, D. and Essed, P. (eds.), *Race Critical Theories*, Oxford: Blackwell, pp. 123–45.

Parrenas, R. (2001) *Servants of Globalisation: Women, Migration and Domestic Work*, Stanford: Stanford University Press.

Parrenas, R. (2005) 'Long distance intimacy: Class gender and intergenerational relations between mothers and children in Filipino transnational families', *Global Networks*, vol. 5, no. 4, pp. 317–36.

Pearce, J. (1992) 'A new Filipino identity', *The Age*, 2 September (online Factiva accessed 12 April 2012).

Perdon, R. (1998) *Brown Americans of Asia*, Sydney: Manila Prints.

Philippine Community Herald. (2008) 'Aussie Pinoys win in NSW local council elections', September, vol. 14, no. 9, p. 1.

The Philippine Star. (2009) 'Full text of "the war at home" by Chip Tsao', 1 April, www.philstar.com/Article.aspx?articleid=454117 accessed 22 April 2010.

Poynting, S. and Noble, G. (2004) *Living with Racism: The Experience and Reporting by Arab and Muslim Australians of Discrimination, Abuse and Violence since 11 September 2011*, Report to The Human Rights and Equal Opportunity Commission, Sydney.

Pratt, G. (1996) 'Inscribing domestic work on Filipina bodies', in Nast, H. and Pile, S. (eds.), *Places through the Body*, London: Routledge, pp. 283–304.

Quimpo, N.G. (2003) 'Colonial name, colonial mentality and ethnocentrism', *Kasama*, vol. 17, no. 3, published by The Solidarity Philippines Australia Network.

Rafael, V. (2000) *White Love and Other Events in Filipino History*, Durham: Duke University Press.

Raj, D. (2003) *Where Are You From? Middle Class Migrants in the Modern World*, Berkeley: University of California Press.

Robinson, K. (1996) 'Of mail order brides and "Boy's Own" tales: Representations of Asian-Australian marriages', *Feminist Review*, vol. 52, pp. 53–68.

Ryan, S. (2009) 'Migration policy changes derail bid to hire Filipinos', *The Australian*, 22 September, accessed 12 April 2011 from Factiva database.

Said, E. (1995) *Orientalism: Western Conceptions of the Orient*, London: Penguin Books.

San Juan Jr., E. (2001) 'Interrogating transmigrancy, remapping diaspora: The globalization of labouring Filipinos/as', *Discourse*, vol. 23, no. 3, p. 52.

Saroca, N. (2006) 'Filipino women, migration, and violence in Australia: Lived reality and media image', *Kasarinlan: Philippine Journal of Third World Studies*, vol. 21, no. 1, pp. 75–110.

SBS. (2008) 'Complaints angel project is exploiting Filipinos', *SBS*, 23 January (online Factiva accessed 12 April 2011).

Schirmer, D. and Shalom, S. (1983) *The Philippines Reader: A History of Colonialism, Neo-Colonialism, Dictatorship and Resistance*, Boston: South End Press.

Soriano, G. (1995) 'Filipino families in Australia', in Hartley, R. (ed.), *Families and Cultural Diversity in Australia*, Sydney: Allen and Unwin, pp. 96–120.

Stratton, J. and Ang, I. (1994) 'Multicultural imagined communities: Cultural difference and national identity in Australia and the USA', *Continuum: The Australian Journal of Media and Culture*, vol. 8, no. 2, pp. 124–158.

Sydney Morning Herald. (1995) 'Anger as Filipina maid hanged', 18 March (online Factiva accessed 12 April 2011).

Sydney Morning Herald. (2009a) 'Gunman kills broadcaster in Philippines', 29 June, http://news.smh.com.au/breaking-news-world/gunman-kills-broadcaster-in-philippines-20090629-d221.html accessed 22 April 2011.

Sydney Morning Herald. (2009b) 'Philippines army, rebels clash kills 43', 13 August, http://news.smh.com.au/breaking-news-world/philippines-army-rebels-clash-kills-43-20090813-eiww.html accessed 22 April 2011.

Sydney Morning Herald. (2010a) 'Baby found in plane bin in Philippines', 13 September, www.smh.com.au/world/baby-found-in-plane-bin-in-philippines-20100913-15783.html accessed 22 April 2011.

Sydney Morning Herald. (2010b) 'Four dead after bus hijack in Philippines', 1 December, http://news.smh.com.au/breaking-news-world/four-dead-after-bus-hijack-in-philippines-20101201-18gmz.html accessed 22 April 2011.

Sydney Morning Herald. (2010c) 'Militant killed in Philippines', 15 May, http://news.smh.com.au/breaking-news-world/militant-killed-in-philippines-20100515-v55w.html accessed 22 April 2011.

Sydney Morning Herald. (2010d) 'Six killed on Philippine election day', 10 May, http://news.smh.com.au/breaking-news-world/six-killed-on-philippines-election-day-20100510-uml4.html accessed 22 April 2011.

Sydney Morning Herald. (2011a) 'Two dead, fifteen hurt in Philippines bus blast', 25 January, http://news.smh.com.au/breaking-news-world/2-dead-15-hurt-in-philippines-bus-blast-20110125-1a439.html accessed 18 January 2012.

Sydney Morning Herald. (2011b) 'Knifeman kills three in Philippine school', 22 October, http://news.smh.com.au/breaking-news-world/knifeman-kills-three-in-philippines-school-20101022-16xqz.html accessed 18 January 2012.

Tolentino, R. (1996) 'Bodies, letters, catalogues: Filipinas in transnational space', *Social Text*, vol. 14, no. 3, pp. 49–76.

Toohey, P. (2007) 'A load of bull', *The Bulletin*, 16 October (online Factiva accessed 12 April 2011).

Tubangui, H., Bauzon, L., Foronda Jr., M. and Ausejo, L. (1982) *The Filipino Nation: A Concise History of the Philippines*, Manila: Grolier International.

Tyner, J. (2009) *The Philippines: Mobilities, Identities, Globalisation*, London: Taylor and Francis.

Vasta, E. (1993) 'Multiculturalism and ethnic identity: The relationship between racism and resistance', *Australian and New Zealand Journal of Sociology*, vol. 29, no. 2, pp. 209–25.

Winant, H. (1994) *Racial Conditions*, Minneapolis: University of Minnesota Press.

Wise, A. (2005) 'Hope and belonging in a multicultural suburb', *Journal of Intercultural Studies*, vol. 26, no. 1–2, pp. 171–86.

Wise, A. (2010) 'Sensuous multiculturalism: Emotional landscapes of interethnic living in Australian suburbia', *Journal of Ethnic and Migration Studies*, vol. 36, no. 6, pp. 917–37.

Woelz-Stirling, N., Kelaher, M. and Manderson, L. (1998) 'Power and politics of abuse: Rethinking violence in Filipina-Australian marriages', *Health Care for Women International*, vol. 19, no. 4, pp. 289–301.

Zaragosa, E. (2008) 'Fil-Aussie, Ariel Satorre runs for councillor', *Philippine Community Herald*, May, vol. 14, no. 5, p. 1.

Figure 2.1 Parade of traditional Filipino costume, Philippine Cultural Day, St Marys, May 2009
Source: Ana Gacis.

Figure 2.2 Filipino Seniors Sonata Concert, Memorial Hall, St Marys, 2010
Source: Ana Gacis.

Figure 2.3 Filipino *turo turo* (point point) restaurant on Main Street, Blacktown
Source: Kristine Aquino.

Figure 2.4 Filipino business hub in Main Street, Blacktown
Source: Kristine Aquino.

Figure 2.5 Grand Final contention at the 2011 New South Wales Filos Championship Cup, Auburn
Source: Kristine Aquino.

Figure 2.6 Filipino symbols inscribed as tattoos among young Filipino basketball players
Source: Kristine Aquino.

3 Coping with honorary whiteness
Aspirant middle-class Filipino migrants

"Filipinos aren't *really* Asians."

These were the seemingly harmless words spoken to me by a previous partner of mine of Anglo background not long before I had embarked on my research for this book. The utterance of this comment came when he was enthusiastically sharing with me his insights into the differences between 'Asians' and 'Filipinos'. To make his case, he argued that barring our 'Asian-looking' appearance, Filipinos had 'non-Asian'-sounding surnames, we did not have any exotic religion or strange cultural practices, and we spoke English as well as if it was our first and only language. Filipinos, he therefore concluded, weren't *really* 'Asians'.

At that point, I was unsure as to whether he was simply pointing out his observation or that hidden deep underneath his comment was the belief that there was something wrong with being 'Asian'. Things, however, became a little clearer as our relationship travelled along. Upon meeting his upper-middle-class family, I was to later find out that my lack of 'Asian-ness' would do well to access their approval. I gradually realised over numerous dinner conversations that his parents liked migrants *but* only certain kinds of migrants. They often expressed displeasure at the behaviour of Lebanese youth, the 'backwardness' of Muslim culture and the dirtiness of crowded 'Asian ghettos', like Cabramatta, in Sydney's western suburbs.

On the other hand, I was apparently no more 'culturally' different to his family with my English skills and 'non-Asian' disposition. My middle-class education and occupation, furthermore, proved that I was 'integrated' and most certainly qualified as an 'acceptable' Other. I remember trying to explain the history of colonisation in the Philippines as a subtle attempt to make them understand that the image of the 'Westernised' Filipino of which they were so approving was born out of oppression and conquest. I also tried several times to gently enquire about their assumptions of 'Asian' people and culture with the hope of making them realise the heterogeneity masked by this overly narrow-minded grouping. As well, I attempted to tell them that not all Filipinos shared my experience of social mobility on the chance that they might re-evaluate what it means to be a 'respectable' immigrant. But my explanations and questions failed to extract any real consideration about the way in which they ordered the world. In retrospect, I should have been much more direct and instead pointed out how 'racist' I thought their opinions were. But I had held back. Aside from wanting to avoid much awkwardness, like many middle-class interviewees who I discovered to have shared similar situations, I felt a sense of relief and even flattery as they rewarded me with acceptance into their 'white world', despite knowing how conditional the appreciation was.

This instance has always served to remind me that there are powerful affective emotions experienced by racialised subjects when receiving recognition from the dominant group. In this chapter, I unpack the concept of middle-class whiteness – its material markers of skin colour and its symbolic associations. Although having white skin is the most compelling quality one can possess to qualify for whiteness in Australia, to be 'white' is also significantly composed of an array of cultural and economic attributes. I engage with the growing body of literature in Australia and the more established field in the US, which interrogates whiteness as a *political, social and cultural construct* that systematically structures privilege in white-dominated societies (Baldwin, 1998; hooks, 1992; Allen, 1994; Frankenberg, 1997; Dyer, 1997; Lipsitz, 1998; Hage, 1998; Sullivan, 2006). While the definition of whiteness in Australia has its foundations in a black/white binary opposition rooted in relations between white settlers and Indigenous people, increased migration from Southern and Eastern Europe, Asia and the Middle East has seen whiteness increasingly measured along a wide spectrum of Otherness.[1] In middle-class Australia, economic markers of social mobility and cultural symbols of 'assimilability' are valued forms of capital and I suggest that their acquisition by racialised subjects can realise modes of *honorary whiteness* – a status of belonging to the dominant group (Bonilla-Silva, 2003; Ong, 1991; Valdez-Young, 2009; Stratton, 2009).[2]

Research into the experience of middle-class racial minorities and racialised immigrants indicates that socio-economic integration into the 'majority society' can, to certain degrees, equalise relations of power (Raj, 2003: 8; also see Espiritu, 1994; Feagin and Sikes, 1994; Matthews, 2002; Stratton, 2009). In part, this is explained by economic theorisations that see class relations as principal determinants of the limited power held by these groups (Miles, 1989; Wilson, 1998; Jakubowicz et al., 1984). In many ways, for numerous middle-class Filipino migrants I interviewed, they communicated a sense of reprieve from racism because of their class achievements. The Filipino migrants in this chapter self-identified as 'middle-class' are university-educated, work in professional white-collar jobs and hold managerial roles. These individuals also see themselves as securing relative financial stability and prosperity.[3] Such socio-economic capital, along with modes of cultural capital like displays of 'middle-class respectability', mastery of the English language and valuing cultural integration, has enabled access to some of the privileges of whiteness and distances the middle class from being an othered 'Asian' or 'migrant' subject. Following the work of Hage (1998), who extends Bourdieu's theorisation of capital into the arena of racism, I locate the Filipino middle class in the 'social field' of the Australian national space where individuals and collective groups can accumulate and deploy varying forms of material and symbolic resources that access modes of belonging to the hegemonic core.[4] I also extend this notion a little further through a discussion of how middle-class whiteness in the Australian context intersects with the system of whiteness within which Filipino migrants are implicated as a result of the Philippines' colonisation. Class and racial markers overlap in Philippine history to define the dominant stratum of society – symbols such as wealth, education, practices of gentility and a capacity to master the coloniser's language. This can also function as an orienting force for the Filipino middle class and signal transnational modalities to racial formations.

But, as the term implies, honorary whiteness fundamentally entails *conditionality*, where the threat of withdrawal of approval is never far away. In spite of economic integration, racial boundaries (phenotypical and cultural) continue to frame notions of 'us' and 'them' in Australian society. As Fanon's (1967) work attests, the inferiority complex produced by racial domination can be most haunting for those who have accessed some positive recognition from the dominant group. Honorary whiteness implies a state of suspended fantasy in which "privilege is tentative rather than absolute" (Valdez-Young, 2009: 179). This chapter discusses the palpable struggle to both manage stigma and maintain respect. In the dual process of self-making and being-made, the experience of middle-class Filipinos illustrates the complex and ambivalent politics of racial, cultural and economic citizenship as they are positioned in between inclusion/exclusion and recognition/misrecognition.

The promises and limits of social mobility

Joseph is in his late forties and works as a senior accountant. He had responded to a call for interviewees I placed on the alumni website of one of the Philippines' elite educational institutions. The Australian chapter of the alumni, which includes elementary, high school and university graduates, is large and remains ever proud of its roots. In the Philippines, the institution boasts attendees who come from some of the country's wealthiest and prominent families. Joseph was a student at the elementary and secondary schools before he and his family migrated to New Zealand, where his father found work as a lawyer with an international corporation. Joseph and his siblings proceeded to finish their schooling at an international high school with other expatriate children. His father had been a proud alumnus of the school as well, attending from elementary through to university. His mother, meanwhile, was from a family with "old money". Despite his family's privilege, however, his father decided to relocate overseas because he was offered a job which paid more money than he would ever earn in the Philippines.

Joseph described their lives in New Zealand as one "typical" of expatriate families; they lived among the expat community in a two-storey house located in a gated community and he and his siblings went to a private school. Joseph then moved to Australia after finishing high school to complete a business degree at a university in Queensland, in the east coast, while the rest of his family migrated to America. After his tertiary studies, he had a choice to either move back to New Zealand to find work, join his family in America, who had become well established, or stay in Australia and carve out a life on his own. He decided to move back to New Zealand, worked there for a large company for seven years and eventually migrated to Sydney, where he gained employment with an accountancy firm. Since moving to Sydney, Joseph has lived around the northern suburbs, a largely Anglo middle-class area, where friends and cousins were settled. He soon met his Filipina wife and they now have two young daughters. At the time of our interview, he had recently relocated his family to an affluent neighbourhood in Canberra, the country's capital, two hours outside of Sydney, after finding a more senior position and a higher-paying job.

Throughout our interview, Joseph's reflections displayed a level of comfort with living in Australia despite acknowledging his sometimes othered status as a 'migrant'. He described his experiences of racism as rare but those which he had experienced he took on board as a way to make himself a "better person" rather than dwell on the victimisation and helplessness. While I think that this indicates the kind of rationalisation that occurs with experiences of racism (the anguish is eventually obscured as one is able to reflect on and reason the experience), it also signals a particular kind of disposition among the middle class to distance themselves from a 'victim' status because they do not see their mobility as congruent with the immobility associated with racism. Joseph felt that the most racism he encountered was in Queensland as a university student in the 1980s. He felt terribly alone not only because he was without family but also because the small city where he was living did not have a large population of non-whites. He felt indirect racism in the form of being constantly stared at on campus, in shopping centres and on the street. He was also well aware of the very open practices of racism in Australia at that time:

> This place was the redneck capital of Australia. Queensland itself I suppose has a reputation for being a redneck place. I actually took my family there, passing by on the way to Brisbane and my wife said exactly the same thing. We went to one of the malls and you just felt people looking at you.

Not until his final year of university did he really find his feet and he described to me the sense of respect he felt he gained upon the completion of his university degree:

> Fourth year my coping mechanism was, 'I'm just going to knuckle down and do well!' And I did well. I topped some of my classes. I got it together again. More than anything, the lesson I learnt that year was that Australians like a winner. If you can show them you're good at something they'll come to you and have some respect for you. If you're a winner they will come to you. So you have to be good at what you do.

Securing a middle-class status, he now also sees his earning capacity and consumption practices as a way to affirm his 'equality': "I hate to say it, but 'things' can also change people's perspective of you. Like material things. If I have what my white neighbour has . . . the car, the house . . . then we're the same." Among Filipino middle-class professionals, their class status constitutes why they feel, for the most part, 'accepted' in Australian society and to a degree shielded from racist experiences. Acquiring a middle-class status is central to how they have become *less* 'Other', forged the feeling that they legitimately 'belong in' Australia and gained a sense of mutual respect. For Joseph, acquiring his degree was a way to overcome his marginality and prove his equal worth. Similar reflections can be found among other middle-class Filipino migrants whom I spoke with. Dialogue around the value of their education, skills and earning capacity is mobilised as proof of 'contributing' to Australian society, which they strongly feel justifies their 'equal' status. Their narratives allude to the assets valued by middle-class Australia as being framed by notions of contribution, competency, respectability and aspiration.

Vivienne, a mother and newly retired in her sixties, communicated a similar story. She lives in an affluent suburb in the North Shore and also understood education and intelligence as a means to deal with racism, especially in the workplace:

> I came to Australia in my late twenties and during the days of bad racism. You saw it in lots of place – on the bus, train, at work. There was one woman at work, she always gave me a hard time, just always criticising my work, and I know it's because I am Filipina. She thinks I'm inferior because I'm from a Third-World place. You know what I did? I worked hard so I can get ahead of her. You use your brains with these people. I'm educated, you know. I graduated as one of the top of my college in the Philippines and then I took courses here. You show your skills to them. She never said anything again once I was promoted above her.

Pamela, a second-generation Filipina working as a finance manager at a major Australian bank, similarly views her education as a way to minimise racial discrimination:

> I worked for a while after high school. But my mum was telling me I had to study, especially because we're coloured, people aren't going to value you, as you are right now. Just imagine if you don't have the education. . . . I think having that helps coloured people minimise experiencing racism.

Recognition through social mobility and middle-class respectability stems from the neo-liberalism that marks capitalist societies today, wherein who deserves to belong is increasingly defined in terms of productivity and consumption. As Sennett (2003: 57) reminds us, respect in today's world is often tied to economic worth and the dignity of labour, in that "the value of hard work define[s] the ethos of the self-respecting citizen." But this neoliberal economic system rarely operates in race-neutral ways. According to Ong (1991: 739), for racial minorities, such as non-white immigrants, "attaining success through self-reliant struggle . . . is a process of self-development that in Western democracies becomes inseparable from the process of 'whitening'." This 'whitening' is made possible through the complex and shifting processes of hierarchisation across racial and cultural difference (Elder et al., 2004; Hage, 1998). In Australia, whiteness was principally associated with the category of British 'Anglo-Saxon' and, in due course, became interchangeable with the term 'Anglo-Celtic' with the arrival of Irish Catholic migrants. While the English Protestant elite remained dominant over Irish Catholics, the core culture of 'Anglo whiteness' ultimately came to define the hegemonic foundation of Australia and was further reinforced after the arrival of migrants from non-English-speaking Southern Europe, who were definitively categorised as 'non-white' and 'ethnic'. In this process, as Ang and Stratton (1998) point out, the categorical construction of 'Anglo' homogenised an array of ethnic difference across migrant groups from Wales, Scotland and Northern Europe, especially Germany. But post-war 'ethnic migrants' were eventually also granted modes of inclusion into Australia's 'white' mainstream. Perera (2005) suggests that the possibility of achieving degrees of whiteness for these migrants was implicitly set in place by the violent dispossession of the Indigenous population. The economic migration into Australia of groups from Southern Europe and the Middle East and later from the Asian region represents the value given to their labour in increasing the nation's wealth, which further renders Aboriginal people as 'worthless' in the social order. In the contemporary context of preferred skilled migration intake, Stratton (2009: 19) contends that acquiring a status of whiteness is further extended to 'middle-class Asians' on account of their social mobility but it rests on the process of granting the status of 'underclass' to 'undesirable' migrants, specifically asylum seekers, who "have come to represent the lumpen, unskilled Other". Such processes signal a "dynamic of racial othering" that emerges from a range of economic and cultural mechanisms "that variously subject non-white immigrants to whitening or blackening processes that indicate the degree of their closeness to or distance from ideal white standards" (Ong, 1991: 751).

Furthermore, such access to privilege can empower immigrants with a sense of their own governmentality over the social order (Hage, 1998). Social mobility has produced a particular disposition among some Filipino middle class when understanding their experiences of racism. Joseph categorised the everyday racism he experienced in Queensland as being carried out by 'red necks' or 'yobos', which are labels commonly attributed to lower-class whites in Australia. He recounted another experience when he and his daughters were targets of racial slurs from a passing car on their walk to school. This kind of racism, once again, he attributed to 'ignorant' individuals:

> Yobos yelling out at you, rednecks staring at you because of your skin colour ... there are just people you can't do anything about, louts who abuse you ... you just don't respond to that, it demeans you to do that.

I suggest that such discourse positions the perpetrators of racism as the inferior Other – backward and uneducated – who haven't quite caught up with the rest of the world. In this way, Joseph stakes a claim to a status monopolised by 'white cosmopolitans' in Australia, who assume a status of being educated, open to the world and "capable of appreciating and consuming" difference (Hage, 2000: 201–203). In the new multicultural order, it is racist perpetrators who are ultimately deviant from the 'norm'. As Joseph sternly proclaimed, "I have the right to be here just as much as anyone else. This is my place. I have earned my place in this country." But while the social mobility achieved by some Asian groups in recent decades has diversified what has always been a traditionally white middle sector (Colic-Peisker, 2011), the broadening horizon of who has access to middle-class prosperity and respectability produces complex processes of recognition/misrecognition and racialised visibility/invisibility.

In a popular online forum for Filipino migrants in Australia, a member initiated a subject titled 'Success in Corporate Australia' and wrote the following:

> I have heard there are many Filipino senior executives in the big corporations such as banks, IT companies, etc. in the US, but here in Australia, I have not heard of any. Do you think we are able to succeed in the corporate world of Australia? Does anyone know of any position such as CEO or Managing Director in high-profile Australian companies or any multinational companies in Australia? Or is it true skin colour and accent are stumbling blocks for us to aim for such high positions in the business world and the highest we can aim for in our career is just middle management?

This forum member's subject matter reflects some very poignant questions that linger in the stories of many middle-class Filipino professionals. As racially marked subjects, regardless of achieving degrees of social mobility since their migration to Australia, it remains uncertain whether they can reach the highest levels of the corporate ladder. Norms of the male white executive were commonly acknowledged among my interviewees and their accounts of racism in the white-collar workplace. Indeed, the corresponding responses to this online post were followed by several admissions by other forum members on the whiteness of executive positions at their places of work. Interestingly, these responses were equally filled with folklore-like tales of un-named Filipinos in Australia who had 'made it', functioning like a coping mechanism to keep the middle class hopeful in their quest for positions of power. The lengthy dialogue on the forum which ensued exhibited the significance of the issue and informs the basis of perhaps the most predominant mode of racism middle-class Filipino migrants experience in the workforce. Subtle racist exclusion in the professional sector regularly comes in the form of repeatedly seeking a promotion but being constantly overlooked despite believing that they possess the required skills and knowledge for the job. Middle-class Filipino professionals speak to unspoken norms of whiteness at these executive-level positions which implicitly discourage certain bodies from considering such heights. At times, they can also be communicated in interactions and practices. Joseph, for example, spoke of the institutional racism he sensed in the corporate sector, wherein he felt like an 'outsider' from the exclusive network of white men connected by their private schooling. While he himself has similar cultural capital as these men because of his own private schooling background and his family's social status in the Philippines, this is not automatically convertible in the context of his migration:

> I wasn't connected with the networks in Sydney. I think Sydney has a private school network, all-boys, all-white club. It's got a history of its own . . . They don't make you feel so welcome, I'll tell you that. Not that they do anything to you, but they don't think much of you.

Andrew, who is in his late twenties and works at a major international accountancy firm as a compliance manager, also described similar experiences. While simultaneously completing a business degree and working in the industry for almost ten years, he has worked his way up from clerical assistant to a major managerial position. In our interview, he expressed his anxiety about reaching partner level at his company and, in general, in the corporate world:

> To get to the next one, which is partner or director level, I think that . . . yes there would be an issue getting to that next level. Most of the partners are middle-aged white men. You have to mingle in those networks. They socialise with middle-aged white men, the people they have meetings with are middle-aged white men. So that's where I think maybe race will be an issue eventually if I ever aspire to be a partner. I would really feel uncomfortable as well if I were taken out to these meetings and they're all middle-aged white men. I think the corporate world is dominated by white men.

Andrew and Joseph, remarking on the visibility of white men as corporate executives in their place of work, experience the hegemony of whiteness through skin colour. The visibility of white male bodies in the networks that enable access to prominent positions in the corporate structure hinders those who do not embody this corporeality from envisioning occupying these positions of power. If they were ever invited to the table, moreover, a discomfort of being 'out of place' would still linger. Another example Joseph shared involved an attempt to enrol his daughters into an exclusive private school in his new affluent neighbourhood in Canberra. The principal made a remark to him which he suspected as being indirectly racially offensive:

> The principal said to me, 'By the way, the houses here are $800,000 upwards. Everyone who lives here is a senior manager or executive, so you know, you draw your own conclusions.' I felt that was a strange comment; why does he think I don't have money? Would he say it to a white person? Maybe he thought I didn't fit the 'type' racially to live in this rich area. So I didn't enrol my kids there.

Filipino middle-class migrants may access the economic dimensions of white privilege through socio-economic mobility; however, they continue to encounter exclusion or marginalisation based on racial and ethnic markers ascribed as either physical and/or cultural difference. In her discussion of Chinese-Australians' negotiation of belonging in multicultural Australia, Tan (2007: 67) calls "racial bodily markers" the "tyranny of appearance", wherein "'Asian looks' . . . serve as a 'cue' denoting perpetual 'foreignness' and 'Otherness' that precludes their unconditional acceptance." Phenotype, furthermore, remains tied to cultural signifiers. This transpired in Andrew's account of the 'white corporate executive':

> I think you need to be seen as a leader and I think it's still hard for people to see an Asian man as a powerful leader in our society. So you can get to a certain level because you're technical, you know a lot of things . . . but to be perceived as a leader, to organise, I don't think they associate it with Asians. . . . I don't even know if it's something I can do anything about. . . . I guess I could change my skin colour? (laughs) So I just feel that I have to try harder than others to get there.

In racialised societies where whites dominate, Bonilla-Silva (2006: 233) argues that a white habitus structures "a racialised, uninterrupted socialisation process that conditions and creates whites' racial tastes, perceptions, feelings and emotions and their views on racial matters." This habitus is produced by the segregated lifestyle that whites live in their neighbourhoods, schooling, occupation and leisure activities. Through this isolation, racial discrimination or bias is often not because the Other is resented but because "positive emotions such as admiration, sympathy and trust are reserved for the in-group and withheld from the out-group" (Bonilla-Silva, 2006: 232). This resonates with Lipsitz's (1998) argument that whiteness is a form of *property* that enables its holder to access exclusive privileges, which then necessarily entails a 'possessive investment' to maintain restricted ownership. For Andrew, education, skills, qualifications and 'know-how' can be accumulated and deployed as cultural capital, which can prove his equal worth via competency. But it can get him only so far. 'Asians' are recognised for their ability to follow orders and display aptitude, but to rule and lead in positions of power is something else. The latter is the domain of 'conquering' white men and a position that his honorary whiteness cannot access. The trauma of phenotypical racism is managed by humour and masks the disturbing consideration that the only option is to change his skin colour.

This habitus of whiteness that structures corporate workplaces is perhaps even more poignantly felt by the middle-class Filipina professionals whom I met. In such cases, they experience multiple marginalisations on account of their raced and gendered bodies. Catherine is a second-generation Filipina-Australian and lives in one of Sydney's most expensive waterside suburbs. With a double degree in media and law, she has worked as a lawyer for large media forms and eventually started her own public relations company. She generally sees racism as having a minimal presence in her life and attributes this to having the liberty to inhabit spaces where 'racist types' are rare. Yet, at the same time, she expressed some uncertainty as to her 'belonging' in this racialised and gendered milieu:

> My work is very international. . . . I guess the people I know and meet, they're well travelled, well educated and are exposed to difference. I choose to be in an environment where you don't experience it (racism) very much. I mean, living here in Mosman – they're well educated, well travelled. They don't look down on me. Well, at least I don't think so. . . . Look, I absolutely think Australia is a racist society – I mean, Pauline Hanson and the phenomenon she became. And you look at our politicians – there's hardly any Asians. You look at CEOs – no Asian women. There's racism without a doubt. So laws addressing these inequalities are so important. . . . I'm all for affirmative action. You know, having a certain amount of women or different ethnicities.

Such experiences articulate the cruelty of misinterpellation: just when equal status is in sight one is constantly reminded that the recognition granted is revocable and narrow in its reach. Mechanisms of recognition and misrecognition simultaneously operate in the process of granting and acquiring the conditional status of honorary whiteness. In accessing economic power, the white ruling class grant racialised migrants levels of invisibility but, at the same time, keep migrant differences visible through conditional acceptance that maintain their perpetual Otherness.

English as cultural capital and the habitus of 'Western-ness'

Beyond the economic capital valued by the white middle class are also other forms of cultural capital. Mastery of the English language is among those forms recognised by Filipino migrants as central to their 'passing' in the 'mainstream'. Indeed, while learning English is a matter of practicality in order to navigate an Anglophone society, it also remains valued linguistic capital – economically and culturally – in the hegemonic order (Harrison, 2012). As such, I suggest the constellation of white skin and Western tongue sees the English language embody a particular intersection between whiteness and 'Western-ness'. For middle-class Filipino migrants, English skills and the 'right' accent enable navigation of everyday life with ease but also strategically allow them to 'blend in' (with white Australia) and 'stand out' (from other Asians), and also claim a sophisticated 'cosmopolitan' identity for Filipinos (who are not commonly seen in this light, rather only as deprived and exploitable).

Among the first generation, when speaking to each other, Tagalog or a Filipino dialect is still the predominant language used in conversation. During my fieldwork at places Filipinos frequent, such as the Blacktown CBD, it is common to hear 'Taglish' – the mode of code switching between Tagalog and English (or a Filipino language and English) – among Filipino patrons of shops and restaurants. But while the first generation continue to speak a Filipino language to each other, inside the home, many parents cease speaking to their children in the native language in order to ensure schooling success. And so, among the second generation, while being able to understand a Filipino language quite well as they hear their parents and older family members converse with each other, it is not uncommon to lack speaking fluency. Rose, a mother in her fifties and working as a project manager for a national corporation, recalled the way she was forced to stop speaking Tagalog to her children upon their migration to ensure her kids' schooling success and broader integration:

> I have three children. We arrived here when they were primary school age in the late eighties. . . . After enrolling them into school, we were told explicitly by the teacher – do not speak to your kids in Filipino anymore. If you want them to integrate and do well, speak only in English. Well, lucky that we speak English very well! But imagine if we are another ethnic person who couldn't speak English? What are they going to do with their kids? It is a little unfair when you think about it.

Furthermore, the use of English in the Filipino community in Sydney is promoted in both direct and indirect ways. At community events, particularly those with a large middle-class base, English is spoken in the official proceedings regardless of how small the number of non-Filipinos in attendance. Also, unlike most ethnic media in Australia, Filipino community newspapers are written in English with only a small section of the publications written in Filipino. The use of English in such ways has produced both advantages and dilemmas. While English as a 'neutral' language may be used to bridge the wide linguistic differences across Filipinos and, in the context of migration, is used as a first language as a matter of convenience, it can also be a strategic way to *perform* an assimilated status to wider Australian society. English fluency is a source for recognition among the many Filipino migrants, as I explore in the discussion to follow, and this is especially among the middle class. Yet, at the same time, the impressive level of English proficiency across the community has created panic around the survival of Tagalog and other Filipino dialects among future generations. This was verbalised in several community events that I attended (ironically conducted in English) and by both first-generation and second-generation whom I had interviewed. In addition, mastery of the English language has also served to make Filipino migrants relatively under-recognised in the mainstream multicultural imaginary that desires to consume the 'exotic'. Thus, there is an inherent tension in balancing the preservation of Filipino languages throughout the migrant generations and promoting the uniqueness of Filipino culture through language without compromising English and the power it yields for achieving integration and publicly performing assimilation.

Bernadette is a young Filipina in her early twenties. She graduated with a law/commerce double degree and had just completed an internship with a major national firm. She observed a large number of students from different Asian backgrounds in her law course; however, she explained that when she started interning for the company her peers were mainly white and male. Out of the thirty interns, she was one of the few females accepted and the only Asian. When asked why she thought she had been accepted amid the norm of whiteness (and masculinity) she spoke about the advantages of the Filipino's grasp of the English language:

> In law school, there were so many Asian students. But when I started working for a law firm, I was the only Asian out of thirty (interns). So it's obvious this place thinks whites fit in with the culture more. Because you know, partners doing the interviewing want someone not just for skills but as well someone they will get along with. Someone to 'fit' the culture. And so what can I say? When you see who ends up making it. . . . you realise what the culture is and who they think fits. The line-up is white or male . . . Compared to other Asians, our English is an advantage. Filipinos, we're the louder Asian race. We're a bit more confident than other Asians. And we don't really have the 'Asian accent' when we speak English.

There is, as Fanon (1967: 18) wrote, a power that mastery of the dominant language offers the racialised subject: "a man who has language consequently possesses the world expressed and implied by that language. . . . to speak a language is to take on a world, a culture." For Bernadette, she feels her grasp of English has allowed her to gain recognition from the partners at her firm. It also extends beyond her workplace to social situations and random exchanges in public spaces, where her English acts as a resource to avoid the casual racism that can be triggered by the inability to speak English or by having an accent that indicates only a secondary grasp of the language. Bernadette's mastery of the host society's language allows her to communicate, contribute and protest in the social spaces that she traverses and inhabits. Moreover, it accesses a level of invisibility, a kind of "subaltern tactic to escape the threat posed by the dominant population" as one attempts to subvert the white gaze (Stratton, 2009: 11). For Bernadette, her English fluency disguises her racialised corporeality compared to, she believes, other Asians whose racial and cultural differences are so much more apparent when they lack English skills.

Arnel is an architect in his fifties. He also raised similar points about navigating the language order of Australian society and elaborated on the manner in which he has built on the nuances of his linguistic repertoire:

> At a place I used to work, they used to make jokes about a Vietnamese colleague with a thick accent. They used to ask me why I didn't have the same Asian accent. I gave them a little history lesson that we learn English in the Philippines and we learn American English. They don't know these things. In a way, it (English) lets you get by. They make jokes about Asians in general, but at least they can't joke about my accent. But then you can't win because they used to ask why do I want to be American? (because of the accent) So then you start to learn the Aussie way of English as well. Use their slangs.

But there is more to the mastery of language than the obvious ways in which it assists with 'getting ahead' and 'getting along'. There is a *pride* in claiming to be 'English experts' that forms a part of the middle class's subjective frames and identity projections that align them closer to 'Western-ness'. Bernadette elaborated: "When I think Filipinos I think westernised Asians. Culturally we're a bit more accustomed with the West compared to other Asians. Speaking English is part of our Filipino-ness." Bernadette's English proficiency is something she sees as intrinsic to her being 'Filipino', where to be Filipino is to be *kind of* 'Western' already. This narrative highlights the ways in which English generates a habitus for the Filipino middle class that can negotiate modes of compatibility with whiteness in Australia. This becomes significant especially because regardless of the economic value assigned to Asians in Australia, physical and verbal markers of 'Asian-ness' continue to be a stigmatised as 'foreign' and 'other'.

There is, then, palpable offense taken by many of my middle-class respondents when it is assumed that they *cannot* speak English as it challenges the mode of recognition their linguistic capital grants. Melita, another second-generation Filipina who works as a lawyer in a boutique firm in Sydney, expressed the frustration and disrespect she felt over the constant misrecognition:

> I went to interstate on holidays with friends. I was waiting to get coffee and it seemed to be taking some time. I asked for it again but the girl was just a bit rude. But I waited patiently. When the girl finally gave me my order, it wasn't what I wanted. I went back to her and said, "I ordered a cappuccino." And she was still quite rude. She insisted that I had ordered it. And then I just went off at her. And then the look on her face – I think she was quite surprised. I think she probably thought I didn't know how to speak English . . . that I wouldn't know how to stick up for myself. She probably thought I was some Asian who couldn't speak English!. . . . You get sick of it. Like, people asking you, "Where did you learn how to speak English so well?" Someone asked me that once. Like really? People are still so ignorant these days?

Civility and the 'good migrant'

Whiteness also structures the multicultural order via the categories of the 'good migrant' and 'bad migrant'. Andrew spoke about his disapproval of Filipinos who speak Tagalog to each other in public. While speaking a foreign language in the presence of others can be construed as impolite, migrants who publicly 'perform' their ethnicity in such ways can often be rebuked for being 'bad migrants', unwilling to assimilate into the 'Australian' way of life:

> At work, I remember going into the lunch room; there were Filipinos gathered and they were speaking Tagalog. That made me feel uncomfortable . . . sort of made me cringe that they were behaving like that. I find it rude that they're speaking a different language when everyone can hear. . . . I would prefer it if they weren't speaking to me in Tagalog. I've heard people complain when people speak their own language. So because of those things, I'm conscious of it.

Andrew's criticism of his Filipino colleagues serves to distance him from their linguistic practices. This allows his repositioning as the 'good migrant' that draws on accumulated knowledge of the codes that determine racial inclusion and exclusion. Tania is in her forties and a university graduate in nursing, currently working as a head nurse at a Sydney hospital. She communicated a similar story:

> Older Anglo nurses don't like ethnic nurses to speak in our own language. Memos are sent out to the whole ward if you speak in your own language. Yes, it's hospital policy that you must speak in English, I understand. But other migrant nurses don't really care if you speak Tagalog to other Filipino nurses, but once a white nurse comes, you better speak in English or they'll tell on you and then a memo gets sent out. I was speaking Tagalog once to another Filipina, just catching up. And one of the white nurses, she's nice and all, told me I'm not allowed to do that and that I should speak in English. So I apologised.

Despite that English is necessary for the working environment in hospital wards, Tania's experience of being scolded like a child for 'doing the wrong thing' and for which she feels the need to apologise displays the fine line between official rules and unofficial modes of discipline to which non-white bodies can be subject. And this can inevitably lead to modes of regulating and monitoring across Filipino migrants. Ever conscious of her use of Tagalog, Tania later articulated strong views around the 'unrefined' ways in which Tagalog or English was spoken by certain Filipino migrants, signalling how delineations between 'good' and 'bad' migrants can often be underscored by implicit discourses around the 'civilised' and 'uncivilised':

> They're so embarrassing. The ones who speak Tagalog on the trains. They're so loud. *Parang mga palengkera* (They're like those women who work at the markets). You know, they bump into you in the street . . . *"Hoy! Kamusta ka na!"* (Hey you! How are you?) at the top of their lungs. Sometimes you just want to die. . . . Sometimes it's not even Tagalog. They're on the train speaking in English but they are so loud and chatty.

Palengkeras in the Philippines are women who work in wet and dry markets called *palengkes*, often found in poor urban areas of Manila, and patrons who work and shop here are the poor lower class. To describe someone as a *palengkera* is to demean that woman's crass manners. For Tania, Filipino migrants who speak Tagalog or English *loudly* in public spaces are embarrassing because they represent lower-classed Filipinos. Tania, instead, positions herself as a different kind of 'Filipino', one who is refined and observes the appropriate conduct in public spaces. Research by Pyke and Dang (2003) identified similar distancing tactics undertaken by middle-class second-generation Asian-Americans who assigned to recent immigrants a lower social status because new arrivals occupied the stigmatised identity of 'Fresh Off the Boat' (FOBs). This term was also used by some of my interviewees, particularly those of the second generation, who feel most pressure to "construct identities in relation to the meanings and standards of the new society" (Pyke and Dang, 2003: 148). To be labelled a 'FOB' was to be perceived as fresh from the 'uncivilised' Third World in terms of speech, dress and manners.

The 'good migrant' status is also further established through self-comparisons with other racialised subjects. Specifically, some Filipino migrants distinguish themselves from Muslim Arabic migrants, who have become the primary targets of racism in Australia. I return to the experiences of Andrew, who expressed unfavourable opinions of Lebanese migrants:

> Cronulla (Riots) targeted Muslims . . . I suppose I could relate to why it happened. Just about Lebanese guys. Just the way they taunt. They're just too different from us. They come from a violent. . . . or I guess. . . . aggressive male culture. . . . the war there (in Lebanon) I guess. But I just can't see people getting that angry about Asians. And I guess they (Lebanese) are less educated. That sounds racist. But they're more the working class. I guess I associate that racism with the lower class.

Another interviewee named Vincent, who is in his mid-twenties and works as an IT manager, articulated similar sentiments:

> I used to live in Lakemba but that was before the Lebanese came in. But thankfully we moved away from there . . . They seem uneducated. Cronulla (Riots) could have happened to anyone, but I guess, you know, the rape stories. You go to the city, to Darling Harbour, you see Lebanese guys in white caps harassing girls. It's their culture. It's not helping them and their image.

These two young men view Muslim culture as synonymous with Lebanese-Australians or other Middle Eastern Arabic youth despite that many of these migrants are also Christian. They interpret Muslim culture as violent and disrespectful towards women, which can be ascribed to common stereotypes perpetuated in popular media (Poynting, 2004). Andrew's and Vincent's association of Islam with Arabic young male migrants functions as a point of Otherness from which they can distance themselves and reinforce their attributes of 'Western civility'. Education too acts as a form of distinction. Implicit in this strategy is the perception of Filipinos as being much more compatible with Australian culture. What is then quite insulting for Vincent and Andrew is when, in certain spaces, they experience the same exclusionary treatment shown to young Arabic men. One such example is the experience of being denied entry into upmarket establishments in Sydney, which they witnessed men of ethnic appearance being subjected to, especially Arabic men. Andrew explained:

> I remember going to one club, it's known for its strict door policy, and the door girl said to me, "Are there any more of you coming?" What's that supposed to mean, you know? And she said, "Just tell your friends that they may have

problems getting in." Or some kind of bullshit excuse. That's when I really get frustrated about the whole race thing. I think that . . . people feel uncomfortable when they're in a place full of Asians because they think it leads to violence. It's like Lebanese guys. They can't get in either. So you can't go there with a big bunch of Asians. As a single Asian you're not as intimidating. Which is why they ask the question, "Are there any more of you coming?" So they know whether to expect any more brown people coming. . . . The way you dress, it has to be of high standard. Dress code is already an issue, but I think you need to be perfect so they can't pick you up on anything. You have to have girls with you also. Preferably white girls.

While upmarket establishments claim they do not discriminate against race or ethnicity, only that they have 'specific' door policies, countless instances of rejection experienced by Andrew and other young Filipino men I interviewed hint at how certain spaces are often invisibly 'whitewashed'. Thus, the hard work in maintaining racial invisibility is again evident in the strategies Andrew deploys as he attempts to gain entry into places that prefer an exclusively white clientele. It is played out through his body – his dress must be impeccable, he needs to perform his middle-class respectability and play down any aggressive masculinity, and he must also have white company to camouflage his skin colour. While in his earlier remarks he states that the Cronulla Riots was something not unexpected because of the 'disrespectful' and 'uncivilised' behaviour of Lebanese Muslim-Australian men, Andrew complains of the way Asian males can also be viewed as having the same tendencies. In spite of his tactics to distance himself from 'undesirable' migrants, Andrew's 'ethnic' appearance and the stereotypes attached to his racialised body are an unwanted equaliser that re-situates him in the same marginal position. The exclusion is so humiliating and disrespectful that he went on to admit, "Now I try to avoid those places where you get that criticism. Where race will be an issue."

Transnational regimes of whiteness

In this final section, I explore how whiteness as an orienting force emerges from colonial racial formations in Philippine society equally as it is produced by the hegemony structuring Australian society. Pugliese (2007: 1) contends that whiteness is often (mis)presented as impacting "for the first time on the bodies and subjectivities of diasporic subjects only once they enter the Australian nation". It stems from a tendency to forget or erase the histories of whiteness that already mark subjects before the migration process. He argues that the theoretical inattentiveness to the histories of whiteness in which migrants are already implicated has become part of the system that allows certain norms of whiteness to be taken-for-granted knowledge. I return to the example of English as cultural capital to highlight the multi-routedness of racial formations. As Mishra Tarc (2013: 365–369) suggests, "race *moves* under the intensification of transnational flows and connections", whereby "historical and colonial manifestations of race shuttle back between and across the macro and micro of geopolitical time and space."

As a mode of resistance for Filipinos in the diasporic context, English carries even more weight when understanding that it is through the mastery of the coloniser's language that the elite and upper-middle-class Filipinos in the Philippines have historically been able to position themselves closer to the sources of colonial power (Rafael, 2000: 165). During the Spanish colonial period and later imperial American rule, to speak Spanish or English in the Philippines signalled education, refinement and privilege. This is perpetuated in the contemporary postcolonial and globalising Philippines. Performing 'Western-ness' through the coloniser's language and displays of civility is deeply rooted in what Rafael (2000) calls 'mestiza/mestizo envy' that emerges from the "Filipino historical imagination" where "the *mestizo/a* has enjoyed a privileged position associated with economic wealth, political influence, and cultural hegemony" (Rafael, 2000: 165). It is through the mestizo/a that power and language most successfully intersect because to "occupy the position of *mestizo/a* is to invoke the legacy of *illustrados*, the generation of mostly mixed-race, Spanish-speaking, university educated nationalists". Later, throughout American imperialism, English replaced Spanish as the valued linguistic capital, entangling English with the privilege of fair skin, civility and wealth. In his essay *Notes on Bakya*, Philippine poet, journalist and screen writer Jose Lacaba (1970) traced how the term *bakya* signalled "the masses" (the *bakya* crowd) and was eventually used in derogatory ways to describe the practices and tastes of the lower class. The word *bakya* literally translates to wooden slippers worn in lieu of shoes by the poor in the barrios. He explained that 'to be *bakya*' is often a judgement passed in the *failed English* of the lower class. In the diasporic context, distancing oneself from loud and crass Filipinos who speak Tagalog or English loudly in public spaces or from embarrassing Filipinos who speak imperfect English with a Filipino accent signals an entanglement with these racial formations. Further, this tactic can enable a dual negotiation across two racial regimes. Because English is valued both in Australia and in the Philippines, middle-class Filipino migrants are able to simultaneously negotiate their position in the racial hierarchy of both social orders. They acquire more symbolic power in the Philippine context as Filipinos who have achieved middle-class prosperity and respectability in the West itself and, in the same process, the racialised class system in the Philippines is reinforced in the diasporic context through the marginalisation of lower-class Filipino migrants who fail to display the same kind of cultural capital. As I detail in the next chapter, this form of marginalisation experienced by the working class is interpreted as a 'kind of racism' that occurs *within* the 'community'.

There is also a related discourse of having "Spanish roots" that strengthens the cultural capital of being less 'Asian' and enables a closeness to the ruling class in Australia. References are made to a Spanish lineage through descriptions of mestizo/mestiza relatives or emphasis given to the influence of Spanish customs in Filipino culture. A few also cited their surnames as proof of their Spanish heritage. And so, while American imperialism might be appreciated through language and education, the Philippines' Spanish colonial history is, on the other hand, romanticised through the idea of mixed Euro-Asian lineage. While Spanish influence can indeed be found in Philippine dress, customs and cuisine, relations between Spanish nationals in the Philippines and *indios* were, in contrast, very minor. Mixed-blood Spanish-Filipinos made up an extremely minute proportion of the population under Spanish rule (Aguilar, 2005). Meanwhile, the legacy of Spanish surnames among the Filipino people, as Filipino-Australian historian Perdon (1998) explains, was the product of the colonising government's initiative to establish a civil register in order to conduct a census of the Philippines. The possession of Spanish surnames is more of an administrative outcome than it is a lineage born from colonial Spanish-Filipino romance. Similarly, in research into the diasporic identities of the East Timorese in Australia, Wise (2006) found varying machinations across racial identities among members of the middle class. Portugues-ness is a prominent point of identification in her respondents' subjectivities that allows the aligning of East Timorese-ness with Portugues-ness as a strategic response to the "history of Indonesian occupation, a way of divesting the Asian-ness in East Timoreseness with Portuguesness, of making a core difference from Indonesianness" (Wise, 2006: 138). These manoeuvres take root in the colonial legacy of Portuguesness being "the marker that differentiated one from being too 'native' or too 'East Timorese'."

It is significant to point out, however, that the definition of mestizo/a in Filipino culture that associates the category primarily with mixed-blood Euro-Asian lineage is ultimately an obscured one. Historically, the majority of who were considered mestizo in the colonial Philippines were the population of mixed-blood Chinese-Spanish or Chinese-Filipinos. While being stigmatised as inferior foreigners by the Spanish, Chinese traders in the Philippines eventually became associated with business and wealth. To this day, Chinese-Filipinos make up a significant proportion of the nation's elite and upper middle class. However, as a result of long-held anti-Chinese sentiments that underlie Philippine society, according to Hau (2014: 76),

> the term mestizo itself in popular usage was stripped of its sociological and historical reference to Chinese and was increasingly ascribed to Filipinos of mainly white (American or European) ancestry whose hybridity indexed the hegemonic power and prestige of 'white' America/Europe.

Therefore, the strategy of aligning one's self with 'Western-ness' in order to distance from 'Asian-ness' is equally situated in the politics of racialisation in Philippine society that is perpetuated across borders through the diasporic operationalisation of the obscured mestizo/a identity as 'European' or 'Western'.

Indeed, these transnational connections across racial regimes of whiteness signal the manner in which, as Maldonado-Torres (2007: 243) explains, *coloniality* survives colonialism – a subjectivity maintained alive in "cultural patterns, in common sense, in the self-image of peoples, in aspirations of self" long after the conclusion of colonial administration. Yet, at the same time, there are also moments when this can be disrupted. The blurry boundaries of racial signification can create *fluid* and *hybrid* positionalities for some of my respondents that point to the ways in which their tactics cannot simply be read as colonial mimicry. Karlo is in his fifties and works as an engineer for a local government council. He recalled to me his first experiences in applying for rental homes and how his English skills (and 'non-Asian' sounding surname) were a point of confusion for white Australians and, while can be tiring to constantly explain, also functions to destabilise (even just for a moment) essentialising forces:

> Back then you heard all these stories that they didn't want to rent to Asians. And I was trying to live in the North Shore because I knew a Filipino couple there. You speak on the phone to them (real estate agents) and they have no idea you're Asian. First, Filipinos have an American accent. Second, Filipinos have Spanish surnames. And then they see you and they're surprised that there is this Asian sitting in front of them. One time the agent actually asked how I spoke English so well. It's offensive but also shows how easily confused they are. . . . they can't place you in a box. Some of my office mates asked me before if I am Canadian or American because of the slight American accent. They can't place you so in a way you're a bit more free. And with Asians, they can't place you either. When Japanese see me, they ask if I'm Japanese. When Chinese see me they start talking to me in Chinese.

Lastly, Pamela explained how she sometimes used 'Taglish', the hybrid mode of code switching between Tagalog and English, as a means of disrupting whiteness:

> You know, you can use Taglish with other Filos and use Tagalog words Aussies don't know. . . . My parents stopped speaking to me in Tagalog when I was a kid. But then the older I got, I wanted to re-learn it. So maybe in my late twenties I started practicing again with my parents. And now I speak it pretty well again. . . . It's important because I want to pass it on to my kids. And I realised it's pretty handy when you want to talk about people secretly. Like *yung mga pute* (like white people). (sniggers) And it annoys the hell out of them.

Conclusion

Whiteness, in its local and transnational manifestation, is negotiated, cumulative and contextual and "is far from being the essentialised, fixed racial category it is often posited to be" (Hage, 1998: 58). In the racial organisation of Australian society, respect and recognition do not come for free. Accumulating varying forms of valued cultural and economic capital gives Filipino middle-class migrants something to leverage and exchange. A white middle-class habitus accumulated through social mobility and reinforced by a habitus of 'Western-ness' from the Philippines' colonial history can acquire a status of honorary whiteness. This status resonates with other similar positionalities, such as the 'model migrant' or 'model minority' or the notion of the 'ethnic success story', and which all (problematically) understand the 'successful' integration of minorities in terms of social mobility. I suggest, however, that the notion of 'honorary whiteness' captures the *conditionality* of this 'integration' that remains underscored by *racial* markers. That the middle class as a 'white affair' is now threatened by the social mobility of non-white middle-class migrants like Filipinos (and other Asians more broadly) comes to be regulated through both direct and indirect modes of racism. And so, part and parcel of this mobility is a precarity, where not having white skin can diminish the capacity to secure unquestioned belonging. Honorary whiteness, in this way, remains relegated to a second-class status as the threat of revocation always lingers and privileges are provisional and never total. Middle-class Filipinos, therefore, endure a palpable struggle of managing both privilege and stigma. Social mobility makes available the same kinds of material and symbolic concessions accessible to the white middle class and enables the reworking of racially stigmatised identities. But the respect remains conditional and revocable. Furthermore, intensifying neoliberal values of meritocracy and its intersections with enduring modes of racialised domination undermine egalitarian tenets of 'equality for all'. Such repertoires of resistance endorse an ethos of privatised considerations – a '"you don't get something for nothing'. . . . enterprise-bargaining-like concept" of how to achieve mutual recognition (Hage, 2000: 29). But for middle-class Filipino migrants, they are necessary tactics to survive the wear and tear of routine racism and signal the compromises and ambivalences of fighting racism in spaces of in-between-ness.[5]

Notes

1 For whiteness in the context of black/white relations in Australia see Cowlish and Morris (1997); Moreton-Robinson (2001); Nicoll (2002); Larbalestier (2004); Shaw (2007). For whiteness in the context of whites and other non-white immigrant groups in Australia see Schech and Haggis (2001); Hage (1998); Monsour (2004); Tan (2007); Perera (2005); Standfield (2004); Colic-Peisker (2005); Matereke (2009).
2 The term 'honorary whiteness' has been used in the US context in the work of Bonilla-Silva (2003) in analysing the 'new racism' in America, particularly towards African Americans; in Ong's (1991) analysis of transnationally mobile Chinese migrants in North America; and in Valdez-Young's (2009) essay on the analysis of popular culture texts and her personal history as a Chinese-American. Stratton (2009) has recently introduced the idea into the Australian context and observes the term in the literature to originally refer to Jewish migrants in the US after their 'assimilation' but more recently also encompasses middle-class Asian Americans. In Australia, he sees the status of honorary whiteness as being granted to middle-class Asians (particularly Chinese) or middle-class South Asians (particularly Indians).
3 I acknowledge that the middle class today is an ever diverse category. Either the term tends to be used to describe the middle sector located in suburban Australia with average household incomes and relative socio-economic stability or it can refer to the more affluent and cosmopolitan upper middle class who occupy professional managerial jobs and who have access to high living standards. In some cases, the term 'middle class' has also been applied to the lower middle sector, who share more characteristics with those considered Australia's working-class 'battlers'.
4 The extension of Bourdieu's theorisation of cultural capital and habitus to the study of race has been most prominent among scholars researching the reproduction of racial inequality through educational institutions (Horvat and Wilson, 1998; Horvat

and Antonio, 1999; Horvat and O'Connor, 2000; Lareau and Horvat, 2000; Horvat and Lewis, 2003). In general, research on the middle-class African-American experience has provided key observations into how the accumulation of forms of capital subverts everyday racism to grant these subjects a degree of equal footing with 'white America' (Lamont and Fleming, 2005; Young Jr., 1999; Horvat and O'Connor et al., 2006).

5 A version of this chapter appears as a journal article: see Aquino (2016).

References

Aguilar, F. (2005) 'Tracing origins: *Illustrado* nationalism and the racial science of migration waves', *The Journal of Asian Studies*, vol. 64, no. 3, pp. 605–37.

Allen, T. (1994) *The Invention of the White Race*, New York: Verso.

Aquino, K. (2016) 'Anti-racism "from below": Exploring repertoires of everyday anti-racism', *Ethnic and Racial Studies*, vol. 39, no. 1, pp. 105–22.

Baldwin, J. (1998) 'On being white and other lies', in Roediger, D. (ed.), *Black on White*, New York: Schocken Books, pp. 177–80.

Bonilla-Silva, E. (2003) 'New racism, colour-blind racism and the future of whiteness in America', in Doane, A. and Bonilla-Silva, E. (eds.), *White Out: The Continuing Significance of Race*, New York: Routledge, pp. 271–84.

Bonilla-Silva, E. (2006) 'When whites flock together: The social psychology of white habitus', *Critical Sociology*, vol. 32, p. 229.

Colic-Peisker, V. (2005) '"At least you're the right colour": Identity and Social Inclusion of Bosnian Refugees', *Journal of Ethnic and Migration Studies*, vol. 31, no. 4, pp. 615–38.

Colic-Peisker, V. (2011) 'A new era in Australian multiculturalism? From working class "Ethnics" to a "Multicultural Middle Class"', *International Migration Review*, vol. 45, no. 3, pp. 562–87.

Cowlish, G. and Morris, B. (1997) *Race Matters: Indigenous Australians and Our Society*, Canberra: Aboriginal Studies Press.

Dyer, R. (1997) *White*, London: Routledge.

Elder, C., Cath, E. and Pratt, C. (2004) 'Whiteness in constructions of Australian nationhood: Indigenes, immigrants and governmentality', in Moreton-Robinson, A. (ed.), *Whitening Race: Essays in Social and Cultural Criticism,* Sydney: Aboriginal Studies Press, pp. 208.

Espiritu, Y. (1994) 'The intersection of race, ethnicity, and class: The multiple identities of second-generation Filipinos', *Identities*, vol. 1, no. 2–3, pp. 249–73.

Fanon, F. (1967) *Black Skin, White Masks*, London: Grove Press.

Feagin, J. and Sikes, M. (1994) *Living with Racism: The Black Middle-Class Experience*, Boston: Beacon Press.

Frankenberg, R. (1997) *Displacing Whiteness: Essays in Social and Cultural Criticism*, London: Duke University Press.

Hage, G. (1998) *White Nation: Fantasies of White Supremacy in a Multicultural Society*, New York: Routledge.

Hage, G. (2000) 'On the ethics of pedestrian crossings or why 'mutual obligation' does not belong in the language.' *Meanjin*, vol. 59, no. 4, pp. 27–38.

Harrison, G. (2012) 'Oh, you've got such a strong accent': Language identity intersecting with professional identity in the human services in Australia', *International Organization for Migration*, vol. 51, no. 5, pp. 192–204.

Hau, C. (2014) *The Chinese Question: Ethnicity, Nation and Region in the Philippines*, Singapore: NUS Press.

hooks, b. (1992) *Black Looks: Race and Representation*, Boston: South End Press.

Horvat, E. and Antonio, A. (1999) 'Hey those shoes are out of uniform: African American girls in an elite high school and the importance of habitus', *Anthropology and Education Quarterly*, vol. 30, no. 3, pp. 317–42.

Horvat, E. and Lewis, K. (2003) 'Reassessing the "Burden of 'Acting White'": The importance of peer groups in managing academic success", *Sociology of Education*, vol. 76, no. 4, pp. 265–80.

Horvat, E. and O'Connor, C. (2006) *Beyond Acting White: Reframing the Debate on Black Student Achievement*, Lanham, MD: Rowman and Littlefield.

Jakubowicz, A., Morrissey, M. and Palser, J. (1984) *Ethnicity, Class and Social Policy in Australia*, SWRC Reports and Proceedings, No. 46, University of New South Wales.

Lacaba, J. (1970) 'Notes on bakya: Being apologia of sorts for Filipino masscult', *Philippines Free Press*, 31 January, pp. 117–23.

Lamont, M. and Fleming, C. (2005) 'Everyday antiracism: Competence and religion in the cultural repertoires of the African American Elite', *Du Bois Review*, vol. 2, no. 1, pp. 29–43.

Larbalestier, J. (2004) 'White over black: Discourses of whiteness in Australian culture', *Borderlands*, vol. 3, no. 2.

Lareau, A. and Horvat, E. (2000) 'Moments of social inclusion and exclusion: Race, class, and cultural capital in family-school relationships', *Sociology of Education*, vol. 72, no. 1, pp. 37–53.

Lipsitz, G. (1998) *The Possessive Investment in Whiteness: How White People Profit from Identity Politics*, Philadelphia: Temple University Press.

Maldonado-Torres, N. (2007) 'On the coloniality of being: Contributions to the development of a concept', *Cultural Studies*, vol. 21, no. 2–3, pp. 240–70.

Matereke, K. (2009) 'Embracing the Aussie identity: Theoretical reflections on challenges and prospects for African-Australian youths', *Australasian Review of African Studies*, vol. 30, no. 1, pp. 129–43.

Matthews, J. (2002) 'Racialised schooling, "Ethnic Success" and Asian-Australia students', *British Journal of Sociology of Education*, vol. 23, no. 2, pp. 193–207.

Miles, R. (1989) *Racism*, London: Routledge.

Mishra Tarc, A. (2013) 'Race moves: Following global manifestations of new racisms in intimate space', *Race, Ethnicity and Education*, vol. 16, no. 3, pp. 365–85.

Monsour, A. (2004) 'Becoming white: How early Syrian/Lebanese in Australia recognised the value of whiteness', in Boucher, L., Carey, J. and Ellinghaus, K. (eds.), *Historicising Whiteness: Transnational Perspectives on the Construction of Identity*, Published in association with the School of Historical Studies, Melbourne: RMIT, University of Melbourne, pp. 124–32.

Moreton-Robinson, A. (2001) 'A possessive investment in patriarchal whiteness: Nullifying native title', in Nursery-Bray, P. and Lee Bacchi, C. (eds.), *Left Directions: Is There a Third Way?*, Crawley, Australia: University of Western Australia Press, pp. 162–77.

Nicoll, F. (2002) 'Reconciliation in and out of perspective: White knowing, seeing, curating and being at home in and against Indigenous sovereignty', in Moreton-Robinson, A. (ed.), *Whitening Race: Essays in Social and Cultural Criticism*, Canberra: Aboriginal Studies Press, pp. 17–31.

Ong, A.W. (1991) 'Cultural citizenship as subject making', *Current Anthropology*, vol. 37, no. 5, pp. 737–62.

Perdon, R. (1998) *Brown Americans of Asia*, Sydney: Manila Prints.

Perera, S. (2005) 'Who will I become? The multiple formations of Australian whiteness', *Australian Critical Race and Whiteness Studies Association Journal*, vol. 1, pp. 30–9.

Poynting, S. (2004) *Living with racism: The Experience and Reporting by Arab and Muslim Australians of Discrimination and Violence since September 11, 2001*, Report to the Human Rights and Equal Opportunity Commission, Sydney.

Pugliese, J. (2007) 'White historicide and the returns of the Souths to the South', *Australian Humanities Review*, no. 42.

Pyke, K. and Dang, T. (2003) '"FOB" and "Whitewashed": Identity and internalised racism among second generation Asian Americans', *Qualitative Sociology*, vol. 26, no. 2, pp. 147–72.

Rafael, V. (2000) *White Love and Other Events in Filipino History*, Durham: Duke University Press.

Raj, D. (2003) *Where Are You From? Middle Class Migrants in the Modern World*, Berkeley: University of California Press.

Schech, S. and Haggis, J. (2001) 'Migrancy, multiculturalism and whiteness: Recharting core Identities in Australia', *Communal/Plural*, vol. 9, no. 2, pp. 143–59.

Sennett, R. (2003) *Respect: The Formation of Character in an Age of Inequality*, London: Penguin Books.

Shaw, W. (2007) *Cities of Whiteness*, Oxford: Blackwell.

Standfield, R. (2004) 'A remarkably tolerant nation? Constructions of benign whiteness in Australian political discourse', *Borderlands E-Journal*, vol. 3, no. 2.

Stratton, J. (2009) 'Preserving white hegemony: Skilled migration, "Asians" and middle class assimilation', *Borderlands*, vol. 8, no. 3, pp. 1–28.

Sullivan, S. (2006) *Revealing Whiteness: The Unconscious Habits of Racial Privilege*, Bloomington: Indiana University Press.

Tan, C. (2007) 'The tyranny of appearance: Chinese Australian identities and the politics of difference' in Khoo, T. (ed.), *Locating Asian Australian Cultures*, Oxon: Routledge, pp. 65–82.

Valdez-Young, A. (2009) 'Honorary whiteness', *Asian Ethnicity*, vol. 10, no. 2, pp. 177–85.

Wilson, W.J. (1998) *The Declining Significance of Race: Blacks and Changing American Institutions*, Chicago : University of Chicago.

Wise, A. (2006) *Exile and Return among the East Timorese*, Philadelphia: University of Pennsylvania Press.

Young Jr., A. (1999) 'Navigating race: Getting ahead in the lives of "rags to riches" young black men', in Lamont, M. (ed.), *The Cultural Territories of Race: Black and White Boundaries*, Chicago: University of Chicago Press, pp. 30–62.

4 Reclaiming rights, morality and esteem

The dignity of working-class Filipino migrants

Amid the hustle and bustle of suburban mothers and their energetic children crowding the food court of a shopping centre in Penrith, a largely white working-class suburb in outer western Sydney, I met with Elvie several times over the course of a month. Elvie is in her late forties and is a cleaner at this shopping complex, and she was available to talk only during her short thirty-minute lunch breaks. In this impersonal setting, surrounded by the noise of children playing and with our eyes always on the clock to make sure she returned to work on time, Elvie gradually revealed to me her family's story of migration to seek a better source of livelihood outside of their rural province in the Philippines. The notion of a 'better life', however, has not quite met her expectations, as she explained the hardships of manual labour, the loneliness she feels from being separated from her family in the Philippines, and the racism that she and some of her children have encountered since moving to Australia.

Elvie and her husband, a former seaman in the Philippines and now a petrol station attendant here, migrated to Australia with their son and two daughters four years ago. She was not very confident with her English and her sentences were punctuated with a lot of Tagalog. She was shy and softly spoken the few times that I met with her and often spoke at length only if I conversed in Filipino. She explained to me how her husband struggled to earn decent money as a seaman in the Philippines so they decided to move to Australia from the encouragement of her husband's brothers who were already living here. Elvie and her family live in Mount Druitt, one of the most socio-economically disadvantaged areas in Sydney. She thinks this area where she and her husband have been able to buy a house is affordable but she does not necessarily feel it is the best place to live in terms of "good schools" for her children and nor does she feel it is the safest neighbourhood.

Elvie told me that this was the second time she was trying her hand at working as a cleaner for the shopping centre. Having been a housewife in the Philippines because there was no work in her small province town, cleaning was one of the only jobs quickly available to her when she arrived in Australia with no qualifications or work experience. However, she found the work quite difficult, stressful and physically exhausting and soon moved to 'on-call' employment in a factory. There, she found the unpredictability of the schedule equally as hard and the income very unstable. She eventually decided to return to her work as a cleaner, where her hours and income were fixed albeit still disliking the "dirty" nature of the job. Elvie's husband continues to work as a shift worker and this restricts the amount of time they can spend together as a family. Additionally, although her eldest daughter was a scholarship holder at a university in the Philippines, upon migrating, she immediately found work in a factory in order to help out the family. Elvie explained migration was also difficult for her youngest child, who had a hard time coping with the new environment, particularly at school. She was bullied, teased and sworn at by her white classmates. She became scared to go to school and Elvie allowed her to stay at home for two weeks until she was advised by teachers that this was not permissible. She eventually moved her daughter to a Catholic school, which she believes is a better environment although the cost of tuition is not ideal.

"You expect here *na masarap ang buhay* (You expect here that life is good). *Pero, mahirap rin dito* (But life is hard here too)." This was one of the things Elvie said in our last meeting and it was clear to me that she was somewhat disappointed about how difficult life could be in Australia. On the other hand, she constantly reiterated that the money which she and her husband earn here also supports their parents and relatives back in the Philippines. This ultimately becomes the major staying point for the two of them. She also found optimism in her eldest daughter's aspirations of eventually returning to university (this time to study nursing) and, in general, the opportunities available in Australia to the rest of her children that the Philippines can no longer promise. Elvie was also very uplifted by the idea of one day being able to retire in the Philippines with her husband when they had saved enough money from working in Australia.

Elvie's story greatly diverges from the life narrative of those which I shared in Chapter 3. She is seemingly constrained in her mobility, choices and access to resources as a result of her class position and this is not uncommon in the lives of the other working-class Filipinos I met. In this chapter, I extend the analysis undertaken previously, by providing a comparative analysis of the working-class experience of everyday racism and the kinds of strategies they deploy as forms of everyday resistance. Inclusion and exclusion take different forms while coping mechanisms across individuals and groups vary according to sociocultural and economic constraints. Those categorised as 'working-class' in this chapter are employed in low-skilled and often low-wage occupations and possess limited higher educational attainment. This group, however, can also comprise of Filipino migrants who have had Philippine tertiary education or who in the Philippines once held high-skilled jobs but have taken on lower-skilled occupations after failing to find work in their relevant field once migrating. This is a consequence of the institutionalised deskilling that occurs in Australia which relegates these migrants to a working-class position, from which it is difficult for many to rebuild. I also include the stories of temporary contract workers who engage in blue-collar labour and possess limited assets while in Australia.

Sennett (2003: 57) observes that one of the main trajectories of "modern secular society is to emphasise the dignity of labour". Citing Weber, he reminds us of the ways in which proving one's self through work has become a principal means to ascertain one's basic worth. But what happens when work cannot provide this dignity? In this chapter, I explore how the bodies and identities of working-class Filipino migrants are racially ascribed through their labour. The literature on the racialised segmentation of the labour market posits that "groups of workers are located within hierarchically organised, racialised labour systems" to produce exploitation of some racial groups more than others and the unequal distribution of opportunities, privileges and rights (Bonacich et al., 2008: 342; and also see Herbert et al., 2008; Kelly, 2010; Maldonado, 2009). In the context of the global Filipino diaspora, the contours of how low-skilled or 'dirty' labour marks the bodies and subjectivities of those who undertake such work have been covered exceptionally and my discussion in this chapter draws from these works (Parrenas, 2001a and 2001b; Espiritu, 2005; S. McKay, 2007; Dyer et al., 2008; Margold, 1995). Specifically, I examine how the structural positioning of working-class Filipino migrants at the bottom of the social and economic ladder renders into varying forms of everyday racism inside (and outside) their places of work. Such processes attempt to subordinate and contain these migrants at the 'bottom of the pile'.

If we recall the contrasting mobility, agency and respect that middle-class Filipinos are able to generate from their cultural and economic capital, someone like Elvie might readily be understood through her victimhood. She does not possess impeccable English proficiency, higher education or economic affluence, some of the things that overlap to represent 'successful' migrant 'integration' and achieve levels of recognition in mainstream Australia. Filipino migrants from the working class endure quite profound material and symbolic disadvantage when compared to their middle-class counterparts. But I wish to show that they are far from being powerless victims. This group engages in a wide range of strategies – at times qualitatively different from those of the middle class – in order reclaim respect. This ranges from formal avenues of complaint to mobilising discourses of rights and morality. Cultural and economic capital is also transnationalised to delocalise identities. I explore here how resistance involves not only self-realisation but also broader notions of justice which highlight the manner in which racism is still about structural inequality as much as it is about stigmatised identity.

"They're upstairs. They're white. We're downstairs. We're not white": racialised subordinate labour

Sebastian is in his early thirties and has worked pretty much all of his adult life in blue-collar occupations. His first job was a valet at a hotel in Sydney, which he left a few years later to work as a machine operator at a furniture factory. He then worked briefly as a concreter for a local government council before entering his current job as a warehouse manager for a clothing company. "You see it, the difference. They're upstairs. They're white. We're downstairs. We're not white." This was the metaphor he used, in a rather prosaic but nevertheless perceptive way, when he described his observations of the racially segmented places in which he has worked. Sebastian elaborated on the subtle experience of discrimination at

Reclaiming rights, morality and esteem 69

his current job at the warehouse, where he is ever acutely aware of his racialised class position:

> I'm in charge of the warehouse and the staff there. At first I didn't think it was about racism. I don't know, it's hard to know. But you feel it, you know? It was the people upstairs. I work downstairs in the warehouse. They (upstairs) pass the buck, give us all the work while they go home on time or *early*. I work downstairs, they work upstairs. I think maybe it's that separation. I just didn't have a lot in common with them. They were all white, from the rich suburbs, snobby. Me and my staff, we're all ethnic of some sort. And they think I have a funny way of speaking because I'm from out west. They think because I'm downstairs I have nothing to contribute. But I'm a manager, you know. They think their job is more important.
>
> When I have ideas, they don't listen. Like my opinion doesn't matter. They don't give me credit. Like you know how you get that piece of paper with all the extension numbers of everyone? All their numbers have their names. When it gets to me it just says 'warehouse'. That really pissed me off. So you know, me and my staff, it's like we don't have names. One time one of the girls upstairs asked one of my staff, he's Filipino too, to clean the toilets. He's not a cleaner! They know that! That pissed me off bad. I went to the boss straight away. It's stuff like that. Sometimes I thought it wasn't racism – but you can't help but think, you know. You see it, the difference. They're upstairs. They're white. We're downstairs. We're not white. Even when I was working in the hotel, parking cars. We're all different races downstairs. Asian, Arabs, Indian. Once again, we're in the basement. The white people are upstairs. You just know how they see us, right?

How Sebastian understands his position in the wider order of things is played out through spatial locations and the bodies that occupy these spaces: Sebastian works downstairs in his building with his other ethnic staff while upstairs in the office are his white colleagues. He complains of the lack of respect he receives in the workplace from the people 'upstairs', who occupy higher-status positions. This disrespect, however, is not simply based on his class status but becomes entwined with his racial identity. His white colleagues working 'upstairs' fail to value him or his non-white staff working 'downstairs' and the instance of his Filipino staff being asked to clean the toilet in particular confirms to Sebastian that his team's position at the bottom rung has become a racialised kind of difference. Furthermore, the lack of respect that Sebastian is accorded is encapsulated by the insult of his name being left out of the company contact list. The failure to give him recognition through an identity and denying his intellectual contribution operate as a mode of symbolic violence (Bourdieu, 1990), which functions to subordinate and confine Sebastian and his team 'in their place'.

He also reported experiencing subjugation working as a concreter for the local government council, albeit in a different way. While at the warehouse he is made to feel like his ideas are not bright enough to be heard, Sebastian described a somewhat opposite kind of misrecognition he received from his work mates in his concreting team:

> The council was advertising for concreters. I never did that kind of job before. But they said that they were willing to train people, and I was willing to learn. Right away, I could tell, there was something different about labourers. It's a mix (of ethnicities) – but a lot of them, you know, real yobos. Not many Asians at all. Not like the jobs I had in the factory or even in the warehouse.
>
> There were three of us in the team. The head guy was a white New Zealander – he was the worst. And the other one was an Australian guy – he could be okay but he could also be really bad. He was pretty much homophobic and pretty racist. All he thought was "Aussie this" and "Aussie that". There were other guys in the council – Australians, Greeks, Maltese. Hardly any Asians. Most of them were nice and I wanted to work with them. But the ones I got, I don't know, maybe it was just bad luck. But they were pretty bad. . . . Talking about stuff like migrants, you see, it's normal for everyone there. And it's not bad all the time. They're just talking, saying their opinions. I have my opinions too. But yeah, the two in my group, man it was bad sometimes.
>
> . . . They would tease other nationalities. Around the time the Iraq War was happening, they would just sit down for a few hours instead of working, in the caravan or the side of the truck and read newspapers and listen to the radio, and make comments about Iraqis, Muslims. They didn't like how Muslims didn't want to integrate. Thought Muslim religion was too different. I mean I get it – they are pretty different. But I found it (their discussions) really irritating.
>
> . . . They just didn't like me. They weren't really teaching me skills. Just leaving me out all the time. They didn't think I was a 'real' labourer. They were all concrete guys. That's their background. But me, I had some other skills they didn't have. I've had a few jobs, you know. And before I got the job, I just came back from overseas. I went to Japan and Philippines for holidays. I reckon, if they think you're better than them, they put you down. All these guys, just concreting. Don't really know anything else.
>
> . . . They just thought I was a fish out of water. I had no concreting background, they thought I knew someone in the council and that's how I got the job. So they thought I was just cruising. But the advertisement, it said they were willing to train and I was willing to learn. I didn't get a free ride. But they still gave me a hard time. I asked for a transfer but it was within my three months' probation. They told the bosses I wasn't any good. So they just got rid of me.

In this instance, Sebastian encounters a completely different working-class milieu among labourers. While he is used to factory and warehouse work, which to him comprise of a lot of 'ethnic' employees, he sees labouring as quite an Anglo-dominated working-class space with different habits, practices and values. The 'race talk', for one, is much more straightforward and open, something many other Filipino men who worked similar occupations observed, and creates for Sebastian a heightened sense of discomfort. Lamont's (2000) research with working-class men in the US and France suggests that this group values straightforwardness and honesty born out of the social, economic and political contexts in which the working class are situated. Assertive (and sometimes aggressive) behaviour associated with working-class masculinities can intersect with a working-class disposition to 'tell it how it is' and can lead to particular kinds of everyday racism. In opposition to the conflict avoidance observed in middle-class contexts, which generate quite subtle racism and subtle responses, Sebastian's experience is marked by candidness around 'race talk' and at times explicit racist attitudes. This suggests that working-class Filipino migrants, particularly men, must navigate a different terrain of openness and outspoken views than their middle-class counterparts.

Sebastian's co-workers' accusations that he had 'connections' in higher ranks of the council form his suspicions that they possibly view him as more 'privileged' and that he has abused the system to get a job. The distance that Sebastian places between himself and his co-workers functions as a form of resistance, just as the middle class positions racist perpetrators as 'backward Others'. In this context, however, the kind of cultural and social capital – cosmopolitanism, networks, variety in talents, and aspiration – that generates levels of acceptance for middle-class Filipinos does not serve the exact same uses for those in working-class spaces. This is not to say that the working class are not aspirational. However, in a competitive and insecure economic environment, they might be particularly sensitive to proving worth through hard work and not through inherited privilege, and respect must be hard-earned. Working-class Filipinos cherish these same values around modesty, honesty, humility and industriousness. Racialised boundaries, however, prevent solidarity between Sebastian and his colleagues and possibly occur within the broader context of fears around 'white decline' that for white working-class Australians particularly connects 'Asian social mobility' with the threat to white dominance (Hage, 2000: 212).

The devaluing of qualifications gained in the Philippines is also a significant process that these migrants identify as a form of subtle racism. It is yet another means by which they are perceived, materially and symbolically, as racialised subordinate labour. While many of the older first-generation Filipinos who arrived in Australia as permanent settlers between the 1980s and 1990s complained of experiencing this disqualification, recently arrived migrants who enter through the temporary worker visa scheme also regularly encounter such exclusion in spite of being specifically recruited as 'skilled labour' and at times sponsored by employers in a field of expertise. As Ho and Alcorso (2004: 238) argue, a misleading narrative of the 'migrant success story' justifies the government's acceleration of the skilled migration program based on the idea that this policy has allowed migrants to achieve "increasingly positive outcomes in the Australian labour market".[1]

Lenny is thirty-seven years old and was the first person whom I had the chance to interview when I commenced my fieldwork. He answered a small announcement that I posted in a Filipino community newspaper, calling for research respondents. Lenny is on a working visa under the skilled temporary migration scheme.

He is employed as an aircraft mechanic, maintaining aeroplanes in a small airport base in semi-rural outer western Sydney. Lenny is what you might call a 'seasoned' contract worker. He has worked in Singapore, Saudi Arabia and the UK before arriving in Australia. His reason for migration, like many other Filipinos like him, is to earn money to support his family back in the Philippines. But his migration to Australia has come at a cost. The racism he experienced from his supervisor here was one of the more explicit that I had come across and he struggled to tell me coherently about the instances of abuse he had suffered. In our interview his voice quivered and, at times, I had to gently prompt him to divulge more detail. Lenny strongly believed that the racism from his supervisor was driven by prejudices around his qualifications from the Philippines, which he feels his boss equated with lower intellect and skills:

> It started because we're Filipinos. They are thinking that they are more knowledgeable than us. It started it off, actually it's not me. It's one of my mates, Ernie. He's Filipino as well and we worked five years in Singapore. I was already one month ahead of him here, he can't really speak English that well. It's our supervisor here, he's British, he's also recently arrived maybe six years ago. It's him who is racist to us.
>
> Every time John (supervisor) would give us a job to do, Ernie will talk to me to check. And John went up to me and said, 'Your mate, is he in aircraft maintenance?' And I said, "Oh, yes. I work with him in Singapore." John wanted to know why Ernie was always asking me about the job. 'Doesn't he know what to do?' That's what John thinks. And he researched the background of Ernie – he worked in the UK after Singapore for only six months and then he was sent out. So he was thinking that Ernie wasn't very good at his job. So it happened that his anger to Ernie moved to me. He's (John) thinking that, don't cover up your countrymen, 'Just tell me who he is. Maybe he's not working at the aircraft. Maybe he's working in the car.' It started from that situation.
>
> . . . He insults us. He's always calling us idiots. 'You don't know what to do.' Like that. But I can do it. I've been doing this for a long time. But John will go to the manager and say, 'The one you hired, he doesn't know anything.' We are very degraded, you know. He swears too much on us. . . . . Just saying, 'What the fuck are you doing? You fucking idiot. You don't fucking know anything.'
>
> . . . So it came one day that he threaten us: "You resign or I will shoot you." He's fed up. He just become fed up with us. We are a bunch of idiots to him. He wants us to be replaced but the company is the one hiring us. They cannot sack us because we're doing the job. If not, we would be sacked because we have three months' probation. We are checked on our jobs. If you make a mistake, that would be enough. It's the supervisor who is thinking we're not good. So he is telling us to resign. It's the only way to get rid of us. He wants people that are the same as him. Same race with him . . . And you know, John is actually my classmate in one of the company course. And he told me, 'If you would pass then how much more would I pass?" So really, he thinks I am lower. Filipinos are lower knowledge and mentality.

The devaluing of Lenny and Ernie's qualifications and work experience based on the belief that Philippine education and Filipino intellectual capacity are inferior manifests itself in the intimidating and aggressive actions of their supervisor. Insults about their intellect and skills, while not explicitly containing content about their 'race', are understood by Lenny as 'racist' because they occur against the backdrop of doubts expressed by his supervisor about whether he and Ernie are really qualified for the role because they do not possess qualifications from Australia. The background check that his supervisor undertakes on Ernie is an act of surveillance on the Other based on the alleged 'untrustworthiness' of Lenny and Ernie to tell the truth. This kind of scrutiny enacted by employers on migrant contract workers is a routinised form of disciplinary power over the bodies and subjectivities of 'Third World' migrant labour (Pratt, 1996). This is a significant difference in the impact of racism on permanently settled migrants, like Sebastian, and temporary labour migrants, like Lenny; the latter are often held to ransom by their company sponsorship on which their employment relies. Racism in the workplace, therefore, is a pressurising force that threatens this group's livelihood and ability to stay in the country. Such surveillance and verbal harassment are acts to degrade Lenny and serve to confine him to an inferior rank.

For working-class Filipina women, there is an added feminised racialisation to class marginalisation. I return to Elvie's story to share another account of how the labour of the working class is inscribed on their bodies and identities:

> *Sa trabaho* (at work), it's okay. Most Australians, some are nice, some are not. Most customers, *kung Australiano or kung iba* (whether Australian or another [race]), some are nice, some are not. But you know, my workmate, Chinese *siya* (she's Chinese), she was told by a customer, *pute* (white), go back to her own country!.... Here at the food court, a lot of parents let their children make a mess. Some of them say sorry but some of them have no manners. They don't care. There's someone who will clean up after them. *Parang* (it's as if) ... they see you as a maid. Asian maid, you know? I know that cleaning is my job. But the respect for you, *wala* (nothing). *Hindi naman sila nasa bahay* (they're not at home). It's public. They have no manners here, even outside. Because they see me, they leave the mess. *Pero, hindi naman ako katulong nila* (but I'm not their personal maid). *Respeto lang, parang walang respeto sa iyo kasi* you're a cleaner (it's their respect, it's as if they don't have respect for you because you're a cleaner). One time, this little boy spilled his drink, and the mother called me. She started saying, 'Clean, clean'... pointing to the table and floor like that (waves her finger around towards the floor). 'You clean.' That's what she did. I know what to do. She thought I can't understand English? The way she told me. No manners.

Elvie's experience as a cleaner raises a few significant points. She is deeply offended by the manner in which one female customer treated her, not only ordering her to clean but also doing so in a way that assumed she could not understand her request because she is an immigrant. The incident encapsulates the lack of respect Elvie is granted not only because she undertakes a 'dirty job' but also because this dirty job has become entwined with her already marginal racial identity. She also mentions that while she has not experienced direct racial slurs herself during the job, one of her colleagues who is also Asian was told to 'go back to her own country' by a customer. It indicates the kind of exposure racialised working-class migrants have to everyday racism, especially those working as cleaners in public spaces or cashiers in supermarkets and the like. They not only are on the receiving end of racism from colleagues or managers but also can suffer abuse (whether direct or indirect) from customers because they constitute the front-line and bottom-rung labour force. That Elvie's colleague who experienced the abuse is also an Asian woman points to the feminised and racialised dimension of this front-line labour, wherein there remains a disproportionate concentration of migrant female labour in low-skilled and low-wage service jobs not only in Australia but also in other advanced industrial economies (Parrenas, 2001a). Elvie and other migrants like her who occupy such a position in the labour market become more vulnerable to higher levels of abuse because it can come from multiple sources and such abuse is premised on multiple marginalisations because of the intersecting stigmas around their race, class and gender.

Elvie's narrative also speaks to racial, class and gender regimes in the Philippine context. She refers to being seen as a maid – moreover, an 'Asian maid', which is racism implicated in wider discourses that circulate about Asian women and their supposed inferiority and servitude. The occupation of a maid in the Philippines is regarded as a lowly position often undertaken by poor rural women who have moved to urban cities for work (Lan, 2003). No doubt the behaviour of customers that Elvie describes is very much insulting and rude. But because maids are not common in the Australian domestic sphere, it could be unlikely that they see Elvie within this frame. In other words, the idea of a 'cleaner' involves different connotations from those attached to the notion of a 'maid'. However, the manner in which Elvie conceives of her status within the 'maid' discourse suggests a particular way in which she understands the situation within dual frameworks. It is not just the rude behaviour of the food court's customers that marginalises Elvie but its intersection with knowledge she holds about the status of her work in the Philippines. It is subtle in her explanation of the difference between the mess created in the private and public sphere; a maid is needed inside the house for mess that is left in a carefree way by one's employers, while a maid is not needed outside, where restraint should be practiced. While such a distinction suggests a criticism of 'uncivilised' Australian habits in the public domain, Elvie feels degraded and shamed that her job as a cleaner is performed like that of a 'maid' and she must enact this role not within the privacy of the home but in the openness of the public gaze.

When asked about her experiences of racism, Elvie's account also included the exclusion she experiences from more 'well-off' Filipinos. This is a significant difference in the experience of Filipino migrants across class contexts. The working class are subject to multiple sources of marginalisation, including their own 'community':

May mga Filipino (There are some Filipinos). . . . *alam mo Pilipino siya pero hind ka babatiin* (you know she is Filipino but she won't greet you) . . . just look at you, but not look at you in the eyes. That happened when I'm in my job. They see you but they don't greet you. You're meant to be ... *kababayan* (countrymen). *Pero* (but) there are some they don't greet you. *Yung mga 'sociale'* (Those who are 'well-to-do'). *Baka mayaman na sila parang ganon* (Maybe they are already rich, maybe that's it). They forget that we are all Filipino.

Elvie describes being 'seen' by more well-off Filipino migrants but it is the kind of 'seeing' that looks right through her and that renders her invisible. It is expressive of the distancing strategies the middle class undertake in order to cope with or avoid their own exclusion. By refusing to meet her eyes or greet her, they hope to keep Elvie unseen and hidden. That she understands this marginalisation from other Filipinos as a mode of racism points to the palpable humiliation such domination brings about as it becomes inseparable from the kind of domination endured from white Australians. For Elvie, it is even "worse" because she believes they are *kababayan* (countrymen) and she hoped for solidarity. This method of intra-ethnic othering (Pyke and Dang, 2003: 425) reflects the manner in which minorities can reproduce racial inequality as they accept the "legitimacy of a devalued identity imposed by the dominant group" by acknowledging that there are negative racial-ethnic traits to their collective identity. Such intra-ethnic boundaries serve "as a basis for monitoring and controlling social behaviour along acculturative lines" (Pyke and Dang, 2003: 153).

Reclaiming rights and morality

The working class redeem respect in quite qualitatively different ways to the middle class. For those I spoke with, respect is pursued through reclaiming rights via formal institutional avenues and also through dispositions that locate them as 'moral' people. Notions of solidarity emerged from their stories which significantly differ from the emphasis on individualism among the middle class.

Unlike their middle-class counterparts, who tend to avoid confronting racism directly, rationalise the experience or deny its occurrence, working-class Filipinos I spoke with were often not shy to make formal complaints to their managers, human resource departments at work, and some had even taken their stories to the media or as high as the Equal Opportunity Commission. In Sebastian's story, he had encountered very candid and honest 'race talk' among the labourers he worked with. While a lot of these discussions, he justified, were 'harmless' expressions of 'opinions', Sebastian observed that at times these could create tension and conflict he could not ignore. He described one particular incident at the council that prompted him to complain to higher management:

> They (his team) kept talking and joking about this one story. There was one Asian guy who worked as a labourer there and he got sacked because he attacked someone with a knife. And they told me one day, "Oh, yeah, we better watch out for you, Sebastian. You Asians carry around knives all the time." And I said, "Yeah, you shouldn't turn your back to me." And then he

just snapped and goes, "Why? Are you going to stab me? Are you threatening me?" I thought we were all just mucking around and he was all serious all of a sudden. And then the last thing he said to me was, "You better watch out, mate, I could be holding a mallet and I could miss and hit you in the head." I told our manager about the incident – that it was bullying and being racist. He started the investigations and my team mates were telling them (management) another story, saying it was only a joke. . . . Once I complained, it was uncomfortable, you know. They knew I was talking to management about them. But what they're doing, it's not right. Can't let them get away with it. At work, it's different when racism happens to you. That's your work, your earning. Most times, it's not worth my energy. But at work, something like that, you have to complain. It's my right. That's what managers are for.

I suggest that whereas much of the routine racism that the middle class endures is understated and elusive, more direct, confronting and threatening manifestations in the experience of some working-class interviewees present the opportunity to identify more clearly the bullying, harassment or 'inappropriate' conduct. Sebastian interprets that his mistreatment is "not right" and is validated by his knowledge that there are *rules* in the workplace about such misconduct. He believes it is his "right" to complain and that this is "what managers are for". There are formal structures in place to which he can appeal and, while he concedes that complaining caused further tension with his co-workers, Sebastian persists because such rules reinforce that it is his 'right' to seek reparation. It is significant to note that aside from having to deal with more identifiable racism, working-class spaces are also far more visibly unionised. According to Merry (1990) in her research about working-class experiences with the legal system, such institutional frameworks allow people implicated in more collectivised systems to interpret problems as relevant to legal avenues of redress and develop a kind of 'legal consciousness'. I suggest this is also a kind of *rights-based* consciousness among my respondents when dealing with racism in the workplace.

Lenny also sought the same avenues of assistance as Sebastian. At our interview, he brought along the letter of grievance he had filed with his employer, which explicitly listed all the acts of racism and general harassment he endured. Like Sebastian's case, Lenny was able to pursue formal avenues of complaint because the abuse was much more open. Lenny as well mobilised a discourse around 'rights' when he explained his reasons for undertaking a more formal mode of action. Moreover, Lenny felt that he has really only learnt about such formal systems of complaint and support since his time working here in Australia:

My first complaint, after so many incidents, was to human resources (points at letter). One Aussie guy, he backed me up. He told me to complain. I was going to resign, but HR help me. They support me, moral support. They told me that this company, we hate bullying. We don't tolerate bullying. We don't tolerate harassment. They're under a duty of care. But even when they told me like that, I'm still scared. I told them I don't want to work with him anymore. Because once he knew it that I complained, I will be a very big target.

... He (supervisor) was called also. So he answered all that (complaints in the letter). They find out that it's true but he says it's only a joke. So he admitted it. But they didn't take it as a joke. He got a final warning that he will be out of the company if he do it again. . . . I felt intimidated, scared. And even the company bring me to the psychologist. They hired a psychologist. They taught me how to forget about it, try to move on. They taught me to stay positive. They put a middle man between us. They told me, 'If your boss will give you a job, then he will talk to this guy.' So I stop talking to John (supervisor), we're not allowed. But I said it still doesn't work, because I still see him, you know. So that's when I was moved. But there were lots of investigations happening, investigations to the people around us, before anything happen.

You know, I didn't know this. In the Philippines, they don't know what bullying is or harassment. Because in the Philippines, if your boss shouted at you at work, that's okay. But here it's different. I'm not aware of that. So the HR manager brought me to training about what is bullying and harassment. So that's when I got an idea. Really, it proved to me that my supervisor is doing wrong. So after the course, the HR manager told me if John shouts at me again, to tell him. So from there, John began to stop. He knew that I knew my rights now.

. . . Australians, they're the one who taught me how to manage this situation. They taught me where to report. That's the problem, if you're new here, you don't know what to do. Even your fellow Filipinos, they're scared.

As a temporary contract worker, Lenny's experience needs to be distinguished from that of Sebastian, who has been living in Australia for much longer. Sebastian has grown accustomed to the explicit rules and regulations in the workplace, which form part of his decision to make a complaint. He is aware of certain rules, having resided in Australia for a long time, and certainly these are tied to his rights as a *citizen*. Lenny, however, is newly acquainted with such systems, which he acknowledged does not exist in the Philippine workplace. Kelly (2010) similarly observes that some Filipino employees in Canada tolerate antagonistic behaviour from managers because they are used to the limited avenues for protest in the Philippines that stem from rigid managerial hierarchies and also a culture of rewarding unfairly based on nepotism and patronage. Therefore, while Lenny has experienced his 'worst' racism here in Australia, at the same time, he has most *enhanced* his sense of rights in the very same context.

This acquisition of knowledge of rights via migration also emerged in an interview with Glenda, a young woman in her late twenties, who works as a registered nurse at a Brisbane hospital in Queensland. She was in Sydney visiting one of my interlocutors, Tania – also working as a nurse – and decided to come along to one of our catch-ups to share her story. Glenda is on a temporary working visa and arrived a year ago with plans of settling in Sydney. She was previously working in the UK at a nursing home for five years and endured terrible mistreatment as a migrant nurse, which she attributed to the status of subserviency attached to her being Filipino and being seen as 'Third World' labour. She had gone through an agency to acquire a nursing job in England and was posted at a nursing home in a rural area. Along with two other Filipinas, she told me that they were "dumped in a tiny caravan" on the site of the nursing home, which, among other things, had no clean running water. Most vivid in her memory was the way that they had to take water from the nursing home by filling up milk bottles and bring them back to the caravan to use for drinking water and for showering and flushing the toilet. Some older Filipina nurses, she also recalled, were forced to sleep in the nursing home and became "24-hour nurses". On their days off, Glenda was unable to rest but was instead forced to leave the caravan to avoid being harassed by their employers to take on extra work. According to Glenda, they had become "maids and cleaners" and had to undertake labour like cleaning the toilets, which was outside the scope of their jobs. Her living and work conditions were so intolerable, she remarked, "It's like we were not even treated like human beings." Glenda escaped from this situation only when she and her Filipina friends met, by chance, a Filipino priest in the city and to whom they told their plight. The priest took them to BBC News and, after being interviewed and exposing the nursing home, they were instantly moved to a hospital with better working conditions. She described migrant nurses as being better received in Australia but notices the slight ways in which exploitation continues to occur. Filipina nurses are often given the most difficult patients, Filipina team leaders are understaffed compared to Anglo team leaders, and doctors tend to take advantage of Filipina nurses by giving them heavy workloads because "they know Filipinas never complain."

But Glenda made clear that she now most certainly complains to supervisors and managers, which she attributed to the exploitation she has suffered in the past: "I know to speak up now after what happened in the UK. It's your right, I learnt that now." Moreover, she feels more confident than before to fight for her rights at work because she has the union to support her. Much like Lenny and Sebastian, Glenda pursues more formal avenues of redress because of the explicit encounters of exploitation or abuse. And, like Lenny, awareness of her rights is relatively new and acquired only upon migration. Even though the mistreatment she experienced in the UK was extremely dehumanising, it was also within the same context that she heightened her sense of rights. This has better prepared her for work in Australia, where she feels confident that the safety of her employment and her welfare are protected by the union. The experience of these three individuals can be telling of the far more egalitarian system that exists in Australia when compared not only to the Philippines but also to other societies. Minorities in Australia, therefore, might be offered more systematic avenues of redress when it comes to racial vilification than those offered in some other countries. While anti-discrimination and equal opportunity legislation tends to act more as preventative measures rather than existing as successful systems of redress (Hollinsworth, 2004), such institutionalised arrangements are, nevertheless, valued by minorities who experience quite dramatic instances of racism despite that retribution is not always successful through these means.

Interconnected with the motivation to use formal regulations is a broader sense of 'rights' as *morality*. For Sebastian, while forms of racism in other settings are not worth his energy, such intimidating racism in the workplace prompts a different response. This is not only because it diminishes his self-esteem but moreover because he feels that it prevents him from functioning in his work "*like everyone else*". This was markedly absent in my interviews with the middle class, who used strategies based on individualism rather than referring to notions of solidarity across all people. According to Fraser (2000), injury to identity is not merely based on depriving someone of 'self-realisation' of esteem or status but is intolerable because it constitutes a form of institutionalised subordination, which signals the violation of *justice*. While the racism Sebastian experiences is bruising to his ego, he also significantly interprets racism as being unfair or unjust against his broader sense of 'rights', which he sees as being accorded to some and not to others. Such rights – within a framework of a shared morality by all – are not conceptualised as "being attached to persons as individuals but as being embedded in social relationships and constitutive of these relationships" (Merry, 1990: 2).

At times, this sense of morality is situated within their religious background, which teaches about 'equality as human beings'. Outside of work, Lenny also sought other means to deal with the racism. Aside from seeing a counsellor at work, Lenny also sought help from his church group:

> I really didn't know what the problem is. I didn't know why it was happening to me, why it kept coming back, being bullied and harassed. It wouldn't stop. You know, I ask, what's wrong with me? . . . I'm attending my church. That was because of my big problem. I just always go to church. Just being around them, being with myself, having peace. It (church) helps me a lot to cope with my problem. The coaching, church . . . all of it help me. At church, they tell you, we're all human. We're all the same. I tell myself that now. In the end, we're all the same to God.

Lamont and Askartova (2002) found the same moral religious resources being used in their study of North African immigrant men in France. To resist racism, these men understand Islam as providing guidelines for moral conduct, including seeing all men as sons of God. This religious discourse on morality is quite different to the formal rationalised version of morality and rights associated with the use of formal legal systems. I suggest that they should not be viewed in opposition to each other but instead as complementary in my respondents' spectrum of rights-based discourses that encompass different sources of morality. Further, social capital is accumulated in this context instead of cultural capital, the latter being more significant to the middle class as coping mechanisms against exclusion. Putnam (2000: 22–23) has argued that churches play an integral role in facilitating social networks and promoting reciprocity and trustworthiness in the form of 'bonding social capital', which comprises inward connections within the group, and 'bridging social capital', which comprises outward-oriented social ties outside of the group "across diverse social cleavages". For Lenny, attending his church and being around his congregation provide him with peace and support. He extends the religious philosophies he learns about equality to people outside of his church, even to those from whom he has suffered abuse, as a way to 'build bridges'.

80 Reclaiming rights, morality and esteem

Notions of humility and modesty also figured in these individuals' stories, especially as measures of self-worth. Some discussed the importance of humility and modesty and often in the context of redeeming respect against marginalisation from more well-off middle-class Filipinos. Elvie spoke about how it is more important to be humble than to have money and status:

> You know, some of those Filipinos who judge you, that's wrong. Ako (me) . . . you just be humble. You don't show off. *Yun ang talaga* (that is really) . . . that's what makes you a good person. Even better than the ones with money. *Mahirap naman nang buhay namin, pero mabuteng tao kami* (our life is hard but we are good people). Looking after your family is the main (thing) that is important.

Being humble serves to elevate the working class *above* the middle class, who they view as valuing the 'wrong' things. Such differentiations of morality are underscored by distinctions between 'the disciplined self' and the 'caring self' – the former underlined by neoliberal ideologies around discipline and responsibility while the latter is accentuated by solidarity and warmth (Lamont, 2000: 3–4). And so, while working-class Filipinos may not have the cultural and economic capital of the middle class, they see themselves as 'good people' who are not domineering. In the context of Elvie's expectations of solidarity between Filipino migrants, money and status violate this 'togetherness'. At the same time, however, while dispositions of modesty and humility attempt to invoke solidarity, such moralising can also subtly function as a source of boundary-making that attempts to denigrate the ethics of the middle class.

Transnationalising cultural capital

Status, however, is still significant to the working class. There is an active investment in their socio-economic capital in the Philippines, which can recoup the injuries of racism experienced in Australia. This is achieved in various ways, from consumption practices to return visits and even simply in the act of migration. I suggest that such transnational processes function as a form of *translocal place-making* (D. McKay, 2006), whereby manoeuvring across transnational social fields enables recuperation from misrecognition and inequality in the local setting by transforming their status in an alternate context. Such participation across localities generates new subjectivities which transcend the fixity and materiality of place and identity because "it is formed in movement and through identification or dis-identification with multiple, complex and simultaneously overlapping localities" (D. McKay, 2006: 274).

Maribeth is in her early forties and arrived in Australia in the mid-1990s with her sons. They settled in St Clair, a small suburb in Sydney's western suburbs. Her husband arrived in Australia first and started off as a factory worker, and Maribeth followed a few years later with their two young sons. Despite graduating in hospitality and hotel management in the Philippines, she needed to earn an income straight away and started working as an assistant nurse at a nursing home. Her employer disregarded her lack of formal qualifications and allowed her to begin work after three days of training. She admitted,

> I wanted a better job actually. Better than nursing home. But I had no experience. I was a housewife. And my degree, they didn't count it here. And I had no experience. I wanted a different job from nursing. But what can I do? I need to earn money. I need to help my husband to survive here. The best job I can have is that one so what can I do?

Maribeth's line of work, much like Elvie's, is a source of marginalisation that emanates not only from workmates or residents in the nursing home but also, in particular, from more well-off Filipino migrants. The latter, she feels, do not know the importance of her work because it involves "dirty work" and, as well, because she believes that it is rare that Filipinos become residents of nursing homes so they do not appreciate the value of her job. Maribeth also shyly confessed that she did not own her home. She felt that a mortgage was a "headache" that her family would only struggle to pay. Instead, she has decided to invest in her economic position in the Philippines, where she owns property with her husband. While Maribeth may be working-class in Australia and cannot afford her own home or other luxuries, in the Philippines she participates in a different class process that sees her advance her status to a relatively comfortable middle-class stability:

> Back home (in the Philippines) you know, we got three houses. We have a little business there. My mother-in-law maintains it. And our houses there, one is an apartment. We ask someone to rent it. So back home, we're lucky. So we work hard now, and we spend the money back home. I will go back there one day.

Buying multiple houses or condominiums and extending existing homes into mansions are some of the prevalent ways in which working-class Filipinos are able to access the kind of middle-class mobility that eludes them in the countries in which they perform their labour. Class identity for such migrants is therefore *transnational* – "class in this usage does not designate a discrete strata or place in a social hierarchy, nor is it seen as restricted to a specific history and geography, or tethered to a unit-linear evolutionary historical narrative" (Gibson et al., 2001: 375). Such negotiations of class also rework their stigmatised racial identities, which have become bound to their stigmatised labour. Returning to Lenny's story, aside from supporting his wife and children in the Philippines by providing them with a nice house and education and enabling his wife the luxury of not having to work, his return visits also provide opportunities to raise his self-esteem that has otherwise been battered by his experiences of racism in Australia:

> They treat me special. Because I have the experience now. You know, living around the world. When I was working there, I'm not making a lot of money.

I was treated differently. My wife is having a bigger salary than me. So my in-laws were saying bad things about me. So you were challenged on that level already. It wouldn't work out if I stay there. So I had to go. But now, they've changed. They're much nicer. When I went back there, I brought my PDA, my digital camera (laughs). They think I'm rich. But I tell them no, I'm just a normal person. But I don't want to be down again there. It's very hard. You have to earn money overseas.

Bourdieu (1986: 483) defines class as being as much about the way one is perceived as it is about material reality. Through Lenny's consumption practices, he performs a class identity on his return trips to the Philippines that implies that he is rich and worldly. It provides a counter-resistance to the status he is assigned in the countries in which he labours. But, most importantly, we see here the kind of respect that Lenny is able to recuperate through such a performance. The treatment he receives from his family has notably changed to one that garners admiration. He has reclaimed a sense of masculinity by resuming the position of 'provider' to his family, which was undermined by his inability to provide for them in the past. This compensates to some degree for the emasculation he experiences in the Australian context, where he is abused, harassed and bullied by his supervisor at work. Aside from the relief he feels from the status he has established among his family and friends through ongoing remittances, for Lenny, return visits act as forms of intermittent respite from the domination he endures in Australia and provide opportunities to revive his depleted esteem.

Similarly, Glenda also engages in similar consumption practices, which become a way to perform her raised class status in order to acquire recognition in the Philippines:

When I went back to visit in the Philippines, we went to SM Mall. My mum was practically begging to be served, but they (sales attendants) all ignored her. She was in *chenelas* (flip flops). I was just sitting down, looking. And there was this young girl who was *mestiza* and looked rich. She was playing with one of the toy piano keyboards and they didn't say anything. But when my nephew started playing, they said, *"Hindi puede yan!"* (That's not allowed). I got so pissed off I bought the keyboard and so many other things! What, just because that little girl has lighter skin than us? And then I went to the manager and told him, "These two (sales attendants), *isabihin mo sila kasi* (you discipline them because) they don't know how much money a customer has but they are treating them like shit. You will lose customers!" And then I showed them my passport with my migration status. And then they were making a big deal and suddenly they respect you.

Glenda's experience accentuates the strong link between economic status and forms of cultural and economic capital that frame racial and class hierarchies in the Philippines. The difference in treatment that her nephew receives compared to the young mestiza girl is underscored by the connections that wealth and whiteness have in the Philippines as forms of cultural capital that generate automatic respect. Her nephew, who is accompanied by Glenda's mother, dressed down in *chenelas* (flip flops), and Glenda and her family being of darker complexion frame the mistreatment they receive in the mall from sales attendants. She is forced to 'show off' her money and buy numerous things to prove they are worthy of the same respect. Interestingly, Glenda also shows them her passport, which states her status as an overseas worker. The latter demonstrates the manner in which the standing of Filipino migrant workers has changed in the local context as the very act of migration (even if it is for low-wage labour) in the Philippines has become a status symbol in itself (Gibson et al., 2001).

There is also a sense of *temporariness* that some working-class migrants feel about their situation in Australia. In Maribeth's and Elvie's narratives they express a wish to return permanently to the Philippines after they save enough money from living and working in Australia (or in the case of contract workers, anywhere else they might migrate for work). Maribeth, for instance, is devoted to advancing her economic position in the Philippines because one day she wishes to return permanently to her 'home' and it becomes a coping mechanism for the subordination she experiences in her life in Australia. Aside from economic activity, she also maintains ties to this 'home' through regular communication over the Internet with her family and friends. Despite not returning to the Philippines in nine years, she claims that this communication is more than enough to maintain intimate connections. These undertakings illustrate something beyond increasing status and capital. Such translocality reformulates one's comportment in the world by being situated in more than one place and produces flexible senses of belonging. Through transnational strategies of investing in a business, purchasing multiple houses in the Philippines and maintaining emotional ties with family and friends, Maribeth re-territorialises her absence from local life in the Philippines through such processes of embeddedness. It is made possible by de-territorialising her sense of belonging to Australia, but at the same time, her morale is boosted in Australia and consolidates her sense of place here via her reworked status in the Philippines. Transnationalising capital, therefore, produces a flexible identity and subverts the limited agency suffered as a result of a lower-class status in Australia and the racism that it can bring.

Conclusion

Disposed to the bottom of the hierarchy based on intersecting racial and class formations, working-class Filipino migrants endure acute structural inequality that in everyday life becomes inscribed on their bodies and their bodily labour, buttressing a range of marginalising practices from the dominant group. Their sense of agency, autonomy and mobility is obstructed in both symbolic and material ways. The theoretical links between racism, migrants and the working class are a well-established area of research, where the prominence of structural or economic understandings of racism has concentrated studies within the working-class sphere (see Raj, 2003). The view that racialised inequality is bound to the inequities of limited access to jobs, housing, education and other resources is, indeed, a persistent reality. In the context of the economic positioning of labouring Filipino migrants around the world, they are particularly susceptible to racialised and classed domination in their host societies. But the stories shared in this chapter also demonstrate that these individuals are not mere victims.

Speaking to the preceding chapter, I have tried to provide a comparative picture of racism and resistance across class contexts. The working class view racism as harmful to their esteem and dignity just as the middle class do. But, in addition, they significantly see racism as a violation of rights. The working class articulate conceptions of justice through their pursuit of rights, which speak to workplaces that are more collectivised. While the middle class subvert racism based on individualism, my working-class respondents' coping mechanisms are often supported by notions of solidarity – a sameness that attempts to eradicate boundaries (but can still also produce negative demarcations). Status and esteem also have value to working-class Filipino migrants but perhaps take secondary priority in their struggle for respect and justice, whereas for middle-class Filipino migrants accumulating status is endorsed in the cultural and economic contexts in which they are implicated. Such distinctions between middle- and working-class experiences should not condemn the practices of one group over the other. Structural and cultural contexts importantly shape differences in the experience of racism and related coping mechanisms. Across both the middle-class and working-class experience, racialised orders endure but strategies of resistance reveal how power is negotiated, showing itself as rarely static but as always circulating in multi-routed ways.

Note

1 Issues in Australia related to the state's skilled migration program are broadly situated within new international discussions of temporary migrant labour issues, such as those undertaken by Sassen (2008), May et al. (2007) and Datta et al. (2007).

References

Bonacich, E., Alimahomed, S. and Wilson, J. (2008) 'The racialisation of global labour', *American Behavioural Scientist*, vol. 52, no. 3, pp. 342–55.

Bourdieu, P. (1986) 'The forms of capital', in Richardson, D. (ed.), *Handbook of Theory of Research for Sociology of Education,* Westport: Greenwood Press, pp. 45–86.

Bourdieu, P. (1990) *The Logic of Practice*, Trans. R. Nice, Cambridge, MA: Harvard University Press.

Datta, K., McIlwaine, C., Yara, E., Herbert, J., May, J. and Wills, J. (2007) 'From coping strategies to coping tactics: London's low pay economy and migrant labour', British Journal of Industrial Relations, vol.45, no.2, pp. 404–32.

Dyer, S., McDowell, L. and Batnitzky, A. (2008) 'Emotional labour/body work: The caring labours of migrants in the UK's National Health Service', *Geoforum*, vol. 39, pp. 2030–38.

Espiritu, Y.L. (2005) 'Gender, migration and work: Filipina health care professionals to the United States', *Revue Europeene Des Migrations Internationals*, vol. 21, no. 1, pp. 1–17.

Fraser, N. (2000) 'Rethinking recognition', *New Left Review*, vol. 3, pp. 107–20.
Gibson, K., Law, L. and Mckay, D. (2001) 'Beyond heroes and victims: Filipina contract migrants, economic activism and class transformations', *International Feminist Journal of Politics*, vol. 3, no. 3, pp. 365–86.
Goffman, E. (1963) *Stigma: Notes on the Management of Spoiled Identity*, Princeton, NJ: Princeton Press.
Hage, G. (1998) *White Nation: Fantasies of White Supremacy in a Multicultural Society*, New York: Routledge.
Herbert, J., May, J., Willis, J., Datta, K., Evans, Y. and McIllwaine, C. (2008) 'Multicultural living? Experiences of everyday racism among Ghanaian migrants in London', *European Urban and Regional Studies*, vol. 13, pp. 103–17.
Ho, C. and Alcorso, C. (2004) 'Migrants and employment: Challenging the success story', *The Journal of Sociology*, vol. 40, no. 3, pp. 237–59.
Hollinsworth, D. (2004) *Race and Racism in Australia*, Victoria: Thomson Press.
Kelly, P. (2010) 'Filipino migration and the spatialities of labour market subordination', in Mcgrath-Champ, S., Herod, A. and Rainnie, A. (eds.), *Handbook of Employment and Society: Working Space*, Cheltenham: Edward Elgar, pp. 159–76.
Lamont, M. (2000) *The Dignity of Working Men: Morality and the Boundaries of Race, Class and Immigration*, New York: Russell Sage Foundation and Harvard University Press.
Lamont, M. and Askartova, S. (2002) 'Ordinary cosmopolitanisms: Strategies for bridging racial boundaries among working class men', *Theory, Culture and Society*, vol. 19, no. 4, pp. 1–25.
Lan, P. (2003) 'Maid or madam? Filipina migrant workers and the continuity of domestic labour', *Gender and Society*, vol. 17, pp. 187–208.
Maldonado, M. (2009) 'It is their nature to do menial labour: The racialisation of Latino/a workers by agricultural employers', *Ethnic and Racial Studies*, vol. 32, no. 6, pp. 1017–36.
Margold, J. (1995) 'Narratives of masculinity and transnational migration: Filipino workers in the Middle East', in Ong, A. and Peletz, M. (eds.), *Bewitching Women; Pious Men: Gender and Body Politics in South East Asia*, Los Angeles, CA: University of California Press, pp. 274–93.
May, J., Wills, J., Datta, K., Evans, Y., Herbert. J. and McIlwaine, C. (2007) 'Keeping London working: Global cities, the British State and London's new migrant division of labour', *Transactions of the Institute of British Geographers*, vol. 32, no. 2, pp. 151–67.
McKay, D. (2006) 'Translocal circulation: Place and subjectivity in an extended Filipino community', *The Asia Pacific Journal of Anthropology*, vol. 7, no. 3, pp. 265–78.
McKay, S. (2007) 'Filipino seamen: Constructing masculinities in an ethnic labour niche', *Journal of Ethnic and Migration Studies*, vol. 33, no. 4, pp. 617–33.
Merry, S. (1990) *Getting Justice and Getting Even: Legal Consciousness Among Working Class Americans*, Chicago: University of Chicago Press.
Parrenas, R.S. (2001a) *Servants of Globalisation: Women, Migration and Domestic Work*, Stanford, CA: Stanford University Press.
Parrenas, R.S. (2001b) 'Transgressing the nation-state: Partial citizenship and "Imagined (Global) Community" of migrant Filipina domestic workers', *Journal of Women in Culture and Society*, vol. 26, no. 4, pp. 1129–54.
Pratt, G. (1996) 'Inscribing domestic work on Filipina bodies', in Nast, H. and Pile, S. (eds.), *Places through the Body*, London: Routledge, pp. 283–304.

Putnam, R. (2000) *Bowling Alone: The Collapse and Revival of American Community*, New York: Schuster.

Pyke, K. and Dang, T. (2003) '"FOB" and "Whitewashed": Identity and internalised racism among second generation Asian Americans', *Qualitative Sociology*, vol. 26, no. 2, pp. 147–72.

Raj, D. (2003) *Where Are You From? Middle Class Migrants in the Modern World*, Berkeley: University of California Press.

Sassen, S. (2008) 'Two stops in today's global geographies: Shaping new labour supplies and employment regimes', *American Behavioural Scientist*, vol. 52, no. 3, pp. 457–96.

Sennett, R. (2003) *Respect: The Formation of Character in an Age of Inequality*, London: Penguin Books.

Velasco, J. (2006) 'Imitation and indigenisation in Filipino melodramas of the 1950s', paper presented to the Asia Culture Forum, Seoul, Korea, 26 October. http://cct.go.kr/data/acf2006/cinema/cinema-Session%201%20-%20Velasco.pdf.

5 'Mail order bride' or loving wife?

Revisiting the experience of Filipina 'marriage migrants'

In 2007, a small theatre production by Filipino-Australian siblings Paschal and Valerie Daantos Berry titled *The Folding Wife* showed around Australia to critical acclaim. In a one-woman show, the performance reveals the story of three generations of Filipina women as seen through the eyes of Grace, the youngest child in the family. The narrative mainly revolves around the migration of Grace and her mother, Delores, to Australia after Delores marries a 'foreigner' Australian man who she believes will grant her a life of riches or, at the very least, a better life than the one they live in their rural province in the Philippines. The matriarch of the family, Grace's grandmother, Clara, is also given voice on stage and embodies the historical sacrifices of Filipina women. The play alludes to several intersecting themes that include the scars left by Spanish colonialism and American imperialism; how such conquests have impacted on the lives of Filipina women who now shoulder much of the economic rebuilding of the country; and how the mass migration of Filipinas in varying circumstances subjects them to other neocolonial forms of domination.

The migration of Filipina women is an integral component of the feminisation of international migration (Ehrenreich and Hochschild, 2006; Parrenas, 2001). As part of the country's economic policies and also broader global processes of neoliberal political-economic restructuring, Filipina women migrate to over 190 countries all around the world, primarily as temporary low-wage workers labouring as domestic help, nurses and entertainers (Tyner, 2009). Alternatively, Filipina women have also long migrated and continue to do so as spouses of men living in countries like the US, Canada, and Australia. In a powerful monologue in *The Folding Wife*, matriarch Clara reflects on how the Filipina woman has been at the centre of social and political change throughout Filipino history – often folding to the needs of her husband, family, community and nation – despite that it often compromises her own desires and aspirations. Such sacrifice (and oppression) is what makes Filipina women 'resilient' – it is "practice" and in their "blood" to "bend and fold into recognisable shapes" (Daantos Berry, 2008). On one level, this resilience is a form of empowerment. In other ways, Clara also signals Filipina women's martyrdom. As a crucial cohort participating in the processes of globalisation, Filipinas are among the chief victims of both the symbolic and physical violence inflicted by globalisation on the lives of those with less power (Parrenas,

2001; Constable, 1997 and 2003; Briones, 2009; McKay, 2005 and 2006; Pratt, 1996; Tolentino, 1996; San Juan, 2001; Espiritu, 2000).

In this chapter, I revisit the experience of Filipina women who migrated on spousal visas to Anglo-Australian men, a topic that has predominated research agendas regarding Filipino migration to Australia (Woelz-Stirling et al., 1998; Cuneen and Stubbs, 2003; Robinson, 1996; Jackson, 1989; Khoo, 2001; Tolentino, 1996; Laforteza, 2006; Saroca, 2006). I cover here some material that has been well established but I also hope to shed new light on the lived experiences of these women. I re-examine the 'mail order bride' stereotype – a label popularised in the 1980s and 1990s at the height of international correspondence relationships between Australian men and Filipina women. The 'mail order bride' symbolised a necessary "construction of the Other in the Australian quest for identity" as mass Asian migration into the country threatened the hegemonic core (Robinson, 1996: 54). As a result of 'Filipina brides' being the first discernible influx of migrants from the Philippines into Australia, this stereotype and its related discourses have become the most predominant archetype associated with the Filipino diaspora in Australia. Today, it continues to form a basis of marginalisation endured by Filipina women who are married (usually) to much older Anglo men. Filipina women who seek out marriages to Western men, and vice versa, are often located in what Constable (2003) calls 'sites of desire' – driven by the West's orientalised understandings of the Filipina woman but also by a postcolonial Philippine fantasy about 'the West' embodied through the 'Western male'.

In this chapter, beyond the exoticisation of the Filipina woman, I explore how the 'mail order bride' stigma also polices broader social mores related to universal (Western) standards of love and intimacy.[1] My analysis of everyday racism moves from the public sphere, like the workplace, to private domains: between a husband and wife, parents and children, brothers and sisters, and between friends. I extend the textual and discursive analysis of the experience of Filipina women married to Australian spouses by sharing the everyday *lived* experiences of these women as told by their own voices. Constable (2003) notes that while media analysis and examination of catalogues or online dating sites are valuable to reading the discourses around the 'mail order bride' issue, such an analysis can be limited to representation that does not delve into the complexity of the women, men and families. In Australia, Roces's (2003) research on Filipina women in remote mining towns who migrated as 'brides' also points out how such readings place a focus on their sexualisation and/or their commodification that, while significant, tends to neglect these women's levels of agencies and complex life trajectories. I aim to highlight the affective dimensions of these women's lives as the focus on discursive analysis has hypersexualised or hypervictimised them into 'unreal' persons – mere reports in the media or subjects and statistics in research studies. This aligns with research on Filipina migration to other places, wherein scholars like Parrenas (2005) and Pratt (2009) have been committed to revealing the emotional side of Filipina workers' migration.[2]

What the overly sexualised readings of 'Filipina brides' or their tendency to be victimised in popular representations have left out are the stories of love, emotions and care that Filipina women nurture and negotiate in their relationships. I attempt to reconceptualise a few things: the idea that these women marry only for migration, the role of their husbands in these women's negotiation of racism, and the manner in which love can come in different albeit legitimate forms. The agency in these women's lives is very much anchored in discourses and gestures of love. And so, although standards around legitimate/illegitimate love form the basis of the racism they experience, sensibilities of love and care also act as a cultural resource to motivate resistance and rework the racialised and gendered stigma of the 'mail order bride' label. While I do not wish to forget that the high rates of domestic violence experienced by Filipina women married to Australian spouses point to significant power imbalances in such relationships and have led to tragic endings for some Filipina wives (see Cuneen and Stubbs, 2003), in this chapter I show that there is a different side to the story that is rarely told.

The making of the 'mail order bride': orientalising discourse

Said (1995: 7) defines orientalism as the manner in which the West manages and cognises the Orient "by making statements about it, authorising views of it, describing it, by teaching it, settling it, ruling over it". Underscoring Western fantasies of 'Asia' is the idea of 'Asia' as weak and passive but at the same time barbaric and menacing. The 'Asian woman' has come to embody in significant ways these discourses – perceived paradoxically as the 'lotus blossom' and the 'dragon lady', which take root in the West's simultaneous desire for and fear of the exotic foreign Other. The Filipina 'mail order bride' epitomises this orientalist frame. This has been the case for countries like the US and Canada, which have had a significant number of Filipinas migrating as spouses of local men since the 1940s (Constable, 2003). For Australia, with its even closer proximity to the Asian region, moral panic around the Filipina 'mail order bride' in the 1970s through to the 1990s was an embodiment of the always looming threat of its Asian neighbours 'invading' Australian borders (Ang, 1996). To stress the case, Filipina migrant nurses began arriving in Australia in almost equal numbers as Filipina women who were migrating as spouses. However, the difference in the visibility between Filipinas married to Australian spouses and Filipina migrant nurses signals the tendency for racialisation to accentuate the most 'deviant' bodies. The aberrant 'mail order bride' poses, more than any Other, the threat of miscegenation, whereby, unlike other forms of immigration "where the newcomers can be ghettoised", these Filipina women are "introduced to the most remote regions into Australian households, giving birth to Australian children" (Robinson, 1996: 54). The 'mail order bride' label was popularised in media depictions underlined by a definition of the Filipina through dichotomous representations of both prey/predator, woman in danger/dangerous woman (Robinson, 1996; Constable, 2003; Saroca, 2006). Filipina brides are positioned as "meek, docile slaves, oriental beauties with shady pasts, passive and manipulable, but also grasping and predatory, using marriage to jump immigration queues" (Robinson, 1996: 54). As Foucault (1981) has theorised, the regulation of sexuality is located in broader civilising processes and the the ways in which 'normal' and 'abnormal' modes of sexuality are marked are key to the structuration of gender inequalities. What the discourse of the 'mail order bride' delineates and through its binary oppositions attempts to discipline is the sexuality of Filipina women – a vestige of colonial ideologies where sexuality has been a defining marker of Otherness.

The status of victimhood is entwined with orientalist ideas of subserviency, docility and naivety. In the 1980s and 1990s, media reporting of domestic violence or homicide of Filipina women who migrated as spouses of white Australian men connected these women's despair, compliance and gullibility to the tragedy that some of them had suffered (Woelz-Stirling et al., 1998 and Cuneen and Stubbs, 2003). The focus of local NGOs and scholarly research on the 'mail order bride' issue during this time also played a significant role in perpetuating a dominant image of Filipinas as weak and victimised. This is part and parcel of early feminist discourse that had shaped understandings of 'Filipina brides' as primary examples of "women's sexual and economic slavery", which lumped them together with trafficked Third World women (Constable, 2000a: 64). On the other end of the spectrum sits the oppositional dialogue that positions Filipinas as opportunistic, conniving and sexual aggressors. Filipina women migrating on spousal visas with men are likened to sex workers from the Third World, in that by appearing in pen pal catalogues, newspaper advertisements or using online dating agencies they are perceived as 'selling' their bodies (Tolentino, 1996; Constable, 2003). Specifically, many of the women I spoke with who are married to Australian spouses complained of being compared to 'bar girls', and this association is rooted in the Philippine sex industry that emerged when the country became a 'rest and recreation' station for US soldiers during the Vietnam War and also when the US established its largest overseas naval bases in the Philippines. Filipina women married to much older Australian men are accordingly seen as marrying only for money and a visa and are stereotyped as suspicious and dishonest 'gold diggers'.

In the Philippines and in the diaspora, such an image is equally prescribed. The ideal Filipina is conceived of as domesticated, demure, sexually passive and docile (Constable, 2003, Brown, 2000; Espiritu, 2003) and 'mail order brides' are viewed as deviant from this norm. The ideal Filipina woman is constructed against the contrasting ideas of white women as immoral and sexually aggressive and thus takes up one aspect of the West's exoticisation and Orientalising of the East in order to reaffirm appropriate femininity.[3] This, however, comes at a cost to Filipina women who are seen to diverge from such standards including those who choose to marry 'foreigners', who conceive a child outside of wedlock, or who separate from their husbands.[4] Jackson (1989: 176–180) in the 1980s made the observation that the

> public image of the 'mail order bride' ensure[s] that Filipinos themselves frequently try to distance themselves from Filipinas in mixed marriages. . . . Any Filipina wed to an Australian, it would seem, is likely to be suspected of being such a bride by her compatriots and probably treated with suspicion until proven otherwise.

It is against these widespread orientalising discourses that the women I interviewed have had to negotiate their lives in Australia. Organised responses from the Filipino community around derogatory media representations of Filipina women emerged as the first forms of community activism among Filipino migrants in Australia. While the women I interviewed concede that things have improved by way of such stigmas, racism continues in various ways that speak back to the 'mail order bride' stereotype across different contexts. This is not only for Filipinas who have met their partners through international correspondence agencies but also for other Filipina women.

Living with the 'mail order bride' stigma

At a coffee shop in a small mall located in a suburb on the south coast of Sydney, I met Cora, Girly and Gemma for morning tea. A friend of mine put me in touch with Cora, who is her sister-in-law, and described Cora and her friends as being part of a tight-knit group of Filipina women who were all married to white Australian men. I recall sitting nervously on the long train ride, unsure of how I would broach the topic of their marriages and route of migration. I was embarrassed to ask them about their relationships, assuming that they too would be shy to talk about the topic, or worse, that they would be offended by something I might say that would be loaded with prior assumptions I had formulated in my mind. I had grown accustomed to (and had regrettably made some of my own in the past) the jokes and suppositions that are associated with Filipina women who marry 'foreigners'. 'Foreigner' is the term used by Filipinos to describe non-Filipinos travelling or living in the Philippines, specifically men courting or married to Filipina women. The term *inday*, translating into the English word 'maid', can be commonly used to describe these women. Speculations abound that these women were most likely 'bar girls' or promiscuous women in their previous lives. The Filipino middle class, from where I had ascertained a lot of these stereotypes growing up, have very entrenched ideas about such women that are carried over from Philippine society and are confirmed by the discourses that can be found in the Australian context.

Cora and Girly had met their husbands through international dating agencies specifically connecting Filipina women with men living in countries like the US and Australia. Girly is forty years old but looks much younger than her age. She has been married to her Australian husband for eight years. She is a full-time 'housewife' and is kept busy looking after three young boys and two girls in their late teens. The friendly young boy she brought along that day was her twelve-year-old son from a previous relationship in the Philippines. The other two boys were at home with their older sisters and these children are from her partner's past marriages to two other Filipinas. Cora is thirty-eight and has also been married to her husband for eight years, and they have two daughters, who were also with her that morning. She works as a cashier supervisor at a supermarket near where she and her family live. She is vibrant and was very accommodating and seemed to trust me because I was her sister-in-law's friend. Gemma is much younger than Girly and Cora and is in her late twenties. She has been in a relationship with her

Anglo partner for three years and they met in Sydney while she was finishing her nursing course. Gemma lives with her partner at a nearby beach suburb.

The racism Cora and Girly recalled came in the form of indirect racism that originates not only from white Australians but also from other Filipinos, from both men and women, and occurs in public and private domains:

Gemma: "I think Australian women don't like Asian women."
Cora: "More competition."
Gemma: "But men, they love Asian girls. Australian women . . . just my instinct I get from them. Just their energy."
Cora: "They're rude."
Gemma: "You can just tell. But when I start talking they realise I can speak English and you're educated. You're not some poor girl from the province."
Cora: "You just feel sorry for people like that. They probably never leave Australia and they live here all their life. They don't want to be swamped by Asians, other countries."
Girly: "For me, the racism was especially because my husband is much older."
Cora: "Yeah, with people looking at you when you're together. It's the same in the Philippines. They look at you. They're just staring at you. They look at you differently."
Girly: "You just get the stares. Just a feeling from white Aussies. They think, 'Oh, another gold digger'. Or maybe I'm the maid. You get it here but in the Philippines they are much more open about it and much more rude. And with me, as well, when I first move here and my husband already had two girls – they didn't like me. They're jealous because the attention of their dad is on someone else. But they had a Filipina mum, but they still don't like me. One of them shout at me that I'm a 'mail order'. Her mum also met her dad this way but she doesn't see it as the same. She hated me in the beginning."

The racism these women experience has not always been verbally expressed but is instead sensed through discomfort from actions and attitudes that communicate disapproval and aversion when they are seen with their husbands in public. They believe that they are seen as (sexual) 'competition' for Australian women or opportunists marrying only for money but also paradoxically mistaken for being deprived and pitiable. In the case of Girly, the stigma of the 'mail order bride' follows her into the home, where one of her stepdaughters acutely conveys her distaste in spite of her own mother meeting her father through a correspondence agency. These experiences go beyond feelings of discomfort but are also debilitating to these women's choices and physical movements. Cora described how her status among other Filipino migrants as a white man's wife led her to initially isolate herself from the Filipino community:

Some Filipinos here too, they look at you. Maybe that's why I didn't want to be friends with Filipinos at first when I came here. You know, what they're thinking, that sort of thing. I met some Filipinas who asked me if I was Filipina and they told me, 'Oh, we're having Filipino parties, you should come!' But I didn't like to at first. But then I met my friend at work who is Filipina and I wasn't too friendly back then. I tried to make more friends with white people than Filipinos. I just say hi to her. But she was so friendly and she introduced me to her friends. I liked them. And these women are also like me, in the same family situation. I met Girly at one of those parties. So I liked them and we have parties like karaoke (laughs).

According to Constable (2003), the decision to marry a 'foreigner' is one of the ways in which an engrained aspiration towards the 'West' imprinted by centuries of colonisation can manifest in contemporary Philippine society. But these women also bear the worst of Filipinos' simultaneous resentment for its conquerors. They are categorised together with Filipina sex workers, who are shamed for selling their bodies to foreign tourists in hostess bars and brothels. Both types of women are judged, in the Philippines and in the diaspora, against 'ideal' standards of Filipina femininity. These women are viewed as proof of decay of Philippine society and culture as a result of Western domination and shamed for assuming the "sexual mores of white women" (Espiritu, 2003: 166). Their disavowal allows for the safeguarding of "Filipina sexual virtuosity and white female sexual promiscuity" (Espiritu, 2003: 166). The shaming of the 'mail order bride' by the Filipino community also speaks to transnationalised regimes of class and race. Being compared to a 'bar girl' or being called *inday* (maid) automatically presupposes Filipinas who marry 'foreigners' are from lower socio-economic backgrounds or poor regional provinces, class stratifications which take on racialised meanings in the Philippine context. To add to the insult, Filipinas who marry 'foreigners' are also financially exploited by their families and friends in the Philippines at the very same time that they are ostracised for marrying white men. Cora explained that one of the reasons she decided to migrate with her husband and daughter to Australia after trying to live together in her home province was because of the stress that was brought on by her family around money:

> My husband and I tend to argue more there. Especially because of family. Family comes over and they want to borrow money. And if you don't give them, you feel bad and I feel pressure as well. So we decided to move away. When we married, it's like I have a dollar sign around my head. Always, just coming over with problems and asking for money.

The status of white men in the Philippines is associated with the "prestige, status and assumed wealth" that take root in racial and colonial relations between the Philippines and its foreign conquerors (Constable, 2003: 122). It provides the basis for which these women are dishonoured by their family, friends and community while simultaneously permitting them to be raised up as people who can provide help and assistance. The contradictory process functions as a mode of material and symbolic exploitation of the Filipina in Philippine society. In the previous chapter, I emphasised the ways in which such a raised status can recoup pride for a migrant. There are, however, immense pressures that come with this position, and this burden is heaviest for Filipina women as they are expected to prioritise their kin and community and this includes the sharing of their income. Ehrenreich and Hochschild (2006) observe that on a much wider level, the feminised South to North migration is partially rooted in the encouragement from family, community and the state for female immigration as they are considered to be more reliable in sending their wages back home than men.

The 'mail order bride' stigma has also been inherited by other Filipinas who have white husbands but did not meet through international dating agencies. Because the stereotype flourishes through the visibility of raced bodies, little distinction is made across these couples. I return to Melinda, whose story I briefly touched on in the introduction of this book. If we recall, Melinda met her husband while he was travelling for business in the Philippines. She migrated to Australia on a spousal visa after a long-distance courtship and they lived in a small country town outside of Melbourne. She described experiencing similar racisms to that of Cora and Girly in both public and private domains:

> My first husband and I went to the local pub and that's where I first experienced being discriminated. I saw this group of elderly Australians, they were women. I was going to smile at them. And you know what they did? They looked at me from head to foot and they . . . (imitates snubbing gesture with her head). They ignored me, you know. And I thought, 'Oh, my god, what is this?' So I told my husband and he said, 'Yes, Melinda, it's because you are Asian. That's why they did that." And he didn't like it and so he spoke to the manager. He said, 'I don't feel good about this, you're my wife!' He spoke to the manager but what can they do? It's their attitude, it's the normal thing. And my husband said to him, 'We won't be coming here anymore.' So we left.
>
> . . . And some of his friends were okay, some of them are not. Actually, there was one friend of his, he was inviting us to his house but my husband sort of warned me, 'This friend of mine, he doesn't really like Asians. So be careful with him.' He made some jokes my husband said about me being from the Philippines. I said to him, 'Okay, darling, don't worry. We'll see what happens.' When we arrived at his friend's house, he was shaking hands with me. 'Oh, you're Melinda.' And I answered him, 'Yes, and you're John. My husband told me that you don't like Asians?' (laughs) Oh, he was so embarrassed! 'Oh, I didn't say that!' That's what he said and he didn't know what to do because there were so many guests. He tried to convince me. 'Oh, Melinda, I didn't say that.' But you know he's kind of winking at my husband, like he is not serious. So I got a feeling that really, I was right. But good, I got him first.
>
> . . . When we went back to the Philippines, we stayed in a hotel. The Filipinos there at the hotel they were looking at us like this, you know (gives a glaring look). You know, a Filipino marrying a foreigner, they were thinking, *'Ano bang classeng babae to?'* (What kind of woman is this?) *Ganon.* (Like that). *'Baka bar girl?'* (Maybe she is a bar girl?). They think it's only bar girls who go with Americans or Australians. . . . Here the same thing happens. The

elderly, when they see a white person, a foreigner, with an Asian woman they probably think 'mail order'. That girl is with him for money. Like in the pub, there was an Asian girl, I think a Filipina. And she was always at the club with a different man. And they just gave her money to play the pokies. They are thinking I am like her.

Sadly, Melinda's husband died from a stroke after only a few years of marriage and she later relocated to Sydney. After a few years, she met her second husband, who is also much older than Melinda and is of Middle Eastern background. He pursued her while frequenting the video store that she used to own in Sydney's north-western suburbs. In her second marriage, despite that her husband was not 'white', Melinda continued to experience racism prompted by her status as a Filipina wife of a much older man who is not Asian:

My second husband, his family, they won't talk to me. And I was wondering why. When I was with them, even though they can speak English fluently, they speak in their language. It's just like us (Filipinos). But then I didn't know that they were also talking behind my back. One of the women in his family, she was very nice to me and very kind. She told me not to mind the others. But she explained that, 'Oh, you know, Melinda, in our minds we were told that Filipinos are, you know . . . it's a poor country, so many problems.' And I said, 'So what?' So they are thinking that you are not good enough! That Filipina women are maids, we're poor, we're desperate. My husband, he's not a bad man but it's his relatives. His sister said something to me that I didn't like. She said, 'You know, Melinda, I must accept you now because you're my brother's wife.' And I asked her why she couldn't just accept me as a person. And she said she couldn't.

Where marriage and family contexts are meant to provide "protection against anomie for the individual" and act as a source of order to make sense of one's life (Berger and Kellner, 1994: 19), racism that filters into these intimate spheres denies these women such comforts. Melinda experiences insulting behaviour from her first husband's friends and the racism worsens in her second marriage when it comes from her husband's family. She also makes mention of the marginalisation from the Filipino community, which doubly acts as a source of stress and apprehension for Filipina women like Melinda.

These widely circulating representations also factor into the experiences of other Filipinas among the second generation, where orientalist discourses that underlie the 'mail order bride' stereotype take form in different guises. I interviewed two sisters – Mary is twenty-seven and works as a solicitor, while her older sister Catherine is thirty-three and works in finance. Both spoke about the frequent racialised and gendered stereotyping they had encountered in the workplace and also other social situations:

Is it racism or exoticism? The men at work have this term, 'emerging markets'. That's their classification for something exotic – usually Asian females. I work for an investment company and it's like a running joke at my work. So they call Aussie girls 'Aussie equities' and exotic girls 'emerging markets'. So they tell me I'm an 'emerging market'. You get stereotyped. There are plenty of guys who like their 'types' – some like blondes and others like more exotic-looking girls. And women I think can also get jealous of Asian women because we're exoticised. And you really don't know whether to take offense or not. Whether it's a compliment or whether you're being objectified.

(Catherine)

There was maybe one incident with my friend who is Vietnamese. We were at a bar in Newtown and my friend is very attractive and dresses kind of 'sexy'. There was this couple, and I think the guy might have been checking out my friend. The girl came up to us and really just started shouting at us and insulting us. Calling us horrible names like 'sluts' and she said to us, 'You Asian girls are so stupid!' My boyfriend had to step in and told her to go away because my friend, she was fighting back and started yelling at her too.

(Mary)

Both of these sisters' experiences, in spite of being second-generation Filipinas, are subtly underscored by discourses that draw on perceptions of the female 'Asian Other' – either as mysterious and exotic beauties or as predatory femme fatales. Mary's experience indicates a more explicit racism that may be likened to the encounters that Melinda endures. On the other hand, Catherine feels an ambiguity about being exoticised. The metaphors that underlie the 'mail order bride' stereotype transmute in varying ways across different contexts experienced by Filipina women and suggest that while Mary and Catherine may be subjected to related representations they are not necessarily seen as 'mail order brides'. In addition, the two sisters also have Anglo partners and were acutely aware of the unfairness of the discourses. However, Mary and Catherine still expressed a disapproval of Filipinas migrating for marriage. They commented on the 'mail order bride' label not in explicitly derogatory ways but instead expressed pity for Filipinas who they believe marry their older husbands out of desperation:

Catherine: "I admit, I judge the (Filipina) women who are with much older men. I do wonder when I see them."

Mary: "People can tell. When I used to work in retail you had some couples come in, obviously they were mail order brides. You could tell not just because of their age but they would always ask their husbands to get them things, (puts on an accent) "Baby, can you get me these?" My friend and I would roll our eyes. But that's me being stereotypical."

Catherine: "I judge them because you look at the guy and he's ugly or old or whatever. And the girl is so young. So they're selling themselves short. I'm embarrassed for them to a degree. I feel icky about it. But I guess if you're in her shoes, you rationalise it. She's probably

	got a better life here. You know, she came from a Third World country. But maybe it's not about embarrassment. It's more, I do feel sorry for them. But you know people don't always marry for love."
Mary:	"I feel pity for them. I also have other non-Filipino friends from high school. . . . one was forced to marry an uncle from Lebanon because it's tradition. Or Indian girlfriends who have had arranged marriages. So I feel bad for them as much as I do for Filipina mail order brides or just Asian women in general who do the same thing."

Catherine and Mary are candid about their opinions. But at the same time, they admit that they can be stereotypical, and I could see that they were using dialogue which is hard to escape when fed by popular discourse (they use the 'mail order bride' term like it is a 'real' and non-offensive descriptor) and which is also informed by their more privileged middle-class position. Mary also compares 'mail order brides' to her girlfriends from 'non-Western' cultures who have had to marry for reasons other than love and hints at what she believes marriage should be based on or what the decision to marry should involve.

Love, economics and the 'care deficit'

In her reflections on the feminised dimension of South to North migration led primarily by female migrant workers in domestic or care fields, Hochschild (2003) argues that there is a 'care deficit' in advanced First World nations that has prompted the 'extraction of care' from the Third World. For instance, Filipinas fill the 'care deficit' in Europe, Middle East, North America and East Asian countries, like Hong Kong, Japan and Singapore, through their labour as domestic workers. In Australia, they migrate as nurses. This 'care deficit' is, in part, an outcome of the changes to women's roles in advanced industrial countries – women now participate in paid employment in larger numbers yet are not adequately supported by the state in the provision of social services or equitable income. Gendered attitudes of men in these societies also continue to reinforce unequal sharing of household duties. Feminised migration today, therefore, sees a "synergy of needs among women – one group, in the affluent countries, needing help and the other, in poor countries, needing jobs" (Ehrenreich and Hochschild, 2006: 180). While Hochschild (2003) speaks of women from the global South migrating for work, I suggest that the concept of a 'care deficit' can also be applied to Filipina women who marry men from these societies, in that such relationships represent an 'extraction of love'.

But this type of love goes not without judgement. In a society like Australia, women have made advances in women's rights and are now omnipresent in the labour force, and no-fault divorce has given further rise to women's independence; this has produced significant threats to hegemonic masculine norms that underlie the institutions of marriage and family. In her research on the experience of Filipina and Chinese women married to American spouses, Constable (2003) suggests that changes to gender power relations in advanced industrial societies have made some men cautious of women who prioritise their career over family. Certainly, while this signals a problem with articulations of hegemonic masculinity, these men also become subject "to dichotomous and reductionist stereotypes as omnipotent, controlling, white/western oppressor, or the reject and loser who becomes an unwitting victim of the 'dragon lady'" (Constable, 2003: 78). Moreover, the marriages are positioned as 'backward' because they are understood as preserving outdated patriarchal relations. Women who enter these 'regressive' relationships then also serve to reinforce the superiority of 'advanced' Western women and signal how "negative stereotypes of women in other cultures are significant in both orientalist and patriarchal discourse" (Robinson, 1996: 60).

Further, the relationship poses a challenge to "ideological constructions of marriage as a love match" (Robinson, 1996: 64). The association of 'romantic love', according to Giddens (1992: 38), emerged as European civilisation discarded the traditional practice of marriage as "contracted, not on the basis of mutual attraction, but economic circumstances". The notion of romantic love has evolved to signify "self-realisation", connecting love and freedom as "normatively desirable states" (Giddens, 1992: 40). In turn, marriages like those of Filipina women and older Anglo men who meet through introduction agencies are positioned as 'calculated' because both parties actively seek each other out through highly rationalised avenues and enter into the relationship with set motives. This process defies the commonly held ideal of love as some form of spontaneous, instantaneous, illogical attraction. But at the same time, such relationships are also understood as involuntary and 'unnatural' because the male is 'undesirable' to his 'own kind', while the woman has 'no choice' but to marry an older white man to escape poverty. The husbands and wives in these relationships are dismissed as illegitimate and dishonest in the failure to conform to ideals of marriage as a romantic association between two free individuals.

Inherent in this ideology is a tendency in advanced economies to separate love from economics, which splits the domestic from the public sphere as the home and family are positioned as a contained and protected space from the "impersonal forces of capitalism and politics" (Constable, 2003: 116). The 'mail order bride' is shamed for bringing together the conflicting spheres of love/economics, private/public, personal/politics. In telling her story, Melinda shared with me how she praised the way her first husband showed respect to her parents in order to woo her, but she was also quite frank that he was rich, which she was well aware would improve her life should she marry him:

> *Na* impress *ako!* (I was impressed!) *Tapos mayaman pa!* (plus he is rich!) *Ay siempre, diba!* (Of course, right!) As if I will say no? *Siempre bakit ka pa maghihirap, eh eto na, mabait na, alom mo naman* he's a nice guy (of course why will I stay struggling, when here he is, he's nice and you know he's a nice guy).

Hypergamy is the practice of women marrying into a higher socio-economic group, and it is important to note that it also occurs in contexts like Australia and white women are stigmatised for the same reasons. However, the racialised visibility of Filipina bodies and their white partners significantly marks them out from other women who engage in the same practices.

Distinguishing between love and pragmatics is rooted in a particularly Western perspective, whereby the separation attempts to 'purify' love from practical concerns. But as Povinelli (2006: 175–176) argues, despite modern-day conceptions, love is ultimately a political event: "it expands humanity, creating the human by exfoliating its social skin, and this expansion is critical to the liberal Enlightenment project." She emphasises that love is often a forgotten force of structuration that has been used to create a "higher civilisational form even though it happens only between two people" (Povinelli, 2006: 178). In other words, romanticised notions of love are not organic but are, historically, another means by which hierarchies of inequality and exclusion are produced and maintained:

> The power of the intimate event of self-sovereignty lay in its ability to connect the micro practices of certain forms of love to the macro practices of certain forms of state governance and certain forms of capital production, circulation and consumption – to make a personal event a normative mission and a civilisational break.
>
> (Povinelli, 2006: 191)

The sexual and emotional relations between Filipina wives and their Australian spouses are illegitimated either because of the calculated and rationalised nature of their 'romance' or because of the assumption that these women do not have genuine freedom and choice in the matter. Those who cannot 'authentically' love are denied equal humanity.

The fallacy of 'marriage for migration'

While some of the women I interviewed certainly marry for economic security, this is not the whole side of the story. These women also migrate *for* marriage because it allows them to fulfil a longing for family and children, which they are not granted in the Philippines for a range of reasons. Filipina women are subject to a multitude of gendered hegemonies in the Philippines around what it is to be not only an 'ideal Filipina' but also an 'ideal wife'. Many Filipina women who find relationships with men outside of the Philippines are often "considered too old, too educated, divorced, or too experienced to be considered good wives" in the local society (Constable, 2005: 12). Cora, Girly and Melinda are all university-educated and emphasised in their stories working hard in their professions and making money for themselves. Cora and Melinda both recalled the way they were treated by Filipino men and also by their own family when they had reached an age at which they were deemed 'too old' to be marriageable material in the Philippines:

> My husband write to me. So we became pen pal partners. And after a year he came to the Philippines for a visit. I had lots of pen pals aside

from him! (laughs) But it just happened that he was the first to come see me and he was 'The One'. I was the same age as you, twenty-seven or maybe younger. I'm too scared to get old. To be an old maid. In the Philippines they say that if you turn thirty and you're not married you're an old maid! My friends were saying, "Come on, you're getting old!" Especially I worked as a teacher, so if you're a teacher you tend to become an old maid (laughs). So we got married there in my province, got a house there, and my first daughter was born there. We lived in the Philippines for three years. I kept working as a teacher and my husband stayed home by himself. He's an engineer, a designer. He worked at home designing and sending things back home but he missed his job here. He couldn't find work in the Philippines.

We decided to move because there is too much stress for us living in the Philippines and we need to make it (the marriage) work so we decided to move to Australia. I didn't resign yet from the school. I just came here first for six months to see if I like it. And I did so we went back there after six months and I resigned from my job so we can live here.

(Cora)

My first husband, we met in the Philippines. He was visiting my hairdresser (laughs). My hairdresser was saying to me, 'How old are you now, Melinda?' I was thirty-three and that's like being a spinster. And she said she had a friend who was there and introduced me to him. So he was in the Philippines looking for shoes for his business. He saw me and we got on well. We talked about the business, asked where I live . . . that sort of thing. And then we became friends. He went back to Australia and would ring me on the phone and you know *ligaw-ligaw* (to court or to woo) (laughs). And he wants me to come here. But I said that I had obligations to the companies I was working for because I had to finish the books at the end of financial year. He said it would be too long! (laughs) So he was so nice.

(Melinda)

In the case of Girly, she told of the way men at her workplace in the Philippines viewed her as 'easy' because she already had a child, which for them implied that she was available to 'sleep around':

I graduated in civil engineering and I worked in the Philippines for a few years. My father said I should get another course because in the Philippines if you have two degrees you're better off, so I also took computer engineering. I had a bright future, you know. But then I end up pregnant. And that's when my father died. I was very close to my dad. And when he died, I was pregnant, it was very sad for me. It didn't work out with my boyfriend because he's Catholic and I'm not. He wanted me to convert so we can get married and I didn't want to convert. It doesn't matter for me if we're two different religions but I didn't want to convert, it made me uncomfortable. When I had my son, my boyfriend just disappeared. We don't have any communication from that moment. I got a part-time job and raised my little boy.

I end up hating men. I don't like to go out with them. And when I had my job they know you have a little boy and they (men) end up courting you because they think one day I'm going to go off with them. That I'm easy. So I thought I don't want to get involved.

I've got a very close friend who likes to email and before they have no email so they have these letters to men from overseas. And she likes going to the US and that's where she is trying to meet men. She got a boyfriend from there. So she put me in the Internet on Brides of Asia. She got my photo and put me on the Internet. And that's when I met my husband. I wanted to go the USA because my friend's boyfriend is from there and she is going there. Anyway, I ended up meeting my husband. He started emailing me. He already had kids too and it's like he understood me. So he went there to marry me in the Philippines.

These women have been shamed in a myriad of ways in Philippine society and signal their marginal position in a largely patriarchal gender hierarchy. But, more importantly, all of these women exercised great agency in their migration. Cora, Girly and Melinda were all fairly independent in the Philippines – graduating from university and working in their chosen professions. Each of them undertook a decision-making process as to whether to migrate overseas. Melinda's first husband desired for her to migrate to Australia sooner but she prioritised completing her work commitments. Cora and her husband made an attempt to live in the Philippines instead of migrating straight to Australia, and during this time she was an equal provider for her family as she continued working as a teacher. Girly, meanwhile, admitted that she did not initially want to marry a 'foreigner' because she acknowledged the difficulties in cross-cultural relationships. Contrary to popular belief that such women marry only in order to migrate or, moreover, equate migration solely with economic well-being, these women demonstrate that this is not always the case. There was hesitancy to leave their home despite knowing that a more financially secure future lay ahead of them overseas.

Motivations to migrate are also associated with fulfilling identities that have been denied to them in the Philippine context – specifically that of a 'wife' and 'mother'. This is not uncommon across female migration from the Philippines, wherein Filipina migrant workers migrate not only for work or income but also to realise autonomy that is often unavailable back home (Parrenas, 2001). While some feminist discourse might view the aspiration to be a wife or mother as a misguided and outdated trajectory for the 'modern' woman, being a wife and a mother and having a 'family' are significant to the Filipinas I spoke with and have been made possible *through* their migration. Girly has two degrees and came from a fairly middle-class family; her father was a doctor and her mother a pharmacist and they both encouraged her to study hard in order to be 'respectable' and financially stable. However, Girly has no qualms about having traded in her career to look after her son, her husband and his children to acquire a different kind of respectability:

> I'm a full-time housewife but it keeps me busy. I never thought my life would go this way, but it's destiny. I had my son and his father left and then I met my husband and it gave me another chance. I'm not working, but I am doing something important . . . taking care of my son and we have a good life here when who knows what things will be like in the Philippines for us. I take care of my husband and our kids and make sure the house is going good and that's decent, *diba?* (right?)

Women like Girly are often criticised for conforming to archaic gender roles. But "often lacking in this critique of marriage and gender relations [is] an appreciation of the ways in which women in different socio-cultural contexts might define liberation" (Constable, 2003: 65). In the literature that examines the 'mail order bride' issue, the longing to have their own families is too often overlooked in preference for the overly sexualised readings of Filipina women's relationships. The idea of 'marriage for migration' needs to be reconceptualised to take into account that some women 'migrate for marriage' in order to overhaul the notions that migration is reducible to economic motives or that marriage is a repressive institution offering limited agency. For migrant women like Filipinas who have married 'foreigner' men, there is a 'transformatory potential' to marriage migration that transcends economic gains (Bulloch and Fabinyi, 2009). For Cora it is *through* her family that she can resist the 'mail order bride' stereotype:

> If it's just you and your husband, people look at you, thinking you're one of the 'mail orders'. But as soon as they see you have kids, they're nice. But if it's just you and your husband, they really look at you differently. But if you have kids they look at your family – they see you as a 'family'. So it's different.

Reframing the 'foreigner' husband

The role of the husbands in relationships with my respondents is also considerably different to the abusive characters that proliferate in media representations. Having stressed that the 'mail order bride' stereotype condemns the relationship and not just the women involved, I suggest that the racism faced by Filipina women who are married to Australian men has profound effects on the lives of the husbands too. Everyday racism is debilitating for not only the target but also those who offer their support to the 'victim'. And so, some husbands also come to play an active role in helping their wives deal with racism. These men, therefore, are 'in it together' with their wives – making sacrifices for the relationship just as much as the women do. Melinda's first husband left his church after she experienced racism from the priest and congregation. He also stopped seeing any friends who displayed racist attitudes towards his wife:

> You know so my husband said, 'Maybe it's about time you stop accepting what they do to you. You should prove . . . you know, just because you're Asian that you're not a liability to this country.' You know what I mean? So I took his advice.
>
> . . . My niece from the Philippines, I adopted her and brought her here. But she got bullied in school and she cannot fight back yet because she can't speak English. And so my husband started to help her. Gave her books for her to read. And gradually she had a teacher who helped children with learning English as a second language.
>
> A week before school finished my niece was crying. She said that they these boys stole all her pens and one of her books they hung on the fence. I went to the teacher and told her the problem. I said, 'Look, this is your problem. This is your responsibility to make sure that nobody is being bullied in this school!' They said that they will look into it. So we went home. And my husband told my niece, 'Don't worry, I will teach you how to fight!' He taught her how to punch and kick. And so when she came back to school in February, the teachers wanted me to come in and talk to me. And you know what the teacher said? 'This girl, she's had a fight with these boys. And they're all crying!' Apparently she hit them! And I said, 'Look, this is what I was telling you about before. They bullied her and now she's fighting back. She's retaliating! So you cannot blame her! You did not do anything about those other boys.'

The power relations in these marriages are much more complex than how they are defined under the 'mail order bride' archetype, where the women are assumed to be powerless. It is commonly emphasised that these women are economically dependent on their spouses, but the ways in which their husbands also find themselves dependent in certain situations and requiring support are rarely discussed. Particularly on return trips to the Philippines, the women I interviewed joked about how ignorant and 'needy' their partners could be. Not knowing the language, customs and surrounds, their wives often need to take control and offer guidance, much like they as husbands might do when in Australia. Cora and Girly shared the following conversation, which illustrates the ways in which power is not merely static but can shift and alternate depending on context:

Cora: "There you are waiting for a taxi and here, you know, everyone is polite and waiting their turn. But there in the Philippines, you have to be quick. Oh, my husband is so slow! I have to hold his hand and push through people to get a taxi. And I'm telling him, "Quick, quick!" and holding his hand. And he doesn't know what's going on. (laughs) . . . And you know, when you're a foreigner there in the Philippines, it's like you have a dollar sign on your forehead. So he needs me there or else they're going to trick him. And the staring is worse in the Philippines. But you know, I stare at them back! Mataray!"[5]

Girly: "My husband, he finds the Chinese rude there in the Philippines. My husband opened the door to a cab there and a China man took it. He grabbed the man by the collar and told him to 'Fuck off!' Oh, my god, I had to tell my husband, 'Don't do that! You know what they'll do to you? Some of these men have knives!' He doesn't know anything and I have to tell him how to act there. I think like Cora said, when you're a foreigner they treat you differently. But I think either they are really nice to you because they think you're rich or they bully you because you don't know anything."

Girly and Melinda also told me how they prefer to leave their partners behind in Australia when they return to the Philippines so they can travel independently without having somebody to constantly look after:

We've been back twice now. But he doesn't like it. It's the weather, too hot and humid. He complains too much and I can't enjoy. And we can't stay inside the hotel all day and night in the air-conditioning! We need to get out. I want to get out! It's better he just stays here so I can see my friends and family.
(Melinda)

He likes going there but it's uncomfortable for him. When he comes with me we have to stay in a hotel and we can't go to my home there. When you go home, you want to see your family in your house and have Filipino cooking. And he doesn't really like Filipino food because he doesn't like pork. And when we go there I have to always be with him all the time. So I like to go by myself. I've taken the kids and they love it!
(Girly)

The resistance to appreciating the culture of their Filipina wives can be read as a form of disrespect, in that these men are willing to marry Filipina women but are not willing to learn about their culture. But for Melinda and Girly, it is significant to note that they negotiate what they think are 'better' circumstances. Instead of tolerating being 'nagged' by their husbands on their trips home, they have willingly opted to holiday on their own. The cross-cultural differences can also go both ways. Melinda had a similar attitude to her second husband in terms of visiting his country of birth in the Middle East:

I don't understand the people there, the language. I would rather a country where they all speak English. Even just a bit. I don't want to go to his country. If it's a week maybe I can put up with it. But a month? No way!

Power relations in these marriages are never entirely equal but shift and vary depending on circumstances. Power, therefore, is not merely a zero-sum condition.

These relationships involve constant negotiation of power, agency and fairness, which rebuts their conventional racialised and gendered depictions.

Confessions of love

Povinelli (2006: 188–190) deploys Habermas's argument that

> the humanist subject was forged out of the intimate recognition that passed between two people in the conjugal household . . . The intimate event holds together what economic and political sovereignty threaten to pull apart . . . conserving the civilizational distinction between the metropole and colony.

In other words, forms of loving and intimacy contribute to the hierarchies through which "people (and societies) might be ranked and evaluated in relation to unmodern Others" (Povinelli, 2006: 188). Normative standards about love underlie the challenge to these women's modes of intimacy. But at the same time, discourses and gestures of love can be the very means by which they make sense of their lives and help cope with the stigma ascribed to their bodies and relationships. In our interview, Melinda looked back fondly at the long-distance courtship she shared with her first husband – how he pleaded with her to come to Australia sooner and sent her books about Australia to prepare her for her migration, and how he wanted to show respect to her parents. She thought he was so intelligent and was very saddened when he died. And while she has experienced problems with her second husband's family, she still also holds fond memories about how she had 'fallen' for him:

> I met him in Sydney. I owned a video shop and I was there behind the counter. And he came in and stuck his head over the counter and asked me, 'What's your name?' This and that. And you know, nobody (customers) really speaks to you here, especially in a job like that. They don't ask you how you are. And we started to be friendly. He came more often. I thought he was going to run out of movies to watch because he would visit so much! (laughs) So you know, *ligaw* (wooing) again.

In both of her marriages, Melinda uses the Tagalog term ligaw, which in its simplest English translation means 'courtship'. However, in Tagalog, the term does not merely refer to a process of dating but encapsulates more affective and emotional dimensions, like passion, desire, fascination and excitement. Similarly, for Girly and Cora, meeting men from overseas through a correspondence agency, while maybe not their first choice to meet their future husbands, was ultimately a genuine avenue to seek out romance and love. Cora spoke about being 'pen pals' with a few men and how she enjoyed meeting and getting to know them in this way because "*they write sweet things to you and you look forward to their writing.*" For Girly and Cora's friend Gemma, who joined us at the interview, she lamented enviously that her friends' stories were more "romantic" compared to her own because they experienced "*love at first sight . . . If a guy likes you they want to come over right away and marry you! I wish I could have done that!*"

These women, therefore, often subscribe to universal notions of love, particularly that of 'romantic love', and they did so long before migrating or being introduced to their partners. It is significant to point out that the idea of 'romance' not only features prominently in Filipino culture because of American influence but also dates back to Hispanic colonialism in the country (Velasco, 2006). Both eras imported theatre and film that primarily portrayed European versions of 'love stories', featuring strong masculine heroes and fragile damsels. And so, just because there is an acknowledgement of the pragmatic motivations for marriage, this does not overshadow the way in which these Filipinas were also marrying for the exact same reasons as their Western counterparts – they too were 'swept off their feet' and 'felt love at first sight'.

Moreover, love is not merely a 'fairy tale' for Girly, Cora and Melinda. Their marriages are taken with every bit of seriousness because Filipino culture places a strong emphasis on the sanctity of marriage. Faeir (2007), in her study of Filipina women working as bar hostesses in rural Japan, found that love was omnipresent in the narratives of her respondents. In spite of initially having an economic relationship with their husbands, love developed slowly and these women were insulted to be seen as marrying only for a visa or financial security because they deeply respected the sacrament of marriage. As divorce is not legal in the Philippines, Faeir (2007: 156) points out that "the pressure to take marriage seriously is legally institutionalised. Moreover, if one believes marriage to be a sacrament and a life commitment based on love, one has little choice but to try to find a way to love one's spouse." But the latter is generally perceived as an 'improper' expression of love because the love is 'forced' or must be 'cultivated' and this standardises love as taking a universal form rather than being expressed and experienced in nuanced ways across sociocultural contexts. In particular, Western notions of romantic love are upheld as 'superior', wherein love is either "present or not from the beginning, rather than viewing it as an emotion that may take different forms and that has the potential to grow and develop after marriage" (Constable, 2003: 128).

Indeed, the women I met were very sincere about their marriages and spoke about the "hard work" it entailed to stay committed to their husbands, to take care of their children and to put their families first. Girly disclosed to me that her husband has had four wives prior to their marriage. She was not, however, ashamed but instead reiterated that she is 'different' from the others because she is far more dedicated to making the marriage work:

> I'm the fifth wife. But he tells me that he doesn't know what happened with the rest of them. He tells me that I'm always the same since we met. Still caring, still committed. I don't change. Well, you know, you shouldn't give up like that. That's what I think.

For Melinda, she has encountered far more resistance from her second husband's family, which has put tremendous strain on their marriage, and she now refuses to see his relatives. However, she was quite stern in pointing out that this was not going to be the end of her marriage:

> My second husband, he's not a bad man, he's also good, but it's his relatives. They want him to marry the same nationality. But my husband said that he had married one like him but it didn't work. And they ended up divorcing each other. Why should he marry another one? He's happy with me. You know, it's a marriage – it's not always a bed of roses. Sometimes it's just hard. Two individuals are different. In the end, we try to agree and we try to care for each other.

These women take pride in their commitment to their marriages amid the marginalisation that their relationships endure. Love is not merely a 'romance', a mere fantasy or 'fairy tale'. Love is about 'sticking' with their husbands, prioritising the family and being the best wives and mothers that they can be. I suggest that these sensibilities of love and care have been central to these women as both a life trajectory *and* strategic resistance. They did not marry merely for migration and to acquire a 'better life' financially. They migrated to realise the goal of marriage, which for them is bound to the value they assign to having children and a family, of being a wife and a mother. But because of their stigmatised status as 'mail order brides', which illegitimates their relationships, they still have to *prove* their capacity to love and to care. From her sister-in-law, Melinda requested respect not merely because she is the wife of her brother but also just because she is another human being. Melinda's yearning is a reflection of the dehumanising effect of the racism that she and other women like her endure. These women's confessions of love assert the interiority deemed necessary to be seen as a modern, autonomous subject.

Conclusion

That Filipina women seek relationships through dating agencies or marry their Australian husbands for financial security or because they agree to being 'housewives' speaks to practices and values denounced through forms of racialised condemnation that intersect with gender and class orders. Beyond Orientalising discourse, the 'mail order bride' stigma serves to regulate wider modes of intimacy and love that are connected to socially constructed ideals about marriage – an institution fundamental to the maintenance of an enlightened and 'civilised' modern society. The policing of intimacy serves as a "defensive retreat from a neoliberal attempt to reduce all our interactions to terms that are compatible with . . . the imperatives of the marketplace" (Johnson, 2006: 4). Intimate life is the "last bastion" of preserving certain kinds of ethics and "saving the claims of private life as source of special values and meanings" (Johnson, 2006: 4). But we cannot forget that certain configurations of love and intimacy create hierarchies of what is 'human' and what is Other and that are bound up in and reproduce broader normative economic and political values. While love might commonly be disassociated from politics, the state or the economy, it is yet another means by which racial projects are created and continually reinforced as a normative horizon. These ideals are maintained through the regulation of 'deviant' bodies, like that of Filipina women married to white men, and disguise the equally pragmatic nature of marriages in contemporary Western societies. This is coupled with pressures from the Filipino community which take root in Philippine social structures and cultural discourses around gender and sexuality and point to transnational circuits of domination. But as a way to manage their 'spoiled identities' (Goffman, 1963), the women I interviewed reclaim love as a way to redeem their 'humanity', which is denied via the dehumanising experiences of racism. They refuse to be seen as victims as they actively negotiate levels of empowerment.

Notes

1 I take inspiration from Constable's (2003) research on Filipina and Chinese immigrant wives within the US and Canadian context. Constable's (2003) work has developed more complex understandings of international correspondence marriages and the stigma ascribed to the relationships and the men and women whom they involve. She particularly goes beyond representational analysis and investigates the life histories of these women to uncover the range of social forces impinging on their experiences and, moreover, the levels of agency and power in their lives.
2 Parrenas (2001) and Pratt (2009) have shed light on the emotions involved in the separation from children felt by Filipina caregivers who migrate overseas for work; the transnational nature of care that is consequently exchanged across borders; or the very experience of 'care work' for Filipina domestic helpers, nurses and even bar hostesses.
3 This appropriation of Orientalist discourse is also common in other Asian countries. For instance, Singapore attempts to gain economically through use of quintessential 'Asian femininity' by its national airline. Singapore Airlines commodifies sexualised and exoticised Asian femininity through its 'Singapore girl', who, Heng (1997: 38) points out, is infantilised as a 'girl' and "never a 'woman', and certainly no mere 'flight attendant', but 'a great way to fly'." Heng (1997: 39) argues that the marketing of Asian femininity is not uncommon among Third World Asian states and that the "legitimation of some feminine identities over others can be a matter of considerable national profit and national interest."
4 One of the most cited cases is ABS-CBN, a Philippine online news website, which featured a story about Filipina 'mail order brides' and described the 'typical' Filipina who takes part in the 'business' as a woman who "believes that marrying foreigner is the ticket out of poverty" (see Constable, 2003: 5). Despite these women risking a "descending hell of spousal abuse or white slavery", they are viewed as persisting with this avenue of migration as an act of despair. The news outlet controversially quotes a Filipina saying, "It is better to be a foreigner's whore than a pauper's wife" (see Constable, 2003: 5).
5 *Mataray* can be likened to 'bitch', 'snob' or, in Cora's case, 'confrontational'.

References

Ang, I. (1996) 'The curse of the smile: Ambivalence and the "Asian" woman in Australian multiculturalism', *Feminist Review*, vol. 52, Spring, pp. 36–49.
Berger, P. and Kellner, H. (1994) 'Marriage and the construction of reality: An exercise in the microsociology of knowledge', in Handel, G. and Whitchurch, G. (eds.), *The Psychosocial Interior of the Family*, New York: Walter de Gruyter, pp. 19–36.

Briones, L. (2009) *Empowering Migrant Women: Why Agency and Rights Are Not Enough*, Surrey, England: Ashgate.

Brown, L. (2000) *Sex Slaves: The Trafficking of Women in Asia*, London: Virago Press.

Bulloch, H. and Fabinyi, M. (2009) 'Transnational relationships, transforming selves: Filipinas seeking husbands abroad', *The Asia Pacific Journal of Anthropology*, vol. 10, no. 2, pp. 129–42.

Constable, N. (1997) *Maid to Order: Stories of Filipina Workers*, Ithaca: Cornell University Press.

Constable, N. (2003) *Romance on a Global Stage: Pen Pals, Virtual Ethnographies and 'Mail Order' Marriages*, Berkeley: University California Press.

Constable, N. (2005) 'Introduction: Cross border marriages, gendered mobilities and global hypergamy', in Constable, N. (ed.), *Border Marriages: Gender and Mobility in Transnational Asia*, Philadelphia: University of Pennsylvania Press, p. 1.

Cuneen, C. and Stubbs, J. (2003) 'Fantasy islands: Desire, race and violence', in Tomsen, S. and Donaldson, M. (eds.), *Male Trouble: Looking at Australian Masculinities*, Victoria: Pluto Press, p. 69.

Daantos Berry, P. (2008) 'The folding wife', in Cheeseman, J., Wendell, P. and Capili, J. (eds.), *Salu-Salo: An Anthology of Philippine-Australian Writings*, Sydney: Casula Powerhouse and Blacktown Arts Centre.

Ehrenreich, B. and Hochschild, A.R. (2006) 'Global woman: Nannies, maids, and sex workers in the new economy', in Ehrenreich, B. and Hochschild, A.R. (eds.), *Beyond Borders*, New York: Worth, pp. 11–27.

Espiritu, Y.L. (2000) 'We don't sleep around like white girls do: Family, culture and gender in Filipina American lives', *Signs*, vol. 26, no. 2, pp. 415–40.

Espiritu, Y.L. (2003) *Home Bound: Filipino American Lives across Cultures, Communities, and Countries*, Berkeley: University of California Press.

Faeir, L. (2007) 'Filipina migrants in rural Japan and their professions of love', *American Ethnologist*, vol. 34, no. 1, pp. 148–62.

Foucault, M. (1981) *The History of Sexuality, Vol. 1: An Introduction*, Harmondsworth: Pelican.

Giddens, A. (1992) *The Transformation of Intimacy: Sexuality, Love and Eroticism in Modern Societies*, Cambridge, UK: Polity Press.

Heng, G. (1997) 'A great way to fly: Nationalism, the state and the varieties of Third World feminism', in Alexander, M.J. and Mohanty, C. (eds.), *Feminist Genealogies, Colonial Legacies, Democratic Futures*, New York: Routledge, pp. 30–45.

Hochschild, A.R. (2003) *The Commercialisation of Intimate Life*, Berkeley: University of California Press.

Jackson, R.T. (1989) 'Filipino migration to Australia: The image and a geographer's dissent', *Australian Geographical Studies*, vol. 27, no. 2, pp. 170–81.

Johnson, P. (2006) 'Making sense of intimacy: A contest between love and friendship', in Cervantes-Carson, A. and Oia, B. (eds.), *Intimate Explorations: Reading Across Disciplines*, Oxford, UK: Inter-Disciplinary Press, pp. 3–10.

Khoo, S. (2001) 'The context of spouse migration to Australia', *International Migration*, vol. 39, no. 1, pp. 111–31.

Laforteza, E. (2006) 'What a drag! Filipina/White Australian relations in The Adventures of Priscilla Queen of the Desert', *Australian Critical Race and Whiteness Studies Association E-Journal*, vol. 2, no. 2, pp. 1–18, http://acrawsa.org.au/files/ejournalfiles/81 ElaineLaforteza.pdf accessed 12 January 2012.

McKay, D. (2005) 'Migration and the sensuous geographies of re-emplacement in the Philippines', *Journal of Intercultural Studies*, vol. 26, nos. 1 and 2, pp. 75–91.

McKay, D. (2006) 'Translocal circulation: Place and subjectivity in an extended Filipino community', *The Asia Pacific Journal of Anthropology*, vol. 7, no. 3, pp. 265–78.

Parrenas, R. (2001) *Servants of Globalisation: Women, Migration and Domestic Work*, Stanford, CA: Stanford University Press.

Parrenas, R. (2005) 'Long distance intimacy: Class gender and intergenerational relations between mothers and children in Filipino transnational families', *Global Networks*, vol. 5, no. 4, pp. 317–36.

Povinelli, E. (2006) *The Empire of Love: Toward a Theory of Intimacy, Genealogy, and Carnality*, Durham: Duke University Press.

Pratt, G. (1996) 'Inscribing domestic work on Filipina bodies', in Nast, H. and Pile, S. (eds.), *Places through the Body*, London: Routledge, pp. 283–304.

Pratt, G. (2009) 'Circulating sadness: Witness Filipino mothers' stories of family separation', *Gender, Place and Culture*, vol. 16, pp. 3–22.

Robinson, K. (1996) 'Of mail order brides and "Boy's Own" tales: Representations of Asian-Australian marriages', *Feminist Review*, vol. 52, pp. 53–68.

Roces, M. (2003) 'Sisterhood is local: Filipino women in Mount Isa', in Roces M. and Piper N. (eds.), *Wife or Worker? Asian Women and Migration*, Lanham, MD: Rowman & Littlefield, pp. 73–100.

Said, E. (1995) *Orientalism: Western Conceptions of the Orient*, London: Penguin Books.

San Juan Jr., E. (2001) 'Interrogating transmigrancy, remapping diaspora: The globalisation of the labouring Filipino/s' discourse', vol. 23, no. 3, p. 52.

Saroca, N. (2006) 'Filipino women, migration, and violence in Australia: Lived reality and media image', *Kasarinlan: Philippine Journal of Third World Studies*, vol. 21, no. 1, pp. 75–110.

Tolentino, R. (1996) 'Bodies, letters, catalogues: Filipinas in transnational space', *Social Text*, vol. 14, no. 3, pp. 49–76.

Tyner, J. (2009) *The Philippines: Mobilities, Identities, Globalisation*, London: Taylor and Francis.

Woelz-Stirling, N., Kelaher, M. and Manderson, L. (1998) 'Power and politics of abuse: Rethinking violence in Filipina-Australian marriages', *Health Care for Women International*, vol. 19, no. 4, pp. 289–301.

6 More than a game

Embodied resistance among young Filipino-Australian street ballers

"You don't see us! You don't see us! You don't know who we are here!"

This was the loud, repetitive rant of a young Filipino man directed at the referee throughout the closing minutes of a heated championship basketball game. Jorell is known on these courts, to his teammates and to the opposition, as the 'hothead' of the team. Standing at a small but stocky five feet, he plays point guard, and he is never scared to stand up to a bigger player who might try pushing him around the court – nor does he ever hold back in arguing with the referees. On that particular night, at a basketball stadium in Clinton,[1] in Sydney's western suburbs, it was the Division 1 grand finals of the weeknight league. Jorell's team, The Knights, is made up of an all-Filipino line-up and they were pitted against a mixed team of white and Filipino players. Jorell was at it all night, relentlessly disputing what he and his teammates believed were 'bad' calls being made by an out-of-towner referee. But as the final buzzer rang and the scoreboard read 34–40, The Knights had lost the championship – one that they had previously won several years in a row.

The source of controversy that night was the opposition's larger-than-life seven-foot Anglo-Australian player, Gerry, and his 'disrespectful' conduct on the court. From the stands, I witnessed the commanding way Gerry manoeuvred on the court. He bullied his smaller opposition with his imposing body and through the smug smirk he would give whenever he held the ball above their heads, as if mocking the Filipino team's smaller size. Jorell and his teammates attempted to counter the physical dominance – as Filipino basketball players often do – through speed, crafty ball handling and fancy footwork. However, even I could not deny the power that Gerry's height and body offer to the game, which is commonly termed the 'sport of giants'. He knew all too arrogantly that once under the ring, he could easily block a threatening shot or reach comfortably for the rebound. But perhaps the biggest disrespect that Gerry showed was in breaching a customary gesture in the game. When you foul an opponent, despite being his challenger, you are expected to help him up and slap his hand, which is an act meant to show that there was no harm intended. It represents the respect a player gives to another in the battle in which they are engaged. Gerry failed to show this respect and there were certainly plenty of times that it was called for. At one point, Jorell stood up against him and a fierce altercation threatened to ensue. The seven-foot centre proceeded to laugh it off – a general indication of how he perceived the challenge posed by Jorell and his teammates.

At a crucial moment in the closing minutes, The Knights tried to catch the opposition's small lead and Leo, their six-foot-two centre, was penalised for throwing the ball in an un-sportsmanlike way at the referee. The technical foul set the team off and they began arguing with the officials that Gerry had done the same thing earlier in the game but was not reprimanded. Gerry is a representative player in a more elite league that recruits only the best and biggest players in the state. This status seemed to form the basis of Jorell's tirade towards the visiting referee, whom he accused of paying too much homage to Gerry's standing by letting him do "whatever he wanted". The unfairness is especially palpable because, despite many attempts, Jorell and his Filipino teammates rarely qualify for such elite-level basketball leagues. I had been told by countless young men on these courts that height and, moreover, an 'undesirable' playing style have worked as a mode of exclusion for many Filipino players who try to make these competitions. Jorell's claims of "You don't see us!", in every way, come to mean his invisibility to the referee, whom he believed recognised only the 'real' basketball player: the one who plays in a more serious basketball league or perhaps even more stereotypically the one with the tall physical build who 'looked' like a 'true' baller.[2]

In this chapter, I explore the intersections between race, class and masculinity among young Filipino men playing in mainstream basketball. I draw from time I spent observing social and competitive basketball games around Sydney's western suburbs, where I got to know many Filipinos, young and old, male and female, who play in these arenas. Basketball is extremely popular among the Filipino community in Sydney. In the Philippines, it is a remnant of American occupation introduced by the Young Men's Christian Association. The sport is passionately followed at the national professional level and played with intensity at the grassroots level, where makeshift hoops are ubiquitous on street corners in cluttered urban streets and impoverished rural provinces (Antolihao, 2010).[3] In Sydney's western suburbs, young Filipino men religiously play social or competitive basketball in various facilities several times a week. Many of these games are coordinated by Filipino organisations and function as spaces where the community can meet, socialise and network. Basketball events are also among the most attended festivities as the sport features at community celebrations where the best teams are pitted against each other to build exciting rivalries (see Figure 2.5).

I grew up in this basketball community. My father founded one of the first basketball clinics for young Filipinos in the 1980s in western Sydney, which at the time had only a small but growing Filipino community. My brothers play basketball along with my male cousins, uncles and friends. I became acquainted with many of the young men at the courts through this personal network, who then introduced me to other Filipino players. Watching countless games from the stands, I established relationships and casually talked over numerous games with players, tournament organisers and court officials and became familiar with the game style of young Filipino men and their interactions with each other, referees and non-Filipino players. In particular, I focus here on stories from young second-generation Filipino males who are aged between their mid-twenties to their early thirties.[4] They shared with me experiences of marginality that slowly made visible an institutionalised whiteness in mainstream basketball at the recreational and elite levels. Moreover, I argue that this is translated into subtle practices and values in encounters with the Filipino male body on the court.[5]

In sport, Carrington (2010) theorises the body as a *racial project*, wherein sporting institutions in postcolonial and migratory contexts produce racial narratives bound to the racial organisation of wider social structures. The body is the central site that enables both "sport (as practice) and race (as ideology). The body serves to make sport 'possible' and race 'real'" (Carrington, 2010: 67). In this chapter, I explore the *embodiment* of racial structures and discourses in mainstream basketball – how 'race' (but also gender and class) is constituted through the body and how racialisations translate into racist practice on and off court. But, as well, central to my discussion is the manner in which these stigmatised bodies deemed 'out of place' negotiate routinised racism. As opposed to avoiding the body, which carries the principal markers of difference as I have discussed throughout the book, these young men daringly *engage with* their corporeality as the site for protest. Jorell's resistance on that eventful night, therefore, extends well beyond Gerry's on-court arrogance but profoundly signals what basketball means to many Filipino men. Jorell cares so much about the game because it is, in so many ways, more than just a game for him and his Filipino peers.

Whiteness in Australian sporting contexts

Australians pride themselves on being a 'sporting nation'. As a prominent institution in the national space, sport is a complex sociopolitical field. In particular, "sport is deeply implicated in the complex interactions and power struggles that surround 'race' and ethnicity" (Adair and Rowe, 2010: 256). This is particularly important when considering how white hegemony in Australia is tied to national identity. Basketball in Australia struggles to maintain a profitable professional league (Dampney, 2008), while cricket and football (rugby union, rugby league and 'Aussie Rules'), rooted in British colonialism, are celebrated as the most popular spectator sports and perceived as iconic of 'Australian life' (McKay and Rowe, 1987). Basketball is widespread only at the grass-roots level in the form of junior mainstream leagues or competitions organised by ethnic organisations. The latter is particularly true for multicultural western Sydney, considered the heart of Sydney's basketball culture. But despite the dedication among young Filipinos and other non-white ethnic youth, they are hardly represented in elite mainstream competition, where junior players are mainly white males. Only with the recent settlement of African refugees in Sydney have a small number of African-Australian men entered development leagues upon being actively targeted by basketball scouts.[6] Soccer is a useful comparison. Its ethnic fan base sustains the professional sporting code in Australia; however, its 'ethnic' association poses problems marketing the sport to the broader public and official sporting bodies have tried to de-ethnicise soccer in Australia in order to boost its national popularity and profitability (Skinner et al., 2008). These cases reflect a history in Australian sports that upholds a white national narrative understated via public rhetoric of sport as the epitome of 'successful' multiculturalism (Rowe and Stevenson, 2006).

In my observation of mainstream basketball leagues, this racial formation is filtered into institutional and interactional practices and values. While racial slurs are still exchanged in sporting matches, these explicit acts are no longer the norm. Instead, everyday white privilege is played out as taken-for-granted 'unearned assets' (Housel, 2007; Hallinan and Krotee, 1993). To be sure, young Filipino men acknowledge that elite sport is extremely competitive and most recreational players will not make it to this level, regardless of ethnicity. However, my interviews with young Filipino men revealed racialising practices (intersecting with class and gender), which I argue sustain a white hegemony in the mainstream arenas of the sport and connect with wider structures of inequality. Bon's story (to follow) is just one of the many that I came across that recount fairly identical feelings of racist exclusion and highlight the racial signification in mainstream basketball. I focus on his biography to tease out with some detail how larger racialising processes work through the body and subjectivity, interaction and practice, in the most complex and intricate ways.

Bon's story

I had asked another player, Vincent, who had become my interlocutor on these courts, to introduce me to Bon, a twenty-five-year-old Filipino baller. I saw Bon frequently at the basketball courts in Clinton, playing in numerous competitions and social games throughout the week. Bon *loves* basketball. He considers himself a pretty sporty guy and regularly contrasted this passion with his schooling, something which he described as having "barely survived". Bon has worked as a labourer since finishing high school, and he explained that he much prefers working out his body and keeping active to having a "sit-down" office job.

At five foot and ten inches, Bon plays point guard – the player responsible for distributing the ball to teammates and creating 'the play' for the point. Bon labels his game as 'physical' and 'aggressive' – something he *needs* to be because there is no room for fear when he is put in charge of leading the team on the court. Accompanying this 'physical' on-court style, Bon has piercings on his left eyebrow and bottom lip and sports a rat's tail at the nape of his neck and, more noticeably, his body is heavily tattooed. Aside from being an aggressive baller, I had been told, he is someone you do not mess with outside of the stadium. Despite admitting to me that he has, indeed, had his fair share of brawls on and off the basketball court, Bon is actually a very sweet and soft-spoken young man. He explained that he was raised in a "pretty rough" neighbourhood not far from Clinton, where he learnt how to stick up for himself and, along with his friends, occasionally ran into trouble with the police as young teenagers.

But beyond having a reputation as one of the 'tough guys' among his peers, Bon is considered one of the *best* players in Clinton. It is not uncommon for Filipino organisers to select him for prestigious exhibitions or to be courted by other Filipinos to join their teams. As I mentioned, I asked specifically to be introduced to Bon. Perhaps out of all the young men who I had watched from the stands, his game is (in the only way I really know how to describe) the most *beautiful* to watch. When Bon brings the ball down the court, especially on a fast break, he looks more like he is gliding rather than running. His feet move so swiftly – changing directions suddenly on the player defending him in balanced, elegant steps. He is also a smart passer and a reliable shooter, which has allowed him to come through for his team in crucial moments.

But despite his obvious talent, Bon has not been very successful in mainstream representative basketball. After trying out for numerous regional teams in the youth league, he made it into only one, which folded after two games. Despite briefly gaining entry, what he remembers most are experiences of rejection by mainstream clubs. While Bon might be praised in the Filipino community for his talents, such dismissal at the mainstream and elite levels deeply hurt because these fields are endorsed by professional and semi-professional leagues. And so, being recognised as a 'good baller', even for Filipino players, is still often underlined by being recognised as such in *mainstream* arenas.

Throughout most of our interview, Bon was hesitant to attribute experiences of unfairness to race. This includes the many experiences outside of the basketball court that he thinks might have been 'racially' motivated. On the one hand, Bon recalled school peers trying to "pick fights", assuming that Asian males are weak and "do not fight back". This stereotype insults him to the same extent as those that posit Asian men as lacking sexual and phallic prowess. On the other hand, he reflected on whether his run-ins with the police can be attributed to him being stereotyped as a member of an 'Asian gang' – a popular anti-Asian sentiment about Asian males when he was growing up. As a young adult, he is occasionally denied entry into establishments in Sydney. Like many other young Filipinos who relayed similar stories to me, this rejection is not uncommon despite strictly adhering to entry regulations. In these contexts, they complain of being stigmatised as 'threatening' to clientele. On one occasion, in order to gain entry into a popular Sydney bar, Bon was forced to cut off his rat's tail in front of the door attendants and other patrons who found amusement in his public humiliation. But even in this situation, he was not quick to say it was 'racism', although I could see through his hesitancy. For a guy like Bon, who is respected among his peers for his physical and mental toughness on and off the court, I can only imagine that it is difficult to admit to the humiliation that racism brings. Basketball provides for Bon an outlet for achievement. But his experiences even on the basketball court are rich with complex racial signification:

> When I was nineteen, I tried out for a representative team in the North-West. And like not to brag, but clearly I was one of the stand-outs there. But you know, the coach said, 'I'll give you a call. Let you know if you made it.' I never heard from him. That day, I used to have braids, I had long socks, I got pretty dark skin . . . I looked different from the white players. I reckon that sort of

had definitely a racist thing. I tried out for three teams. I even tried out all the way in the North Shore. Same thing. The guys there, man . . . they weren't aggressive like how we (Filipinos) play. Same thing . . . I was playing good. Didn't hear from them. I just kept trying.

. . . Not getting in, it's a lot of things. It's about who you know. The parents need to know the coaches or you have to know the coaches. Or someone's gotta vouch for you, tell the coach you're a good player. Me and my brothers, we didn't know anyone. All those white parents know each other.

. . . Size matters. Filipinos aren't really the biggest guys so it's hard to play against Aussies 'coz they're a lot taller. Filipino games are just faster than white ballers' games. They play differently. They like to set up . . . you know [run] plays and all that. Textbook basketball. Because they're a lot bigger they tend to play more an inside game. . . . play their big guys, play near the basket. So it's hard for Filos to get in there and try to stop them 'coz they're too big.

. . . I learnt basketball from my brothers and my dad, playing out on your driveway. You learn watching NBA on TV. All those white players, they get schooled, they know those coaches. So Filipinos aren't 'by-the-book', they see us as street ballers. Our style . . . lots of white coaches, that's not what they look for. You make a fancy move and make the basket but they don't want to see that. So even if you score, they say, 'I don't want you doing that stuff.'

Bon's experience on and off the court signals everyday racisms based on paradoxical discourses that take root in historical conceptions of Asian masculinity. Effeminisation of Asian males is a construction from Western imperialism's positioning as the 'masculine conqueror' to the 'weak feminine' East (Khoo, 2003; Eng, 2001; Kim, 2005). For the Philippines, according to Espiritu (2003: 56), its colonisation "had less to do with Filipinos' incapacity for self-government and more to do with imperialists' desire to cast themselves as men who wielded power". Such discourses write themselves today on labouring bodies of Filipino low-wage migrant workers around the world (S. McKay, 2007). In Australia, effeminisation translates into the lack of recognition given to Asian men in sports and is elaborated in stereotypes around Asian 'nerds' or the 'backward and patriarchal' Asian man (Morris, 2006; Lucas, 1998; Nilan et al., 2007). This othering of Asian masculinity buttresses dominant modes of white masculinity that prioritise physical build and strength and connect Australian manhood with sexual dynamism and phallocentric desire (Carden-Coyne, 1999; and Connell, 2003). On the other end of the spectrum, threatening labels about Asian maleness preserve 'civilised' ideals of white hegemony. This was conjured up in the colonial fear of the 'Yellow Peril' invading Australia after the influx of Chinese goldminers and reproduced in white moral panic around Vietnamese gangs in ethnic enclaves, like Cabramatta, in Sydney's south-west, in the 1980s (Dreher, 2007). Filipino masculinity has not been at the centre of these discourses largely because of the hyper-visibility of Filipina women in the Australian imaginary.[7] A small body of work on Filipino male migrant identities elsewhere confirms similar stereotypes (Espana-Maram, 2006; S. McKay, 2007; Manalansan, 2010).

I suggest that these broader discourses play out in material and affective ways on the basketball court to organise and order bodies into hierarchies of worth. A number of different issues emerge from Bon's narrative around the racial meanings underscoring basketball: from the practices of exclusive white middle-class networks governing mainstream basketball to racialised corporeal differences across players and the operation of embodied racialised, classed and masculine dispositions on the court. In unpacking these different issues, I anchor my analysis to the differences between *textbook basketball* and *street ball* to interrogate the kinds of racialisations (ascribed or reclaimed) operating through the sporting body. Textbook basketball is a 'technical' style of play involving higher percentage shots, a methodological dribble, and learning and applying rehearsed plays from the clipboard. It is a style regularly mastered in basketball clinics. On the other hand, street ball, as its name implies, is basketball played on the streets – on concrete courts in council parks and open back lots of public schools. It is played three on three and utilises a half court. The game style emerges from unconventional schooling through informal pick-up games and is characterised by improvised and flamboyant moves. All of the Filipinos whom I interviewed at the courts around western Sydney made crystal clear that the playing style of street ball is highly disapproved of by coaches and selectors in mainstream basketball leagues. Despite any talent that Filipinos may showcase on the day, they may be automatically dismissed at recreational mainstream games, and especially in representative trials, because their bodily performances do not project 'technical' training.

I argue that these two different styles of play take on racialised distinctions in mainstream basketball. They embody different modes of *habitus* (Bourdieu, 1990) – modes of sporting bodily competence and disposition generated through bodily and intersubjective interaction with the physical environment and historical forces. Habitus "manifests in our actions, our modes of appearance and through bodily hexis or bodily bearing – posture manners, ways of speaking and dressing" (Noble and Watkins, 2003: 522). Through this lens, I show that the different value assigned to textbook basketball and street ball signals a connection between larger structures of power relations and modes of everyday intimate inhabitance and interaction on the basketball court.

'Dirty' Filipino street ballers: constructions of undesirable racial habitus

In Bon's narrative, when street ball is played in mainstream competitions, it is deemed 'illegitimate' and 'undesirable' as textbook basketball is the endorsed bodily performance. The preference for rationalised and controlled sporting bodily dispositions takes root in Western civilising processes. Elias (1986: 163–165) traces the application of rules, rationalisation and restraint in modern sport to the systematic attempt to control the use (and enjoyment) of violence in society. Further, Bourdieu (1978) sketches this evolution to white bourgeois realisation of political, cultural and economic power in industrial capitalist societies. This history connects with the corporatisation of sport that normalises calculated play

118 *More than a game*

in order to produce systematic wins (Jackson and Andrews, 1999). In Sydney, organised basketball competitions, especially at elite representative level, involve costly court fees, registration, training, uniforms and travel. Basketball clubs are also unequal in their resources. The North Shore and North-West regions – two representative teams where Bon has tried his hand – are affluent areas, and financial capacity produces strong basketball clinics, quality refereeing and first-class facilities. Recruiters dedicate much of their time getting to know the talent in these areas and are brought into regular contact with the players' parents, coaches and tournament organisers. These areas are also less ethnically diverse, which means very few players from non-white backgrounds compete in these tournaments. Consequently, such networks are largely maintained as *white* associations. In contrast, Filipino basketball players reside and play basketball in the Blacktown region – a more socio-economically disadvantaged area and also among the most ethnically and racially diverse.[8]

These insulated networks can function to produce a 'white habitus' (Bonilla-Silva, 2006) and are similar to the kind produced in white middle-class spaces, such as the corporate sector discussed in Chapter 3. In mainstream basketball, I suggest that selection practices favouring textbook basketball endorse a white hegemony as it is an exclusive white middle-class bodily disposition *implicated in* and *produced by* the white networks of mainstream basketball. The inequality of opportunity experienced by Bon is part and parcel of the ways in which sporting authority in white-dominated societies is structured: it is composed of white owners, coaches and judiciary committees (Carrington and McDonald, 2001). Long and Hylton (2002: 99), in their research on the experience of black players in grassroots and professional rugby clubs in the UK, observed the "hierarchy of privilege between black and white people" in organised sporting contexts. Key committees are composed of an "array of white faces", which for non-white racialised bodies come to represent the whiteness of 'the establishment' – "a white establishment that is allowing black players to play the game" and a "whiteness that is exercising authority to discipline them" (Long and Hylton, 2002: 99). This hierarchy operates to limit the agency and freedom of black and other non-white athletes both on the field, where they confront biased referees, and at judiciary hearings that have no black or ethnic representation. It is through these networks that processes of power work to reinforce the hegemonic whiteness in the sport. Non-white bodies are hence limited in their opportunities because they are constantly confronted by authority which lacks diverse ethno-racial representation. For many young Filipino ballers, this is how they understand the establishment of mainstream basketball in Sydney as they are regularly confronted by visibly white networks at elite Sydney clubs who do not take notice of their skills and talent.

But more significantly, white habitus frames the disciplinary practices of referees and other officials who engage in signifying practices that connect with corporeal affective responses to intersubjective encounters. I remember distinctly, during my time as a spectator, witnessing a white referee publicly scold a Filipino player in a heated match: "*This ain't a Filipino league. Play properly!*" A response to the 'aggressive' bodies of Filipino ballers on the court, it is one of

More than a game 119

the many examples I observed that signal subtle racialised rules about 'rightful' bodily performance. Bon further elaborated on the regulation of Filipino bodies in mainstream basketball:

> At the trials, you score but you do it with a fancy move, the coaches . . . it's not what they're used to. We're street ballers to them as in we're not traditional. And we're dirty street ballers to them. Not that we play dirty but you know, we're more physical . . . and okay, we know how to cheat without being caught (laughs). Filos, man, we're just aggressive.
>
> None of us even try for representative competition anymore. They just don't like our style. They like textbook players – you know, set up plays and that. They think Filos are too all over the place. But we just play differently, you know – we play fast, we play hard and like I said, we're not 'by-the-book'. We didn't learn that way like them white players do.

Historical processes of power construct black and white male bodies as the principal points of reference in global sporting culture – black bodies are admired for their corporeal power and white minds for their strategic abilities (Carrington, 2010). The location of 'intermediary' Asian bodies is ambiguously negotiated along this range (Yep, 2012; Thangaraj, 2010; Johal, 2001). The global commodification of basketball stars like Michael Jordon positions basketball as a 'black sport' (Anderrson, 2007). NBA players Yao Ming and Jeremy Lin are the only celebrated Asian players. In the aftermath of the 2012 'Linsanity', Leung (2013: 55) argues that Lin's talent was originally bypassed in the NBA because being Asian did not fit the racialised image of elite basketball players. Furthermore, the status of Asian-Americans as 'model minorities' is an undercurrent in sporting reports that attribute Lin's rise to fame not to skill or physique but to diligence and brains.

I suggest that Bon's body is marked as 'out of place' in the spectrum of racialised, sexualised and classed masculinities in sport. The most popular conceptions of street ball emerge from poor black US neighbourhoods, where the theme of 'life on the street' is used in international basketball advertisements to commercialise the connection between urban roughness and hyper-masculine swagger (Maharaj, 1997). 'Swag' is a mode of masculine performance "associated with the dominant pose of urban black men who, through hip hop and other cultural forms, have influenced the expressions of masculinity amongst non-blacks as well" (Wang, 2012: 6). As a mode of racial posturing and borrowing, Bon too embraces swagger in his personal style. His body is adorned with piercings and tattoos and his hair is braided in cornrows. His fancy and daring moves on the court also epitomise a tough and cocky bravado. The media features black professional basketball players acting out this street ball swagger via dress, 'trash talk', flamboyant dunks and celebratory dances. It is (on the surface) acknowledged by the sport as an acceptable mode of masculinity. However, on Filipino bodies, swagger is read differently by mainstream clubs. Stereotyped to lack the physical build and hyper-masculinity on which racialised representations of the black body are premised, Bon is seen to merely *mimic* black maleness. Bon alluded to the physical differences between white and Filipino sporting bodies. While height is not everything in basketball, it is valued bodily capital in the 'sport of giants'. For Filipino ballers, emasculation can occur vis-à-vis the preference expressed for more 'capable' and 'stronger' racialised bodies that work through wider discourses on effeminate Asian masculinity. Specifically, rejection based on body size reinforces understandings of Filipino bodies as inferior and capable only of cheap labour. Therefore, while not necessarily seen as weak, Filipino bodies are neither respected as powerful or cool.

But Bon is also simultaneously reduced to his bodily aggression via persistent Cartesian dualism that reiterates in sport "the intellectual as the higher faculty and the physical as the lower" (Louis, 2002: 115). 'Textbook' basketball and 'street ball' entail quite different bodily labour. Wacquant (1995: 73) defines bodily labour as the "highly intensive and finely regulated manipulation of the organism whose aim is to imprint into the bodily schema . . . postural sets, patterns of movement, and subjective emotional-cognitive states". In the sporting context, bodily labour is what makes someone a 'competent' practitioner of a sport. Textbook training is a way to remodel the bodily movements and cognitive capacities of the athlete to play the game in a less risky manner in terms of shot making and passing. Such movements and plays are calculated and rehearsed in training sessions for execution in competition. The style of street ball also involves significant bodily labour but, in contrast, the training involves developing a 'feel' for the moment. Textbook players also use these same sensory judgements; however, for street ballers, the body and mind are primarily tooled around *improvisation* from which 'knowledge' about 'what the moment calls for' is developed and constantly harnessed. But because of its visible flamboyance, 'street ballers' are perceived as lacking the 'thinking' component on the court in terms of calculated and rationalised tactics. As Bon described, Filipino ballers are defiled as 'dirty players'. The 'aggressive' and 'fancy' style Bon speaks of refers to the assertive bodily rhythms of Filipino basketball players as they find ways to manoeuvre around larger bodies, while improvisation lends itself to bodies ducking and penetrating during points. Seemingly failing to exercise strategy and discipline, Filipino ballers are concurrently cast as 'all body, no mind' as street ball is misconceived as irrational and 'brute physicality'.

Such schemata and practice that mark Filipino bodies as 'matter out of place' (Douglas, 1966) reveal an established order where white subjectivities discipline non-white bodies into line. Whiteness as an entrenched hegemonic norm allows white bodies to "sink comfortably into space but curtail the everyday bodily practice of non-white bodies" (Lobo, 2013: 458). If habitus is the embodiment of social location, street ball can come to represent the materialisation of recklessness and waste. Maharaj (1997: 99) contends that although 'the street' is commercialised in popular culture, it is ultimately pathologised as criminal and its inhabitants problematised beyond social and economic control. This is particularly true for African-American males in the US, signalling the racial signification in sport that maintains profound racial inequalities. Despite rewarding black men in sport, 'black swagger' continues to be problematised in professional sporting realms and ordinary black males remain socially and politically powerless (Wang, 2012; Louis, 2002).

Similarly, moral panics persist around western Sydney's economic poverty and 'cultural backwardness'. Compared to the middle-class body, the 'Westie' body is "perceived as the grotesque body" and materialised by the West's "menacing youth" (Powell, 1993: 30). Bon embodies this 'undesirable' habitus through his personal style but more significantly through his 'dirty' bodily comportment. For Bon, his aggressive play is a harmless assertive engagement that includes pulling 'sneaky' tricks in the game. But such performance, beyond signifying practice, is *felt* through intimate bodily contact as provocative, uncontrollable and 'out of place'. Bon's bodily hexis 'cheats' the game rules and physically breaches the symbolic codes governing the haptic senses of white middle-class bodies that inhabit the social and material environment in different ways.

Street ball as embodied resistance

Yet, Bon chooses to remain a street baller despite knowing his style to be the source of misrecognition and exclusion. I suggest street ball is a mode of *embodied resistance* – a habitus that offers possibilities for redemption of respect and dignity. For Bourdieu, "the somatisation of power relations involves the imposition of limits upon the body which simultaneously constitute the condition of possibility of agency" (McNay, 1999: 104). As a *generative* rather than determining structure, habitus highlights how identities and bodies inhibited by hegemonic forces also attempt to *negotiate* power. Expressive practices through bodily style and comportment open up opportunities to undermine domination.

By aligning with a non-white masculinity such as black masculinity, Bon can stand *in opposition* to hegemonic white masculinity. This negotiation speaks to Gilroy's (1993) theory that modes of blackness have evolved to speak to experiences of subalternity across different groups. Thangaraj (2010) also documents this tactic among young South Asian–American ballers via employing black aesthetics to assert a 'politics of difference'. But blackness is not merely emulated – it can be actively given different meaning by its appropriators. For instance, the tattoos of many Filipino players at Clinton express their ethnic background (see Figure 2.6). Bon has on his left arm symbols of the sun and three stars from the Filipino flag arranged in a tribal design. On his right forearm, he has an intricate drawing of Philippine hero Lapu Lapu, the first native to resist Spanish invaders. On his upper back, Bon displays a giant cross cradled in between two angel wings and his Filipino surname is emblazoned through both symbols:

> Yeah, I've always wanted some work done. I dunno, something you just have to do. It's a guy thing. Tattoos tell your story. I always wanted something about my background. I wanted something that I wouldn't regret. The one with Lapu Lapu, he's such a big hero. There's a big statue of him in Cebu City, where I'm from – looks exactly like the one I got. He's got the big-ass sword too. He fought off the Spanish. And my surname, well, you know I'm proud of that. Family is everything. And yeah, all my tattoos are about being Filo. You gotta be proud of that too.

122 *More than a game*

Body tattooing is often interpreted as acts of empowerment and modes of transgressive politics (MacCormack, 2006 and Fisher, 2002). For marginalised bodies, tattooing can be especially meaningful because

> skin is a marked surface inscribed with texts of race, gender, sexuality, class and age ... The tattoo is an addition to the surface ... [complicating] the already complex sense of immediacy between the internalisation of social discourse ... and the externalisation of self as an enacting entity in the world.
>
> (MacCormack, 2006: 59)

Thus, tattooing can *reinforce* difference as a way to regain power over corporeality that is regulated by outside forces. Bon, for example, acknowledges on his skin the history of Spanish colonisation and *indio* resistance, allowing him to reclaim *pride* in his historically subjugated body. But while signifying symbols are important in destabilising discourse, more significantly, the tattooed body does something to the material field in which it traverses. It alters forces and other bodies by producing affects that unsettle bodies and their functions. For the young men at Clinton, branding the bodies performing the (seemingly) 'black style' of street ball into *Filipino* bodies disrupts – visually and haptically – white/black binary oppositions of racial and masculine categories in sports. It also distinguishes these young men from homogenising 'Asian' categories. Murphy, a young Filipino-Australian tattoo artist, explained:

> Because our tribal tattoos look like Polynesian tattoos, sometimes Islanders will come up to you and ask why do you have Islander tattoos? But then I tell them that I have a Filipino tribal tattoo. They don't know Filipinos have tattooing traditions. They're shocked.[9]

Thus, as MacCormack suggests (2006: 79), tattooing can be understood as "an experiment in being, a body among other bodies ... Tattoos both invite and resist the gaze of others ... looking in fascination, as an opening up to being affected, transforms looking and knowing to seeing and thinking."

Equally, street ball is not a simple duplication of the game played by African-Americans. The Philippines has its own version that has flourished since American occupation. For example, the 'circus lay-up' – an unconventional shot that is usually forced after being jammed in the air amid defenders – has become a celebrated move in Filipino basketball (Bartholomew, 2010: 16). Young Filipino men in Clinton master the style of no-look passes and body-twisting tricks from their fathers, older brothers and uncles who grew up playing basketball on street corners in the Philippines – a sport that Antolihao (2010: 478) argues has become a "spectacle of subaltern struggle" popularised from a colonial tool of pacification to a sport for the masses. Bon takes pride in Filipino ballers' dissident bodies and commented, "*White guys think we're aggressive but they can't call it, can't see what we're doing exactly.*" This style serves to undermine norms defining 'skill' and 'race'. These dexterities are no novelty, as one white Australian player, Jonathon, who frequently plays against Filipinos stated:

> I ask them all the time, why don't you guys play reps? They're good . . . a little dirty, sneaky but they're good ballers. Filos are real quick and tricky. Probably the refs hate their game, too aggressive than what they're used to calling. And Filos argue with them all the time (laughs).

How street ball functions to rework dismissive stereotypes is further illustrated by the conversation ahead that I shared with another young Filipino-Australian who lives in Clinton. Leo lives within walking distance to a couple of courts around Clinton and works as a train station attendant. He had reported the same kinds of racisms that Bon experienced. When he talked about the playing style of street ball, it became even clearer to me how it provides redemption from the injuries of racism:

Leo: "Okay, like a trained play or textbook baller when they're dribbling the ball, there's no show-off kind of play. Just do-what-you-gotta-do. No dribbling under the legs or cross-overs. Just get to that spot and pass the ball. If it was a street baller, if someone was guarding him, he'd be trying to dribble all over the place and try to get around them. . . . rather than just protecting the ball. So a textbook baller, they just protect the ball, not a lot of dribbling, just walk it over. Pass if you're in danger. If that was a street baller, he'd go all the way. He won't pass. He'll dribble all over the place to get around the players and take it to the basket himself. A trained player, he'll look for other players. But a street baller, he'd take it himself because he's gotta be the big hero. He wants the glory, you know." (laughs)

Researcher: "Is that really smart, though?"

Leo: "I dunno about smart . . . (pauses) It's not about being 'smart'. It's something more. It takes a lot to . . . create, you know . . . Like, create a way to get the basket. I like the Filo games because it's more exciting. Some moves we can come up with . . . pretty amazing, hey. Street ball is a bit sneaky. A bit dirty. (laughs) Makes the game interesting . . . Put it this way, textbook is still good basketball. But you know, street ball . . . it's faster, you don't really know what's going to happen. There's something more to it than just practice, practice."

So a street baller must find ways to 'create' the shot or play amid the bodies guarding his path to the ring. This creativity is in the elaborate and obscure manoeuvres that these young men push their bodies to undergo in practice and in competition. Throughout my time spent on the stands, watching countless social and competitive games, I witnessed some pretty amazing things. Bon's combined quickness and grace stood out to me from the very beginning. But one of my most favourite things to watch was his attempts to drive the ball to the ring, where he displayed no fear by *manipulating* his body – gracefully ducking, turning, bending – to get around the other players in his way. Street ball is not entirely selfish play, either. Some of the most impressive moves I saw involved creative exercises in passing the ball to produce an assisted score. Paul, a quiet young man from the Penrith area, is another dedicated basketball player at Clinton, and caught my eye with his inspiring play. He regularly showcased his talent not through shooting but through remarkable no-look passes that seemingly weave through the opposition to reach his teammate, who appears almost surprised when he catches the ball. This kind of assist is difficult to master even by professional players (and certainly not encouraged in elite leagues), but at Clinton, courageous players like Paul enjoy its risks. There is an element of uncertainty that you feel in the pit of your stomach while watching these kinds of plays, especially in close heated games as these seemingly spontaneous passes, shots and cross-overs appear likely to fail in their endeavours. Indeed, sometimes they do. But I eventually came to understand that this is the very *excitement* that many of the young men speak of when you play street ball. The improvisation and risks taken in being creative produce the *possibility* of amazing feats. These 'performances' are what reputations are built on – producing *pride* in and *respect* for the player who dares to push his body to the limits.[10]

And these young men pay due respect to each other's bodily labour. While their game style is dismissed at mainstream leagues as illegitimate, they are valued very differently among Filipino ballers on the courts at Clinton. The chaotic nature of street ball is, in contrast, *celebrated* among players and spectators as inspiring, exciting and entertaining, whereby the lack of routine and predictability is the very basis of respect, transforming these skills into a form of *subcultural capital* (Bourdieu, 1984) – capital that may not be converted in the fields of power that structure hegemonic values and practices in mainstream basketball, but instead given claims of legitimacy in other settings. There is, in Leo's words, a 'glory' in street ball that cannot be achieved in the routine and practiced movements of textbook play. While the logic of rehearsed plays and simple movements on the court increases the likeliness of a win, Filipino ballers ultimately prefer to remain 'street ballers' because textbook basketball is experienced as too robotic, monotonous and tame. The creativity, aggressiveness and hazards of street ball give young Filipino men a chance to be 'the hero' – a status that is denied them not only in mainstream basketball but also in other everyday spaces. While 'showing off' might be disapproved of by mainstream coaches, it becomes an important way for Filipino ballers to feel valued. Street ball transforms exploited Filipino bodies into *creative* Filipino bodies. What is deemed 'improper' behaviour allows Filipino ballers to "carve niches of autonomy" (Espana-Maram, 2006: 8).

Body building is another mode of rewriting these scripts. Together, the visibility of buff and heavily tattooed bodies on these courts strongly conveys a sense of masculinities 'on show'. Leo stands, almost lankily, at six feet and two inches in height and is one of the tallest Filipino players competing at Clinton. As if self-conscious about his weight, one of the first things he explained to me when we sat down for an interview was that he was trying to "work out" his body so he could be a stronger player on the court. For the centre position that he plays, the body building is understandable. But aside from his personal goals to be a 'stronger player' there is a wider culture of body building that is strongly fostered in the sporting space he inhabits. It is not uncommon to hear 'body talk': lengthy discussions around what kinds of weight exercises and nutrient supplements best enhance the muscular build; expressions of collective approval over who has recently 'bulked up'; and playful jibes over who is 'out of shape'. For many Filipino ballers, 'working out' at the gym is not simply about fitness or refining the body for basketball but also about bodily aesthetics as a form of protest masculinity, which Connell (2003: 112) defines as "not simply observance of a stereotyped male role. It is compatible with respect . . . a sense of display". Rippled abdominals, toned chests and sharply defined biceps are some of the ways to lay claim to the dominant notions of modern masculinity and counteract stereotypes around effeminate or sexless Asian masculinity.

Racialising space: communities of resistance

Lefevbre (1971) theorises space as a construct of socio-economic, cultural and political discourses which can be regenerated and negotiated by individuals and communities. I suggest that the stadium in Clinton, where I spent most of my fieldwork for this chapter, serves as a space where Filipino ballers gain recognition which is denied in mainstream leagues. Such individual notions of respect are not only personal but also tied to the respect that the Filipino 'community' desires. There is a particular team who plays a pivotal role in this process. Bon, Leo, Jorell and Vincent are all part of the team Pare[11] – a team that is well known in these surrounds for being 'the best' in the area. They have won most tournaments in Clinton – both mainstream and those coordinated by Filipino organisations – and do so in consecutive runs. Moreover, they are distinctly known as a *Filipino team* and its members pride themselves on being an 'all-Filipino' line-up. Kane, the team's captain, is always on the hunt for new Filipino talent or is constantly attempting to convince existing stand-out Filipino players at Clinton to abandon their team and play with Pare. His team desires to prove that they do not rely on larger white players to strengthen their game and take pride in the fact that most of the team members (barring one) have no formal training but are instead street ballers. The dominance by Pare works with the other tactics of embodied resistance to significantly construct the Clinton courts as a distinctly 'Filipino' space. I suggest, therefore, that these young men are not in the game merely for individual glory. Their choice to remain an essentially 'Filipino team' illustrates how they locate themselves within a community that is also in search of visibility and appreciation.

I witnessed one particular event that encapsulated how important the courts at Clinton are to these young Filipino men and the community to which they belong. A few months after completing my fieldwork, Vincent invited me to watch a highly anticipated basketball game. A professional team, as part of a comeback tour, was staging an exhibition game at the very courts where my respondents play.

Vincent and a handful of other Filipino ballers were selected to join an assembly of mostly white basketball players who compete at elite representative mainstream levels. The event was targeted to the Filipino basketball community that live in the neighbouring suburbs. The lead-up to the exhibition game consisted of constant advertisements on Facebook from the promoter and posters on announcement boards at the stadium, which featured Vincent's name and also his captain, Kane, to attract the night's audience. Vincent and Kane were also featured on the front page of a few local newspapers in Clinton. On the night, the Filipino national anthem was sung at the opening proceedings of the game to a crowd of mostly Filipino locals from around the area and of course the regular players at the stadium. While many were there for the professional team, because of the significance that this space holds for the community who uses it, they were mostly present to support their local Filipino stars.

After building the hype around the Filipino ballers who would contest the exhibition game, what happened on the night was something that perhaps even I did not expect, despite becoming well versed in the kinds of disrespect that Filipino ballers endure. The exhibition's promoter had brought in a well-revered semi-professional coach to direct the Clinton assembly and what transpired that night reaffirmed all of the stories that I came across from the young men I had gotten to know. Vincent and Kane, along with the other chosen Filipino players, humiliatingly sat on the bench for much of the game. The coach ignored his Filipino line-up and opted to reuse the tired and cramping elite players as if the rest of his bench was invisible. This also did not go unnoticed with the crowd, who began to murmur in the stands about the wasted Filipino talent. It was, however, in the final two minutes of the game that the worst kind of insult was added to the deepening injury. With the professional team in a stretched lead, the coach finally turned to his Filipino players and, with a look of resignation, ushered all of them onto the court to play. The disappointment and bitterness were palpable among the crowd. But in the very little two minutes that these players had, Kane made a remarkable point in classic street ball style. Against professional athletes, he drove the ball to the ring, twisting and turning around the larger bodies guarding him. The audience were suddenly on their feet. *This* is what they had come to watch.

Despite Kane's brief moment of glory, the consensus after the exhibition game, as the Filipino crowd piled out of the stadium and into their cars, was disappointment. I felt it too and it cut deep. After talking to Vincent a few days later, I found that he shared the same feelings of hurt, anger and embarrassment:

> I knew I wasn't going to get any major court time. I mean it's a pro team. But I didn't expect that (kind of treatment). I mean, the last two minutes of the game? Really? All the Filos came to watch us. We're on the front page of the papers. And then we get put on court in the last two minutes when there wasn't any hope left for the game. Like we were nothing, you know. I don't know why the promoter got that coach. He's one of those coaches that don't . . . like, well, you know, don't respect Filipino players. He just kept using those white players he knows who play reps in his area. I mean I didn't expect to do anything

amazing, but at least use us to refresh those other players, let the other guys rest, you know. Last two minutes . . . like that's what our nationality is worth on the court?

And so the true damage that night was not to Vincent's personal ego. The decisions made by the coach in that game (and the non-action from the promoter) were not only an insult to the reputations of Vincent and the Filipino players who are respected in that stadium but also equally hurtful for the Filipino community, who takes pride in the young Filipino men who put their heart and soul into carving out a space where Filipinos can finally be respected. The hard work in building their reputations has allowed Filipinos to become a part of the stadium's history in Clinton. Moreover, the recognition Filipino ballers gain from the other basketball players, tournament organisers, referees and spectators who occupy this space comes to construct the *legacies* of these young men and the community they represent. Such legacies will linger on at the courts in Clinton among new generations of ballers, even when their owners are finished with the game. This is what was almost carelessly taken away from them that night.

The courts at Clinton are an unlikely 'sacred' space of resistance for the Filipino community in Sydney, where Filipino ballers have attempted to create an autonomous space to escape what hooks (1992) describes as the 'terrorising white gaze'. The stadium at Clinton is a rare place where the race, ethnicity, class and masculinity of Filipino ballers finally do not matter. The space assumes the role of a 'Filipino institution' within an antagonistic white environment and provides a sense of ontological security for its marginalised members. In retrospect, the violation of this sanctuary is the reason for the anger, disappointment and hurt that the crowd, including myself, felt that night. The collective significance that the local Filipino community attaches to the stadium as a 'Filipino space' speaks back to what Sivanandan calls 'communities of resistance' (cited in Carrington, 2002: 280). Such spaces of 'autonomy' outside of mainstream spaces are strategic sites for the articulation of wider struggles for recognition and where 'community' is constructed, repaired and celebrated.

Conclusion

The body and its comportment are a significant site through which ideas of 'racial difference' are materialised and generate certain kinds of exclusionary practices from the dominant group. The kinds of everyday racism endured by Filipino ballers on the basketball court reproduce the racisms they are subject to in other contexts, where they are stereotyped either for being too effeminate or for being too violent. These racialisations intersect with the policing of hegemonic versions of white middle-class masculinity in Australia. But these stories also give flesh to a mode of resistance against racism. Beyond re-signifying practices, street ball can disrupt the status quo in material ways, where the body "has the potential to loosen the hold of race", to loosen "the grip of whiteness" (Lobo, 2013: 463). This embodied resistance can dislodge the experience of racism from a victimhood status the way formal political anti-racism often fails to do.

There are, however, complexities and limitations to resistance on the ground. While street ball can interrupt the stability of whiteness, it does not simply overthrow unequal power relations. For instance, the increased participation in basketball of newly settled African immigrants to the Blacktown area, especially at the courts at Clinton, is a site of emergent racial politics in this basketball community. The derision of 'acting too black' is evolving as a means to assert 'Asian' assimilation into Australia for young Filipinos in order to distance themselves from African immigrants, who are incipient targets of popular racism. And so, in the complex system of differentiation that structures everyday life, the relationship between domination and resistance is not dichotomous but involves more complex processes of negotiation.

In a recently published book about the Philippines' "unlikely love affair" with basketball, Bartholomew (2010: 14) calls Filipinos' passion for the game an inspiring "against all-odds devotion". For the young Filipino men who I got to know at Clinton, their love for the game in the diasporic context is no different. Despite being regularly told that they are not good enough for elite basketball leagues because of their body size or skills, these men continue to play and persevere. For someone like Bon, who is stigmatised in racialised, gendered and classed ways, street ball takes on deeper meaning because, unlike whites, he must play in the face of threatening powerlessness. With its continued illegitimacy in mainstream basketball, street ball as embodied resistance functions as an unofficial text to wage an underground guerrilla battle, allowing Bon and other young Filipino men to survive racism, daily, against the odds.[12]

Notes

1. The name of the locality has been changed.
2. 'Baller' is popular slang for 'basketball player'.
3. Boxing is also popular in the Philippines (Espana-Maram, 2006). Especially since the overwhelming success of international boxer Manny Pacquiao over the last decade, it closely matches the national status of basketball.
4. As a result, the themes I explore here around masculinity reflect the concerns of this particular group. While the issues I explore in this chapter around the body and masculinity certainly speak to broader issues experienced by other Filipino migrant men in Australia, my analysis is very particular to the experiences of these young men in the context of the sporting arena. I thus acknowledge that other concerns around masculinity unrelated to the body are also experienced among Filipino men – such as my discussion in Chapter 4 of first-generation Filipino migrant men whose inability to be the main provider for their families is seen as a form of emasculation. Additionally, I interviewed young Filipino-Australian men who do not participate in basketball and actually distance themselves from what they feel are hyper-masculine stereotypes of Filipino men that have emerged from the very context I am exploring in this chapter. Thus, while it is outside of the scope of this chapter, I acknowledge that such alternative experiences are also important to acknowledge and investigate.
5. I distinguish between 'mainstream' basketball leagues that operate and basketball leagues run by organisations from the Filipino community. Mainstream basketball leagues include both recreational tournaments and representative regional teams at the local and state level.
6. The active recruitment of young African men to development leagues, local and abroad, shows signs of the racialisation of black athletic prowess studied in the Australian

context among Indigenous Australians (Coram, 2007; Hallinan and Judd, 2009; and), in the US with African-American men (Louis, 2005) and in the UK among Afro-Caribbean men (Johal, 2001 and Carrington, 2010).
7 Filipino diaspora studies is predominated by the experience of Filipina migrants, attributed to the feminisation of international migration that is significantly composed of Filipina women.
8 During Bon's youth, Blacktown did not have a representative team due to financial limitations. Today, it has developed junior representative teams and there is positive development at these levels in terms of Filipino talent.
9 For Filipino tribal tattooing traditions see Salvador-Amores (2002).
10 At this juncture, I want to be careful not to position street ball as exciting and creative but more or less un-calculated play. This risks drawing on the mind/body split that similarly underscores the way mainstream leagues devalue this style of play in preference for the conscious tactical style associated with textbook basketball. The act of 'playing' as 'second nature' can often erase the long and "tedious process of learning that second nature" (Noble and Watkins, 2003: 527). A 'feel' for the game is "never just a feel for 'the game', but a feel for the ball, the pitch, the uniform, the other players, the coach, the referee, the spectators, the temporality of the game" (Noble and Watkins, 2003: 527). All of these things involve past experiences in training and in competition. And so, while street ball might involve more improvisation or more 'feel' than textbook basketball, such senses are still regulated by *accumulated* 'know-how'. Contrary to the assumption that street ball involves purely random bodily movements, which forms the basis of dismissal that mainstream basketball clubs direct at the 'free-for-all' style in which Filipino ballers engage, consciousness and training exist in this style of play. To be sure, even textbook players engage in some forms of improvisation just as street ballers do. Sutton (2007), drawing on the philosophy of Dreyfus' phenomenology of expertise, has theorised extensively on the process of how one 'plays' a game 'competently' and the role of memory and reasoning in the bodily actions of a player in the heat of competition. He argues that to be a 'competent' player at any sport, training is essential and remembering movements, ball handling, kicks, positioning, footwork and so on is vital. However, such conscious 'thinking' on the field, court and pitch is more like "training wheels" that a competent player abandons after some time because "a slow transition from novice status through competence to genuine expertise involves . . . gradually relinquishing one's reliance on explicit rules" (Sutton, 2007: 768). Instead, according to Sutton (2007: 764–769), the moment of 'playing' involves a "flexible performance" of both consciousness *and* unconsciousness – what he calls *embodied intelligent action*. And so, in the context of this chapter, while one group might engage in conscious tactical play more than the other because of differences in training methods and structural opportunity, they can still share in the same sensory techniques. And so, what becomes important is interrogating how these styles come to be *socially constructed* as racially distinct and the nuanced demarcations it creates between disciplined/undisciplined, civil/uncivil, clean/dirty bodies.
11 The team name has been changed. *Pare* is a Tagalog term that males use to address other male friends.
12 A version of this chapter appears as a journal article; see Aquino (2015).

References

Adair, D. and Rowe, D. (2010) 'Beyond boundaries? "Race", ethnicity, and identity in sport', *International Review for the Sociology of Sport*, vol. 45, pp. 251–7.

Anderrson, M. (2007) 'The relevance of the Black Atlantic in contemporary sport: Racial imaginaries in Norway', *International Review for the Sociology of Sport*, vol. 42, no. 1, pp. 65–81.

Antolihao, L. (2010) 'Rooting for the underdog: Spectatorship and subalternity in Philippine basketball', *Philippine Studies*, vol. 58, no. 4 pp. 449–80.

Aquino, K. (2015) 'More than a game: Embodied everyday anti-racism among young Filipino-Australian street ballers', *Journal of Intercultural Studies*, vol. 36, no. 2, pp. 166–83.

Bartholomew, R. (2010) *Pacific Rims: Beermen Ballin' in Flip Flops and the Philippines Unlikely Love Affair with Basketball*, New York: New American Library.

Bonilla-Silva, E. (2006) 'When whites flock together: The social psychology of white habitus', *Critical Sociology*, vol. 32, p. 229.

Bourdieu, P. (1978) 'Sport and social class', *Social Science Information*, vol. 17, pp. 819–40.

Bourdieu. P. (1984) 'The forms of capital', in Richardson, D. (ed.), *Handbook of Theory of Research for the Sociology of Education*, Westport, CT: Greenwood Press, pp. 46–58.

Bourdieu, P. (1990) *The Logic of Practice*, Trans. R. Nice, Cambridge, MA: Harvard University Press.

Carden-Coyne, A. (1999) 'Classical heroism and modern life: Bodybuilding and masculinity in the early 20th century', *Journal of Australian Studies*, vol. 63, pp. 138–49.

Carrington, B. (2002) 'Sport, masculinity and black cultural resistance', in Sugden, J. and Tomlinson, A. (eds.), *Power Games: A Critical Sociology of Sport*, London: Routledge, pp. 267–91.

Carrington, B. (2010) *Race, Sport and Politics: The Sporting Black Diaspora*, London: SAGE.

Carrington, B. and McDonald, I. (2001) 'Whose game is it anyway? Racism in local league cricket', in Carrington, B. and McDonald, I. (eds.), *'Race', Sport and British Society*, London: Routledge, pp. 49–69.

Connell, R.W. (2003) 'Australian masculinities', in Tomsen, S. and Donaldson, M. (eds.), *Male Trouble: Looking at Australian Masculinities*, Victoria: Pluto Press, pp. 9–21.

Coram, S. (2007) 'Race formations and the aping of the Australian Indigenous athlete', International Review for the Sociology of Sport, Vol. 42, No. 2, pp. 391–409

Dampney, J. (2008) 'Spirit likely to vanish from NBL', in *Sydney Morning Herald*, 25 November, http://news.smh.com.au/spirit-likely-to-vanish-from-nbl-20081125-6hdi.html accessed 28 August 2013.

Douglas, M. (1966) *Purity and Danger: An Analysis of Concepts of Pollution and Taboo*, Routledge: New York.

Dreher, T. (2007) 'Contesting Cabramatta: Moral panic and media interventions in "Australia's heroin capital"', in Morgan, G. and Poynting, S. (eds.), *Outrageous! Moral Panics in Australia, Australian Clearing House for Youth Studies*, Hobart: ACYS, p. 111.

Elias, N. (1986) 'An essay on sport and violence', in Elias, N. and Dunning, E. (eds.), *Quest for Excitement: Sport and Leisure in the Civilising Process*, Oxford: Basil Blackwell, pp. 150–74.

Eng, D. (2001) *Racial Castration: Managing Masculinity in America*, Durham: Duke University.

Espana-Maram, L. (2006) *Creating Masculinity in Los Angeles Little Manila: Working Class Filipinos and Popular Culture, 1920s-1950s*, New York: Columbia University Press.

Espiritu, Y.L. (2003) *Home Bound: Filipino American Lives across Cultures, Communities, and Countries*, Berkeley: University of California Press.

Fisher, J. (2002) 'Tattooing the body, marking culture', *Body and Society*, vol. 8, p. 91.

Gilroy, P. (1993) *The Black Atlantic: Modernity and Double Consciousness*, London: Verso.

Hallinan, C. and Judd, B. (2009) 'Race relations, Indigenous Australians and the social impact of professional football', *Sport in Society*, vol. 12, no. 9, pp. 1220–35.

Hallinan, C. and Krotee, M. (1993) 'Conceptions of nationalism and citizenship among Anglo-Celtic soccer clubs in an Australian city', *Journal of Sport and Social Issues*, vol. 17, no. 2, pp. 125–33.

hooks, b. (1992) *Black Looks: Race and Representation*, Boston: South End Press.

Housel, T. (2007) 'Australian nationalism and globalisation: Narratives of the nation in the 2000 Sydney Olympics' opening ceremony', *Critical Studies in Media and Communication* vol. 24, no. 5 pp. 446–61.

Jackson, S. and Andrews, D. (1999) 'The globalist of them all: "The everywhere man" Michael Jordan and American popular culture in postcolonial New Zealand', in Sands, R. (ed.), *Anthropology, Sport and Culture*, Westport, CT: Bergin and Garvey, pp. 99–117.

Johal, S. (2001) 'Playing their own game: A South Asian football experience', in Carrington, B. and McDonald, I. (eds.), *'Race', Sport and British Society*, London: Routledge, pp. 153–69.

Khoo, T. (2003) *Banana Bending: Asian-Australian and Asian-Canadian Literatures*, Montreal: McGill-Queen's University Press.

Kim, D. (2005) *Writing Manhood in Black and Yellow*, Stanford, CA: Stanford University Press.

Lefevbre, H. (1971) *Everyday Life in the Modern World*, New York: Harper.

Leung, M. (2013) 'Jeremy Lin's model minority problem', *Contexts*, vol. 12, no. 3, pp. 52–6.

Lobo, M. (2013) 'Racialised bodies encounter the city: 'Long Grassers' and asylum seekers in Darwin', *Journal of Intercultural Studies*, vol. 34, no. 4, pp. 454–65.

Long, J. and Hylton, K. (2002) 'Shades of white: An examination of whiteness in sport', *Leisure Studies*, vol. 21, pp. 87–103.

Louis, B. (2002) 'Brilliant bodies, fragile minds: Race, sport and the mind/body split', in Alexander, C. and Knowles, C. (eds.), *Making Race Matter: Bodies, Space and Identity*, New York: Palgrave Macmillan, pp. 113–31.

Lucas, R. (1998) 'Dragging it out: Tales of masculinity in Australian cinema, from Crocodile Dundee to Priscilla, queen of the desert', *Journal of Australian Studies*, vol. 22, no. 56, pp. 136–46.

MacCormack, P. (2006) 'The great ephemeral tattooed skin', *Body and Society*, vol. 12, p. 57.

Maharaj, G. (1997) 'Talking trash: Late capitalism, black (re)productivity, and professional basketball', *Social Text*, vol. 50, pp. 97–100.

Manalansan, M. (2010) '(Re)locating the gay Filipino', *Journal of Homosexuality*, vol. 26, no. 2–3, pp. 53–72.

McKay, J. and Rowe, D. (1987) 'Ideology, the media, and Australian sport', *Sociology Sport Journal*, vol. 4, no. 3, pp. 258–73.

McKay, S. (2007) 'Filipino seamen: Constructing masculinities in an ethnic labour niche', *Journal of Ethnic and Migration Studies*, vol. 33, no. 4, pp. 617–33.

McNay, L. (1999) 'Gender, habitus and the field: Pierre Bourdieu and the limits of reflexivity', *Theory, Culture and Society*, vol. 16, pp. 95–117.

Morris, R. (2006) 'Growing up Australian: Renegotiating mateship, masculinity and "Australianness" in Hsu-Ming Teo's behind the moon', *Journal of Intercultural Studies*, vol. 21, no. 1–2, pp. 151–66.

Nilan, P., Donaldson, M. and Howson, R. (2007) 'Indonesian-Muslim masculinities in Australia', Faculty of Arts Papers, University of Wollongong.

Noble, G. and Watkins, M. (2003) 'So, how did Bourdieu learn to play tennis? Habitus, consciousness and habituation', *Cultural Studies*, vol. 17, no. 3–4, pp. 520–38.

Powell, D. (1993) *Out West*, St Leonards: Allen and Unwin.

Rowe, D. and Stevenson, D. (2006) 'Sydney 2000: Sociality and spatiality in global media events', in Tomlinson, A. and Young, C. (eds.), *National Identity and Global Sports Events: Culture, Politics, and Spectacle in the Olympics and the Football World Cup*, Albany: SUNY Press, pp. 197–214.

Salvadores-Amores, A. (2002) 'Batek: Traditional tattoos and identities in contemporary Kalinga', *Humanities Diliman*, vol. 3, no. 1, pp. 105–42.

Skinner, J., Zakus, D. and Edwards, A. (2008) 'Coming in from the margins: Ethnicity, community support and the rebranding of Australian soccer', *Soccer and Society*, vol. 9, no. 3, pp. 394–404.

Sutton, J. (2007) 'Batting, habit and memory: The embodied mind and the nature of skill', *Sport in Society*, vol. 10, pp. 763–786.

Thangaraj, S. (2010) '"Ballin" Indo-Pak style: Pleasures, desires and expressive practices of "South Asian American" masculinities', *International Review for the Sociology of Sport*, vol. 45, no. 3, pp. 372–89.

Wacquant, L. (1995) 'Pugs at work: Bodily capital and bodily labour among professional boxers', *Body and Society*, vol. 1, no. 1, pp. 65–93.

Wang, O. (2012) 'Living with linsanity', *Los Angeles Review of Books*, http://lareviewofbooks.org/essay/living-with-linsanity accessed 14 October 2014.

Yep, K. (2012) 'Peddling sport: Liberal multiculturalism and the racial triangulation of blackness, Chinese-ness and Native American-ness in professional basketball', *Ethnic and Racial Studies*, vol. 35, no. 6, pp. 971–87.

7 Conclusion

Residing in the city where I undertook my fieldwork, I had anticipated that I would, once in a while, cross paths with some of the Filipinos who had participated in my research. But to my surprise, it rarely happened. While I had gotten to know quite closely a few of the Filipinos who became interlocutors or interviewees, as months passed after 'officially' concluding my fieldwork, we began to lose touch. As I went to ground to write this book and recounted their stories on paper, I often wondered how each of them was travelling along in their lives. I wondered, as well, whether they ever pondered what had become of this project.

It was probably only a good two years after my fieldwork when I finally experienced my chance encounters. I bumped into Melinda, whose story features in Chapter 5, at a café in the city, where she was having lunch with her husband. While I remember all my respondents well, I was so pleased to see Melinda as her story had stayed with me for a long time and I never forgot her feisty determination to confront racism. Melinda also seemed happy to see me. As if I was a long lost daughter, she stood from her chair and embraced me. She introduced me to her husband and told him that I had interviewed her for my book. Like a proud parent, she boasted to him that I was "doing good things" for the Filipino community. Melinda and I chatted about how my work was coming along and I updated her that I was in the throes of writing. She encouraged me to "work hard" and to keep up the "important job" that I had taken on.

The other person whom I had a chance to see again was Leo, one of the young Filipino ballers I had gotten to know at the basketball courts in Clinton. He was a guest at a Filipino wedding that I attended. He too asked about my work and, at that point, I enthusiastically told him that I was very close to finishing my first significant draft. I also reported to him that whenever I presented my research on Filipino basketball to academic peers or to the public, many found his world a source of inspiration. The smile on his face reminded me of the pride that I have tried to capture in Chapter 6 around the significance of basketball to the young Filipinos who play this game. Later in the evening, as a post-wedding celebration, much of the wedding party (mainly young Filipinos like Leo and myself) headed to a local bar by the beach. I enjoyed a few drinks with some of the other guests and on my way out found Leo outside of the establishment, sitting on his own. I was to find out that he had been denied entry into the premises and had argued at great length with the security and door attendants that his friends were inside, including his wife. They refused him entry despite not being any tipsier than the other guests who were allowed inside. They simply said to him that he "looked like trouble". He began reminding me of our interview and how this "always" happened to him. After yet another humiliating experience of being forced to stand rejected on the street, he also reminded me that I had to "stop this".

Many of Filipinos I had interviewed never really asked me why I was doing this research, let alone tell me that they expected anything significant to come out of it. But my encounter with Melinda and Leo signalled to me that for some, while not explicitly articulated, they felt that in some way or another sharing their story was going to 'do something' about racism. Encountering Melinda and Leo again at the time that I did set in motion some necessary reflection about what I hoped to achieve with this book. In this concluding chapter I address two areas that my work might have some implications – the political and the personal. These are interconnected threads that have been running throughout this book, sometimes in union and other times in tension.

Implications for theoretical and political debates on 'race', racism and anti-racism

As Hall (1997: 7) reminds us, while "having been shown the front door, [race] tends to sidle around the verandah and climb back through the window . . . there is always something about race left unsaid." In Australia's multicultural order, this remains ever the case. There is a continued need to better understand the "work of 'race' in practices of racism" as non-racialism has become an obstructing force in formulating productive anti-racism projects (Lentin, 2016: 45). By interrogating the processes of *how 'race' is made* (both as constructed difference or sameness) in the everyday lives of Filipino migrants in Sydney, this book hopes to have shed light on some of the resources through which racism finds its force. In Australian society, 'race' continues to be brought into being through distinctions between white/non-white bodies across different spatial and temporal contexts, and which are ascribed meanings through complex cultural, economic and social mechanisms. I emphasise that this racialisation exceeds signifying practices but intensely constitutes, alters and organises bodies and subjectivities in material and affective ways. As Fanon (1967: 112) wrote, the body and psyche are "sprawled out, distorted, recoloured, clad in mourning" in the process of being constituted as a raced subject. This is a much more violent process than those that mark out 'cultural difference'. And so, 'race' needs sustained theoretical, empirical and political interest not because it is 'real' but because there is a reality to the ways in which it is experienced in everyday life by those marked by its forces. 'Race' remains tied to a structural system of power and privilege rooted in a brutal history of oppression, which (re)surfaces no less cruelly in contemporary practices of more subtle domination.

Racism persists for varying reasons, especially structural institutional ones. But this book hopes to have shown how racism also endures through the ways in

Conclusion 135

which structural power and historical systems filter down to mundane practices engaged by ordinary people. While not all racial meanings are enacted into 'racist practice', I have focused on those that Filipino migrants experienced as forms of racialised denigration, marginalisation and domination: from jokes about 'mail order brides' to denying someone entry into certain premises because he or she is 'Asian'-looking; from staring at (or ignoring) someone because her skin colour does not 'fit in' to emotionally intimidating a co-worker because of an assumption that Filipinos do not complain. These accounts of racism emerge from the perspective of the marginalised and dominated and it is not to say that shedding light on the operation of racism via this standpoint can explain everything about the dynamics of racism. But I argue that it can reveal particular kinds of knowledge accumulated by lives lived 'on the outside' which need to be taken seriously as points of access to understanding the complex contours of racism today. There is a deep-seated experience of 'race' for those constituted by its forces and their lives bear the most telling scars of the physical and psychological damage inflicted by racism. Through an exploration of *everyday racism*, racism reveals itself as being entrenched in our social system and not operating as some kind of abstract force or mere residual effect of other conditions of inequality. I extend that it must also be understood as being produced through transnational fields of power which signal the deep historical contingencies and the complex trajectories of racism in everyday life.

But respect is acquired in varying ways just as much as racism prevails. Through an examination of Filipino migrant lives, we can see that respect is not merely granted because the dominant endow such recognition of their own accord. Those who are dominated *struggle* for it – they *resist*, every day and often through unremarkable means, being subjugated and victimised. Outside of formal politics, everyday resources are used to subvert and negotiate racism by those who continue to be subject to racialised domination. Through the case studies I have presented, degrees of 'equality' can be achieved through socio-economic mobility and middle-class respectability, rights are reclaimed by using legal avenues of redress and upholding moral ground, racial stereotypes about 'mail order brides' are resisted through loving relationships, and effeminisation of the Filipino male is confronted through bodily protest. At times micro power relations can be overturned by such tactics. For example, whiteness in all its perceived fixity can be penetrated in everyday life or oppressive class boundaries or gender roles can be transgressed through transnational means that delocalise such positions. I expand in a moment about what micro resistance signifies for the transformation to racialised macro relations of power. I first emphasise, though, that regardless of whether broader hegemonic norms are transformed or sustained, the quiet humdrum of 'getting along' in a racially demarcated society is not just because of actions of the dominant – individual or institutional – but also because the marginalised have learnt how to *survive* domination.

In focusing on resistance from the marginalised, however, I stress that I do not promote that combatting racism be the responsibility of those who are racially tyrannised. I argue that paying more attention to the resistance undertaken *from below* – what de Certeau (1980: 6) classifies as the domain of the Other, the movements "in the enemy's field of vision" – can meaningfully reveal the "gaps in power" that exist in enduring structural orders and are often found in the intricacies of everyday life. Scott (1990) similarly theorises resistance in everyday life as a mode of 'history from below' which produces 'hidden transcripts' that operate under the 'official transcripts' enforced by the dominant. The practices in speech, dress and appearance among the Filipino middle class, consumption practices in the Philippines undertaken by the Filipino working class, the confessions and gestures of love among Filipina women married to white Australian men, and the denunciation of 'textbook' basketball as boring and predictable among young Filipino ballers – all of these are modes of resistance that reposition subjects outside of a victimhood status. Such resistance in everyday life, according to Scott (1990), constitutes an *infrapolitics* engaged by the dominated outside of formal political institutions and organised social movements which should be understood as not only private individual stories of resilience but also importantly indicating the dynamic intersections of macro and micro systems of power.

Indeed, the range of strategies engaged in everyday life reveals the *complexity* of struggles against racism in *lived* experiences. Surviving the wear and tear of routine racism does not always involve the objective of a 'non-racist' order and the equalising of power relations. For example, the struggle for recognition has often been critiqued as being insufficiently concerned with 'equality', especially when compared to the aims of redistribution. Because recognition involves the struggle for self-realisation, equal outcomes are not always achieved in highly individualised and identity-based struggles. For instance, among middle-class Filipinos, their efforts to redeem respect and honour can entail processes that marginalise other migrants, including other Filipinos, and strengthen existing unequal racist arrangements, local and transnational. In this way, the kind of recognition that is achieved does not contribute to an egalitarian order despite that the Filipino middle class may achieve mutual respect from and (degrees of) equal standing with the white middle class. The working class, in comparison, desire recognition too but the road they undertake through legal or formal avenues of redress is combined with a redistributional justice that certainly helps realise 'ideals' of equality where perpetrators of racism are reprimanded and victims of racism compensated in material and symbolic ways. This kind of resistance appeals more to official anti-racism initiatives that already exist in the legal structures and policies that are designed to balance out power relations. However, different structural and cultural contexts do not make the latter strategy possible in every situation. Everyone is implicated in different milieus that make available (and attractive) certain kinds of resources for fighting racism. In the middle-class context, saving one's esteem might matter more than redeeming rights, and so strategies based on individualism 'work best' to resist racism because of the resources made available by neoliberal structures that promote status and merit. The formal avenues that are used by the working class also exist in middle-class spheres but they are culturally valued in different ways within such spaces. They are not useless to the middle class but are perhaps not as useful. It is maybe in the stories of young Filipino basketball players who engage with their difference that resistance appears in its idealised form – as acts of sabotage and disruption. However, because street ball more or less acts as subcultural capital, whether such tactics can shift broader relations of power also remains a question.

In his book *Race Rebels*, Kelley's (1994: 4–10) analysis of black working-class resistance to racialised domination in America is also inspired by Scott's work on infrapolitics, and he argues that

> We have to step into the complicated maze of experience that renders 'ordinary' folks so extraordinarily multifaceted, diverse, and complicated. Most importantly, we need to break away from traditional notions of politics. We must not only redefine what is 'political' but question a lot of common sense ideas about what are 'authentic' movements and strategies of resistance. . . . Politics is not separate from lived experience or the imaginary world of what is possible; to the contrary, politics is about these things. Politics comprises the many battles to roll back constraints and exercise some power over, or create some space within, the institutions and social relationships that dominate our lives.

As opposed to discounting the ambivalence of quotidian modes of resistance against racism detailed in this book, I argue we situate them more precisely within anti-racism politics and as forms of anti-racism 'from below'. I suggest that the notion of *everyday anti-racism*, the ways in which individuals respond to racism in their day-to-day lives, offers an important theoretical and political arena to illuminate how routine racism is negotiated across different temporal and spatial contexts and through varying identity struggles. At times, such everyday responses can problematically reproduce larger racial formations. But it can also be about interfering with, even just for a moment, the status quo. Conceptions of anti-racism, I argue, cannot only be about fighting the broad identifiable racisms at the structural and institutional level where anti-racism attempts to achieve 'equality for all'. Anti-racism must take into account the small-scale and subtle racisms occurring in people's lived experiences which produce contradictory and ambivalent positionalities. As part of advancing anti-racism research and praxis, we need to probe more into the repertoires of material and symbolic resources used to negotiate the messiness of everyday life, to better account for the hard and complicated labour of fighting racism on the ground.

Implications for Filipino migrant lives

While many Filipino migrants I met were quite happy with their settlement in Australia, these individuals did not need to dig too far from the surface to reveal the subtle and not so subtle modes of exclusion, marginalisation and domination that they endure. The 'Filipino' in Australia continues to be constructed as a raced subject – an identity and body assigned racialised value through historical, structural, discursive and intersubjective processes. This racialisation and the racism it can produce profoundly shape how they can see themselves as 'Australian'. Certainly, being 'Filipino-Australian' can embody a mode of hybridity that enables a multiplicity and fluidity of positionalities in diasporic contexts. But accounts of racism in this book reveal the weights of 'race' that must necessarily be negotiated in the process. And, indeed, Filipino migrants subvert racism in varying ways and often via means that do not involve dramatic conflict or controversy. Currently, Filipinos are the fourth largest group of recent migrant arrivals to Australia, making this group one of the fastest and consistently growing migrant populations in the country. And so it is important not to forget that Filipino migration to Australia is incomplete and the stories and images presented here are only (part of) the story so far.

I hope that the lives detailed in these pages have not simply provided the interface through which to examine sociological concepts and problems. I have tried to communicate the complexities of individuals and that of a collective 'community', and I hope this book has provided a small platform to give voice to both their suffering and conquests. These struggles are each personal and distinct but are, as well, not fragmented. Through sociological analysis, I have tried to provide a framework to understand the everyday injuries Filipino migrants experience in a world that attempts to tell them that these are insignificant grievances based on their subjective 'feelings'. Regardless of the nature of everyday racism as a private individual event, varying forms of humiliation, domination and misrecognition are shared across class and gender, migration status and migrant generation, which draw on dynamic historical transnational systems of power. Such critical engagement with how modes of domination subtly manifest in their everyday lives has the potential to form the basis of a *collective struggle* that can hopefully respond to the different circumstances and challenges of the 'Filipino' in Australia. As Honneth argues (1995: 161–164) in the struggle for recognition,

> The motives for rebellion, protest, and resistance have generally been transformed into categories of 'interest', and these interests are supposed to emerge from the objective inequalities in the distribution of material opportunities without ever being linked, in any way, to the everyday web of moral feelings. . . . Hurt feelings of this sort can, however, become the motivational basis for collective resistance only if subjects are able to articulate them within an intersubjective framework of interpretation that they can show to be typical for an entire group . . . as soon as ideas of this sort have gained influence within a society, they generate a subcultural horizon of interpretation within which experiences of disrespect that, previously, had been fragmented and had been coped with privately can then become the moral motives for a collective struggle for recognition.

I wish to end this book with the voice of one of the many Filipino migrants who shared their struggles and dreams with me. It is they who ultimately deserve the final word on the pains endured in the diaspora but also on the hopeful possibilities that lie ahead:

> Lots of Filipinos think patience is not our best quality. *Pero matiyaga tayo. Totuo yan.* (But we are patient. This is true.) Think of all the sacrifices we make, migrating here and migrating there, migrating everywhere. And then the feeling of being a second-class citizen when you get to wherever you are going. It's really a very tough situation for many Filipinos. *Pero matiyyaga at matapang yung mga Filipino.* (But Filipinos are patient and tough) We're still young here, you know. And we're still growing. More Filipinos, always coming to make Australia 'home'. . . . I want to see how far the Filipino can go in Australia. I think we can really go far.

References

de Certeau, M. (1980) 'On the oppositional practices of everyday life', *Social Text*, vol. 3, pp. 3–43.

Fanon, F. (1967) *Black Skin, White Masks*, London: Grove Press.

Hall, S. (1997) 'Race, The Floating Signifier', transcript of Lecture at Goldsmiths College, London, Media Education Foundation. www.mediaed.org/transcripts/Stuart-Hall-Race-the-Floating-Signifier-Transcript.pdf.

Honneth, A. (1995) *The Struggle for Recognition*, Cambridge: Polity Press.

Kelley, R. (1994) *Race Rebels: Culture, Politics and the Black Working Class*, New York: The Free Press.

Lentin, A. (2016) 'Racism in public or public racism: Doing anti-racism in "post-racial" times', *Ethnic and Racial Studies*, vol. 39, no. 1, pp. 33–48.

Scott, J.C. (1990) *Domination and the Arts of Resistance: Hidden Transcripts*, New Haven: Yale University Press.

Index

American imperialism 18, 59, 87
anti-Asian attitudes 7; Asian immigrants 26–7; Asian males 115–6; Asians in Australia 22–3, 31; anti-discrimination laws 10, 78
anti-Muslim sentiment 26
anti-racism 28; conceptions of 137; everyday life 6–11, 136
Aquino, Benigno 'Ninoy' 21
Asian-ness 43, 55, 60
assimilation policy 24
Assisted Passage Migration Scheme 23
Australia: Filipino migrants in 2–3, 137–9; Filipino migration to 21–7; immigration 22–7; multiculturalism 9, 25–6; national identity 25; post-war migration from Philippines 31–2; racio-ethnic diversity 23–4; researching Filipino migrants in Sydney 3–6; whiteness in sporting contexts 113–17
Australia's Federation 22–3

baller 112, 128n2
basketball: in Australia 113–17, 128n4–5; Bon's story 114–16; 'dirty' Filipino street ballers 117–21; recruitment of African men 113–14, 128–9n6; resistance for Filipino community 125–7; sport of giants 111; textbook, *vs* street ball 117
basketball players: Filipino 111–13; Filipino community 125–7; Filipino symbols as tattoos 42; Filipino team for community 125–7; 2011 New South Wales Filos Championship Cup 42
Bell Trade Act 34n5
benevolent assimilation 20
Blacktown 52; business hub 41; Filipino basketball players 118, 129n8; Filipino heartland 4; Filipino *turo turo* (point point) restaurant 41
Bourdieu, Pierre 44, 69, 82, 117, 121, 124
body: race and the body 9; middle class bodies 50, 58; working class bodies 68–9; Filipina bodies 89; Australiansport and racialised bodies113–17; basketball 113, 114–16; body building 124–5; manipulation in sports 122–4; racial difference 127; as racial project 113; soccer 113–14; tattooing 42, 121–2

care deficit, female migrant workers 97–9
case studies: civility and 'good migrant' 55–8; English language and habitus of 'Western-ness' 52–5; mail order brides 91–7; middle-class Filipino migrants 11, 43–5; social mobility 45–52
capital: cultural 11, 45, 50, 51, 52–55, 60; linguistic 52, 58–9; racism and capital 44; socio-economic 44, 52, 67; social 71; sub-cultural 124
Catholic missionaries, Philippines 18–19
Centre for Philippine Concerns 28
Chinese-Spanish or Chinese-Filipinos 33n3; mixed-blood 19, 60
class: definition 82; middle class Filipinos 44; working-class Filipinos 80–3*Colombo Plan, The* 23
colonialism 10, 60–1; British 113; European/Western 11, 21; Hispanic 106; racialism and 19; Spanish 87
coloniality 60
community: Filipino ballers 125–7; Filipinos 5–6, 33, 92–4; racialising space 125–7
conditionality 45, 62
convict transportation 22
Cronulla Riots 26, 57–8

Index

culture 7, 97–8; Australia 24–5, 57; basketball 113; body building 125; Filipino 53–4, 57, 59–60, 104, 106; Irish Catholics 48; Muslim 43, 57; Philippines 21, 30–1, 77, 93; popular 11, 62n2, 120; race and 7–8, 11; sporting 119

differential inclusion 21
Displaced Persons' Resettlement Scheme, The 23

Economics, Filipina migrants 97–9
embodied resistance, street ball as 121–5
English language 52–5
Equal Opportunity Commission 75
ethnicity: language of culture and 8; migrant 55, 58; racio-ethnic diversity 23–4; sporting events 113–14, 127; term 7
everyday anti-racism 10–11, 137
everyday racism 3, 5, 9–12, 26, 135, 138; basketball story 114–16, 127; blue-collar labour 68–75; mail order bride stigma 88; middle class experience 50–52; working-class experience 67–8, 71, 74

Filipina: as abused domestic help 27, 34n6; brides 2; domestic helpers 34n7; feminised racialisation and class marginalisation 73–5; servitude and submission 34n8; stereotypes about 2; term 12–13n1; *see also* Filipina marriage migrants; mail order brides
Filipina marriage migrants: confessions of love 105–7; fallacy of 'marriage for migration' 99–102; feminisation of international migration 87–9; husbands role in relationship 102–5; living with 'mail order bride' stigma 91–7; love, economies and care deficit 97–9; making of 'mail order bride 89–91; racialised condemnation of 87–9, 107–8; *see also* mail order brides
Filipino 11; America's little brown brothers 20–1; community 5–6; competing representations 27–32; early history of 17–21; hostile and opportunistic 29–30; identity 6; inferior and 'Third World' 30–1; parade of costume 40; submissive and victimized 27–9; term 12–13n1; Western, integrated and invisible 31–2; working-class stories 11–12
Filipino-Chinese: mestizo 19, 33n3, 59; mixed-blood 19, 60

Filipino migrants: aspiring middle-class 43–5; in Australia 137–9; habitus of Western-ness 52–5; mastery of English language 52–5; researching, in Sydney 3–6; social mobility and racism 46–52; transnational regimes of whiteness 58–61; *see also* working-class Filipino migrants
Filipino Seniors Sonata Concert 40
Filipino-Spanish, *mestizo* 19, 33n3
Folding Wife, The (theatre production) 87
folk, understanding racism 13n3
Fresh Off the Boat (FOBs) identity 56–7

general knowledge of racism 13n3
George III (King) 22
Good Neighbour Councils 24

habitus 51, 52, 55, 61, 117, 120
hacienda system 18
Hanson, Pauline 25, 52
honorary whiteness 11, 44, 62; term 62n2
Howard, John 26
hypergamy, Filipina migrants 98–9

identity: Filipinos 6; Fresh Off the Boat (FOBs) 56–7; working-class Filipinos 80–3
immigration: Australia 22–6, 31; females 94; Filipino 89
Immigration Restriction Act 23
inday (maid): shaming of mail order bride 93; term 91
Independence Day Ball 32
indios 18–19
institutional racism 26, 49

Jordan, Michael 119

Keating, Paul 25

Lacaba, Jose 59
Lapu Lapu 121
Lin, Jeremy 119
love: confessions of 105–7; Filipina migrants 97–9; intimate life 107–8; *see also* mail order brides

McKinley, William 20
Magellan, Ferdinand 18
mail order brides 2; business of 108n4; controversy 3, 29; decision to marry a foreigner 93–4; Filipina migrants 87–9; Filipino migration to Australia 21–7;

living with the stigma of 91–7; making of 89–91; role of husbands 102–5; shaming by Filipino community 93; stereotype 12, 28, 88, 95–7; stigma of, for Filipina women 88–9, 94; *see also* Filipina marriage migrants
mainstream media: Filipina women 30; Filipino migrant workers 29–30; news reports 34n8; reports of Filipino exploitation 28–9
mainstream politics, New South Wales (NSW) 32
Manila Men, Philippines 22
Marcos, Ferdinand 21, 24
marriage: fallacy of, for migration 99–102; international correspondence 88, 91, 92, 105, 108n1 *see also* mail order brides
mestizo/mestiza 19, 33n3, 59
middle-class Filipino migrants 43–5; social mobility 45–52
MIGRANTE Australia 28
Ming, Yao 119
mis-interpellation 33
morality 75–80
multiculturalism 9, 25–6; multicultural society 33
Muslim Arabic migrants 26

national identity, Australia 25, 113
neo-liberalism 30, 47
New South Wales Filos Championship Cup (2011) 42
New South Wales (NSW) 4; Filipino Women's Working Party 28; mainstream politics 32
non-interpellation 33
Notes on Bakya (Lacaba) 59

orientalism: definition of 89; mail order bride 89–91, 107, 108n3
Otherness 27, 44, 51, 52, 57, 90

Pacific Islanders Labourers Act 23
Pacific War 23
parade, Filipino costume 40
People Power movements 21
Philip II (King) 18
Philippine Australian Community Services Inc. (PACSI) 28
Philippine Community Council 32
Philippine Cultural Day, parade of Filipino costume 40
Philippine Revolution 19, 20

Philippines: boxing 128n3; description of 17, 33n1; economy 21, 34n5; idea as 'Third World' 30–1; institutions 33–4n4; languages 17–18, 33n2, 52–3, 55–6; mestizo 19, 33n3; sex industry 90; Spanish in society 18–19; Spanish roots 59–61
Philippines Community Herald, The (newspaper) 32
political debates, race, racism and anti-racism 134–7
post-war migration, Philippines to Australia 31–2

race: everyday life 6–1; everyday race making 17; racio-ethnic diversity 23–4; racism and anti-racism 134–7
Race Rebels (Kelley) 137
racialisation: basketball 117; black athletic prowess 128n6; body 113, 127; feminised 73; Filipina migrants 89; Filipino migrants 30, 31, 134, 138; politics in Philippine society 60; term 9
racial formations 17
racialism: colonialism and 19; non- 134
racism: against Filipino street ballers 117–21; end of 8; everyday 5, 12, 26, 135; everyday life 6–11, 136; experiences of 4–5; Filipino middle-class 46–52; folk understanding 13n3; husbands helping mail order brides 102–5; mail order bride stigma 91–7; resistance of 135–7; working-class Filipinos 68–75, 84
resistance: 'from below' 135–6
rights, working-class Filipinos 75–80
Rizal, Jose 19

situational knowledge of racism 13n3
social mobility, middle-class migrants 45–52
Spanish roots, Philippines 59–61, 87
street ball: body building 124–5; as embodied resistance 121–5; manipulating body 122–4, 129n10
street ballers, 'dirty' Filipino 117–21
swag: black swagger 120; masculine performance 119
Sydney: basketball in 12, 111–13, 115–18, 121, 127; Cronulla Riots 26, 57–8; English use in Filipino community 53; immigration 23, 46; mail order bride in 91–2, 95; middle-class stability 13n2; Filipino migrants in 3–6, 11, 29, 31; working-class in 66, 68

Index 143

Tagalog language 18, 33n2, 52–3, 55–6, 59, 61, 66, 105, 129n11
Taglish (Tagalog and English) 52, 61
Tarc, Mishra 58
tattooing, body 42, 121–2
temporariness, sense of 83
Third World: idea of Philippines as 30–1; intelligence and 47; migrant labour 73, 77; uncivilized 57; women 90, 97, 108n3
transnational racial formations 10
Tsao, Chip 27

understanding, sociological 13n4

Vietnam War 90

war on terror 26
Western-ness: habitus of 52–5, 61; language and civility 59–60
'White Australia' policy 7, 8, 23, 24

white habitus: disciplinary practices of referees 118–19; Filipino basketball players 118–20
whiteness 9–10; Australian sporting contexts 113–17; civility and 'good migrant' 55–8; Filipino social mobility 45–52; habitus of 51–2; hegemony of 50; political, social and cultural construct 44; property 51; transnational regimes of 58–61
women *see* Filipina marriage migrants
working-class Filipino migrants 11–12; dignity of labour 66–8; notion of better life 66; racialised inequality 83–4; racialised subordinate labour 68–75; rights and morality 75–80; sense of temporariness 83; stories of 11–12; transnational class identity 80–3
World War II 23

Yellow Peril 29, 116
Young Men's Christian Association 112